WHOSE HISTORY?

WHOSE HISTORY?

The Struggle for National Standards in American Classrooms

LINDA SYMCOX

Teachers College, Columbia University
New York and London

Published by Teachers College Press, 1234 Amsterdam Avenue, New York, NY 10027

Library of Congress Cataloging-in-Publication Data

Symcox, Linda.
    Whose history? : the struggle for national standards in American classrooms / Linda Symcox.
        p. cm.
    Includes bibliographical references and index.
    ISBN 0-8077-4231-7 (pbk. : alk. paper) — ISBN 0-8077-4232-5 (cloth : alk. paper)
    1. History—Study and teaching—United States.   2. Curriculum planning—United States.   3. Education—Standards—United States.   I. Title.
    D16.3 .S96 2002
    907.1'073—dc21   2002018895

ISBN 0-8077-4231-7 (paper)
ISBN 0-8077-4232-5 (cloth)

Printed on acid-free paper

Manufactured in the United States of America

09   08   07   06   05   04   03   02   8   7   6   5   4   3   2   1

To my husband, Geoffrey

Contents

Acknowledgments

ALTHOUGH WRITING A BOOK is a task done in relative isolation, the book itself emerges through relationships with others over a period of years. I am grateful to Professor Charlotte Crabtree, Director of the National Center for History in the Schools, University of California, Los Angeles, for her loyal mentoring and thoughtful collaboration throughout the seven years I worked with her at the National Center for History in the Schools. Her energy, passion, and commitment to the work were truly inspirational.

I also wish to thank all of the friends and colleagues across the country whose lives converged with mine during my tenure at the National Center for History in the Schools. Their enthusiasm for the work of the Center and their invaluable contributions as authors, presenters, and participants in the National History Standards Project will not be forgotten. Their work and insights are very much a part of this book.

This book began as my doctoral dissertation. Without the encouragement of my doctoral committee at UCLA, there would be no book. I am grateful to my graduate advisor, James Catterall, for his unwavering guidance, support, and encouragement throughout my doctoral studies and beyond. My thanks also go to all the members of my committee for the sound advice they offered along the way: Megan Franke, Anne Gilliland-Swetland, Russell Jacoby, and Jeannie Oakes. I owe special thanks to Jeannie Oakes, whose encouragement and kind words inspired me to send out a book proposal. My appreciation goes to my friend James La Spina, who also encouraged me to send out a proposal and gave me words of encouragement during the writing process. Thanks also go to professors Kris Gutierrez and Rachel Fretz, whose encouragement first led me to pursue this topic for my dissertation.

At Teachers College Press, I wish to thank Brian Ellerbeck, Executive Acquisitions Editor, for his positive response to my original manuscript and constructive guidance throughout the publication process, as well as Catherine Bernard, Associate Acquisitions Editor, for her thoughtful editorial guidance as I prepared the manuscript. Thanks also go to Ami Norris and Nancy Power, for their efforts in promoting the book, and to Aureliano Vázquez, Jr., for overseeing the title through the production process. In addition, I wish to thank the two anonymous readers who recommended my proposal for publication and provided sound advice for improvement.

Most of all, I am grateful for the support of my family. I thank my two sons, Alexander and Adrian, and my mother, Betty Silvers, for their patience with the author, who was all too often preoccupied with this project. Finally, I wish to thank my husband, Geoffrey Symcox, who, as a veteran involved in the Standards project, offered his invaluable insights and served as my most important sounding board as we discussed this project over a period of several years. I dedicate this book to him.

Introduction

Who controls the past controls the future; who controls the present controls the past.

—George Orwell, *1984*

ON JANUARY 18, 1995, THE UNITED STATES SENATE passed, by a vote of 99 to 1, a non-binding resolution condemning the recently published *National Standards for History*, a seemingly innocuous document outlining curricular goals for the study of history in the nation's schools. This vote of censure was taken after only the most cursory debate, and without the benefit of a single public hearing. Few of the senators had even seen the document, let alone read it. Senator Slade Gorton, moving the resolution, excoriated the offending document: "This set of standards must be stopped, abolished, repudiated, repealed. It must be recalled like a shipload of badly contaminated food."[1] The Senate resolution not only condemned the *Standards*, but also cut off all future funding to the organization that oversaw their development, the National Center for History in the Schools at the University of California, Los Angeles. The intent of the resolution was clear: It stipulated that national standards "should have a decent respect for the contributions of Western civilization, and United States history, ideas, and institutions, to the increase of freedom and prosperity around the world."[2] Clearly, the *National Standards for History*, even though they had been sponsored by the National Endowment for the Humanities and the U.S. Department of Education, and even though they had been developed by a nationwide collaboration of academic historians, education specialists, and K–12 schoolteachers, had failed the political litmus test imposed on them by the Senate. They were deemed un-American.

This vote of censure represented the culmination of two months of heated national debate, which had begun even before the Standards were

1

released. As luck would have it, publication of the nation's first-ever standards for the teaching of history in the schools coincided with the election of the first Republican congress in forty years. Although many moderate Republicans were in favor of national standards, many of the more conservative members of the 104th Congress, heady with an electoral victory delivered in a large part by the Christian Coalition, were eager to prove their patriotism and their attachment to traditional values. By assailing the *Standards* as un-American, the new conservative leadership of Newt Gingrich, backed by its pundits in the press, could parade its ideological credentials and simultaneously use the *Standards* to attack the government agehcies responsible for funding their development.

This book examines how the National History Standards Project (NHSP; 1992–1996), which produced the *National Standards for History*, became a major battleground in the nation's culture wars, the ongoing battle to define the nation's cultural identity, which ebbs and flows with the tides of political change. During the 1980s and 1990s the culture wars heated up: Intellectuals and policymakers alike became embroiled in heated public debates over national and cultural identity. Many of these debates centered on the issue of how to make traditional educational canons more inclusive and reflective of the nation's growing diversity. Although most of the canon debates played out in the arena of higher education, the publication of the *National Standards for History* in 1994 launched an acrimonious controversy over how to teach our national past to K–12 students, thus shifting the locus of debate.

To understand what was at stake in this controversy, I trace the genealogy of the National History Standards Project, from its origins as a neo-conservative reform movement during the early 1980s, through the drafting of the *Standards* during the early 1990s, to the controversy that erupted in 1994–1996 and its aftermath. I examine how the peculiar politics of educational reform sparked a culture war between liberal academics on the one hand and conservative policymakers on the other. During the eighteen months of controversy, the debate over *what* history—and more importantly, *whose* history—should be taught in the schools resonated through the halls of Congress, the national press, the academy, and the nation's schools. History suddenly became headline news.

The *Standards* controversy serves as a case study that illuminates the broader issue of how educational policy is made and contested in the United States. It reveals how policymakers and opinion-makers, including academics, pundits, politicians, and the press, used their positions to advance particular intellectual and ideological agendas, and how their contending efforts drove curricular policy throughout the 1980s and

1990s. Drawing upon the methodology of intellectual history, I situate this case study within the broader intellectual history of the times, focusing on the academic debates over social history, world history, multiculturalism, established canons, national identity formation, cultural history, and the definition of "liberal education." From this analysis I conclude that the controversy over the *Standards* was inherent in the very nature of the process that produced them. The *Standards* were the product of recent historical scholarship that challenged traditional conceptions of the nation's history. The historians who helped draft the *Standards* drew on the "new social history," with its rallying cry of "history from below." In the 1960s social historians had conquered the high ground in their profession and created a new research agenda centering on broad social movements and the contributions of those formerly excluded from the grand historical narrative, such as slaves, women, and the laboring classes. Once uncovered, these anonymous lives could not easily be incorporated into the traditional patriotic narrative of a shared and glorious past whose onward march had been determined solely by the actions of great leaders and generals. Here lay the seeds of conflict. Traditionalists feared that the new social history, embodied in the *Standards*, would supplant traditional history in the K–12 curriculum and undermine the patriotism of the nation's youth. The debate that erupted over the *Standards* in 1994–95 pitted traditionalists, who favored a single grand narrative celebrating a shared and triumphant national past, against revisionists, who favored a more pluralistic rendering of our nation's history, with fewer heroes.

A further aim of this study is to analyze in detail how educational reform movements play out in practice. The NHSP offers a particularly good vantage point for an analysis of curricular reform because of the drama that surrounded it and the high-profile personalities involved in it. Its rise and fall provides us with a close-up of the inner workings of educational reform, the play of political forces, and shifts in policy. The NHSP also provides an abundance of empirical evidence to test current theories about how knowledge is created and legitimized. Theorists such as Michel Foucault, Thomas Kuhn, Michael Apple, and Hayden White have examined this issue from different perspectives, but have rarely attempted to anchor their hypotheses to specific people, places, and events. This study attempts to establish empirical connections between theory and practice. Through close analysis of the pronouncements and written texts generated by the different participants of the NHSP, it demonstrates empirically the subtle interplay of knowledge and power that theorists such as Foucault usually describe only in broad outline.

The question of how power legitimates knowledge is a central concern in Michel Foucault's work. In a series of studies, Foucault looked at various institutions in order to describe the nature of power in society, which he located in what he called "discourse." He refused to discuss power in terms of outright repression; rather, he preferred to describe the subtle mechanisms by which power affects discourse, voice, and daily life. By analyzing how power relationships played out in such institutions as prisons and hospitals, Foucault challenged the assumption that power emanates solely from government, armies, legislative processes, or law courts. Rather, he believed that there are numerous loci of power, each propagating a competing truth with its own justification. Thus, for Foucault, power is always a discursive relation rather than something that a person or group wields or bears. Foucault believed that "history is differentiated and fragmented into particular discourses, and that each fragment has a threshold, a process of birth and an equally complex process of disappearance that can be analyzed and described".[3]

This broad social vision for a more nuanced definition of power helps to illuminate curricular research. Foucault argues that power is used to legitimize knowledge: to decide which knowledge or truth is the correct one. The rise and fall of the NHSP, I believe, bears out his argument. This study shows how the individuals who initiated the movement for standards in the humanities used their public and private positions to create a new discourse in humanities education, a deliberate counter to the liberal discourse then emanating from the university. It was this new discourse that led to the NHSP, and it was this new discourse that, in the end, procured its downfall. By analyzing participants' writings and published speeches, I demonstrate how reformers in various positions of power worked together to create these new discourses.

Thus I argue that by the early 1980s two competing discourses about history education were set on a collision course. In 1983 the report *A Nation at Risk* set the conservative agenda. This agenda was then fleshed out by research conducted by private intellectuals working mostly at conservative think tanks during the 1980s. The other discourse, ultimately embodied in the *Standards*, was articulated by liberal academics trained in the new social history. Debate escalated between the two discourses during the 1980s and early 1990s, polarizing the contenders into irreconcilable camps. Upon the publication of the *National Standards for History* in October 1994, these two discourses clashed in a dramatic public confrontation heightened by the charged political atmosphere surrounding the Republicans' sweeping victory at the polls.

But it is important to remember that the standards movement of the 1980s and 1990s is only the most recent of a succession of reform cycles that periodically arise in response to intellectual, social, and political events. My findings suggest that the 1994 counterattack by conservatives against the *Standards* was merely one episode in an ongoing struggle to regain control of the curriculum from liberal educational reformers, which had begun in earnest with the election of Ronald Reagan, but whose antecedents can be traced much farther back, to the early decades of this century.

In order to study the complex interactions among reformers and their constituents in the government, the academy, the press, and private institutions, I bring to bear historiographical methods that are relatively new in the field of education. One such method is a variant of prosopography, or collective biography. By analyzing the interactions of key participants in the reform movement over a number of years and how their professional lives converged and intersected, I show how individuals and groups form shifting alliances in pursuit of their aims; how these networks coalesce, dissolve, and form again along new lines; how centers of power and legitimation are created; how consensus is forged or breaks down. I also draw on the methodology of intellectual history and a close reading of texts to situate the NHSP within the broader intellectual and cultural debates of the times and to establish links between ideology, power, and reform.

PERSONAL ROLE IN THE PROJECT

Before I begin my historical analysis of the National History Standards Project, I must first describe my personal role as the project's assistant director, and the impact this has had on my research. As a principal in the project, I acquired firsthand knowledge, including the chronology of events, the building of consensus, the successive drafts of the *Standards*, and the political maneuverings around them. I was directly involved in every phase of the project, from helping the principal investigator, Professor Charlotte Crabtree, write the grant proposals submitted to the National Endowment for the Humanities (NEH) and the U.S. Department of Education (DOE), to organizing and overseeing many of the *Standards*-drafting workshops (particularly those in world history), representing the project nationally at conferences and on television and radio talk shows, defending the project during the eighteen-month period when the *Standards* were under attack by Congress and the media, and, finally, helping with the process of re-drafting the *Standards* in the aftermath of the crisis. My experiences within the project gave me insights into the process of setting a national educational reform, with all of its political overtones, and I acquired a unique perspective to guide my research.

However, in 1996, when I left the NCHS, I was still too close to the project and reeling from the effects of the prolonged controversy to be able to broaden my perspective beyond composing a memoir. With this limited view, it seemed obvious that the American political climate had undergone a sea change with the election in 1994 of the first Republican Congress in more than forty years. I had observed politicians such as Newt Gingrich and Senator Slade Gorton, as well as pundits such as Lynne V. Cheney, Rush Limbaugh, John Leo, and Charles Krauthammer, riding the rising conservative tide. For them, the history *Standards*, tarred with the brush of excessive "political correctness," made a convenient target. I watched as politicians and pundits proved their patriotism and their fiscal conservatism by assailing them. Not only did the *Standards* represent postmodernism run amuck, they contended, but also the squandering of taxpayers' dollars by the National Endowment for the Humanities and the U.S. Department of Education.

EVOLUTION OF TOPIC

This was the personal narrative about the *Standards* project that I had constructed at the time. However, my present research questions have evolved far beyond my original concerns about the inner workings of a particular educational reform. For my doctorate in education I decided to research the origins of the NHSP project, hoping to broaden the historical context by enlarging its temporal framework. By tracing the intellectual pedigree of this project I hoped to learn more about the reform cycle within which the NHSP was embedded. This exercise, however, opened, quite serendipitously, another perspective. As I read the foundational documents that led to the standards movement, I became interested in the relationship between knowledge production and power, and how this relationship affects curricular policy. By following the genesis of the project, I was able to see who held political power at various stages of the reform, and how those wielding power were able to use their positions to define normative knowledge. I began to ask questions such as: Who gets to decide policy? How do reformers win the public over to their cause? How do they legitimize their reforms? How do reformers coalesce to work together—or fail to do so? How do politicians use the "bully pulpit" to influence educational policy? What is the role of the media and public intellectuals in the process? What were the intellectual and ideological positions that informed the NHSP, and where did they come from historically? What knowledge, and whose knowledge, was considered legitimate and accepted as the basis for reform at various stages as the NHSP evolved? In what ways did public institutions, private institutions, and the press serve as platforms for reformers of different stripes? How did reformers derive and exercise power from these various sources? What discourses, narratives, and rhetorical devices did reformers create for themselves and for others in order to legitimize their ideas about what history should be taught? What was the role of consensus in the legitimization of knowledge? How was consensus achieved during the NHSP, then shattered, and finally reconstructed?

These questions led me to revise my original analysis. While I still feel that the 1994 attack on the *Standards* was largely the result of political opportunism, I now understand that the attack was merely an episode in a neo-conservative struggle to control the curriculum that had been going on for over a decade. I now grasp the essential paradox inherent in the standards-setting process: the attack on the *Standards* was the logical outcome of their complex genesis. The very conservatives who had pushed for higher academic standards in history in the hope of shoring up traditional canons felt cheated—understandably—by the end product, masterminded by their intellectual adversaries. From their point of view, they had lost control of the standards-setting process and therefore the *Standards* embodied all of the multicultural excesses they abhorred. This resulted in their violent reaction when the document was published late in 1994.

BOOK OVERVIEW

This history of the National History Standards Project is broken down into the following chapters. Chapter 1 provides the context and antecedents for this study. It describes the interplay between intellectual movements, political factors, and reform agendas. The chapter situates the NHSP within its historical context: the cyclical battles over the American curriculum fought since 1900. Chapter 2 traces the paradigm shift that took place in the historical profession between 1960 and 1990.

During this period historians changed not only the subjects of their research, but the questions they asked. This mapping of historiographical trends helps situate the standards reform within the broader intellectual currents of the times, and sets the stage for the conservative reaction that followed. Chapter 3 shifts ground to analyze the political climate in which the call for reform was first uttered. Here I trace the genesis of a neo-conservative movement in the humanities that developed during the Reagan and Bush eras, and that still dominates the reform agenda today. I then analyze the culture wars that erupted between liberal reformers and neo-conservatives. Chapter 4 traces the history of the National Center for History in the Schools and the National History Standards Project, which were created in response to the conservative call for reform, but ended up in the hands of historians who did not share that vision. Chapter 5 describes the two-and-one-half-year consensus process by which the National History Standards were constructed, and shows how the liberal discourse began to reassert itself. Chapter 6 recounts how this consensus unraveled under criticism from conservatives who had initiated the reform project and how a new consensus was then established. In conclusion, Chapter 7 offers a reflection on the NHSP, and on the lessons that may be learned from it about the political pressures that overshadow curricular reform.

1

History Repeats Itself

*Reform Cycles and the
Social Studies Curriculum*

IN 1989 PRESIDENT GEORGE H. W. BUSH summoned the nation's fifty governors to an unprecedented education summit in Charlottesville, Virginia. The goal of this meeting was to find remedies for a perceived national educational crisis, which had been identified six years earlier by the National Commission on Excellence in Education in its report *A Nation at Risk*.[1] At this historic meeting, the governors developed the National Education Goals, which the President adopted a year later. The development of internationally competitive standards for educational excellence now became national policy. Goal Three, out of the six education goals defined by the governors, identified history as one of five core school subjects for which challenging national achievement standards should be established. Thus history education was assured a prominent place in national education reform. In the wake of the governors' summit, bipartisan support grew for development of "world-class" standards in education. In 1991 Congress passed Bush's America 2000 Act,[2] calling for national standards, and in 1994 Congress sustained support for national standards by passing Clinton's Goals 2000: Educate America Act.[3]

THE NATIONAL HISTORY STANDARDS PROJECT

It was in this climate of bipartisan collaboration that the National History Standards Project was launched. In 1992 Lynne V. Cheney, Chair of the National Endowment for the Humanities, and Diane Ravitch, Assistant Secretary of Education for the Office of Educational Research and Improvement at the U.S. Department of Education, both strong advocates for national standards, joined together to fund the National Center for History in the Schools (NCHS), budgeting $1.6 million to develop a broad consensus defining excellence in the teaching and learning of history in the nation's schools.

Armed with these funds, the NCHS went to work to develop comprehensive standards for American and world history. The National History Standards Project represented an unprecedented collaboration among public school teachers, state social studies specialists, school superintendents, university historians, professional and scholarly organizations, public interest groups, and parents' and teachers' organizations, all of whom devoted sustained time and energy to the success of this project. Under development for thirty-two months, the *Standards* were the product of a national forum in which ultimately hundreds of educators pored over, disputed, revised, and refined numerous drafts of the documents. By October 1994, the *Standards* books were in press, with a general feeling throughout much of the educational community that national consensus had been achieved, and that the *Standards* represented a blending of the best historical scholarship and best teaching practice that this nation had to offer.

This apparent consensus over the *Standards* was destined to unravel even before the books were off the press. On October 24, 1994, Lynne Cheney, one of the project's co-funders, wrote an opinion piece in the *Wall Street Journal* lambasting the soon-to-be-released *Standards*, charging the authors with writing a "politically correct" version of the American past, riddled with extravagant multiculturalism, at the expense of a more traditional history celebrating America's many triumphs and heroes. With this single article, Cheney launched a prolonged and passionate controversy over our nation's past that would rage for eighteen months. The controversy came to a head on January 18, 1995, when the United States Senate passed its resolution condemning the recently published *National Standards for History*. However, such controversy was not unique in the annals of American educational history.

THE HISTORIC STRUGGLE FOR THE AMERICAN CURRICULUM

Throughout the twentieth century successive waves of reformers, textbook publishers, curriculum commissions, and national boards have fought battles over the content of the curriculum. Parents and community members have frequently joined in because traditionally the curriculum has been the primary site for each generation to define itself and transmit its values to the next. Christine Sleeter and Carl Grant describe this struggle from a postmodern perspective: "debates about curriculum content can be understood broadly as struggles for power to define the symbolic representation of the world and of society, that will be transmitted to the young, for the purpose of either gaining or holding onto power."[4] Many other theorists, such as Michel Foucault, Michael Kirst, Michael Apple, Stanley Aronowitz, Henry Giroux, Joel Spring, and Peter McLaren, have come to the same conclusion: that knowledge is a valued commodity, defined by those with power and dispensed to those without.[5]

However, from time to time the curriculum itself becomes a vehicle to challenge those power relationships and to transform society.[6] If we analyze the historical struggle over the curriculum, two competing themes emerge, waxing and waning with the tides of political change. Social control competes with social justice; individual rights compete with collective rights. At the heart of this curricular divide lies the question: Is the purpose of schooling to maximize individual potential, or should schools be an instrument of social reform? Are these two goals compatible? Since the answer to this fundamental question taps into our deepest beliefs about human potential and social responsibility in a democracy, the curriculum has, and always will be, contested terrain.

Although society will always be fundamentally divided over what knowledge and whose knowledge should be handed down from one generation to the next, public debates over the curriculum usually arise when the larger society undergoes accelerated political or social change. One such reform movement occurred in the late nineteenth century, when the twin pressures of rapid industrialization and urbanization dramatically transformed the social role of schools. Traditionally, rural Americans had relied upon the family and community for the transmission of social values, and teachers were selected for the degree to which they mirrored the values of the local community. When rapid industrialization and mass immigration brought millions of people to the cities, schools were suddenly called upon to mediate between the urban family and the complex and impersonal world outside it.[7] With this change in the social role of schools came a national battle over who would control the curriculum. Society displaced its fears and hopes onto the school curriculum, and a new Progressive reform movement arose to meet the challenge of social change.

Over the decades curricular scholars and educational historians have identified cyclical patterns that these reform movements have historically followed.[8] Successive waves of curricular reform periodically wash over the American educational landscape in response to intellectual, social, and political events. The standards movement of the 1980s and 1990s is the most recent of these recurring waves of reform. Usually reform movements begin as responses to a perceived threat, and usually they reflect shifts in the political climate. For example, liberal eras such as the 1930s and 1960s focused national attention on child-centered curricula and educational equity, while conservative eras such as the 1890s and 1950s focused attention on the nation's struggle for economic or military survival, and therefore on how students can be taught to meet those challenges. The National History Standards Project falls into this latter category of conservative reform. Fear that America was embarking on a downward economic spiral, and that Japan was rising inexorably, spawned the reform for higher academic standards, including the NHSP.

According to educational historian Herbert Kliebard, the four curriculum forces that would shape the American curriculum had already emerged by the beginning of the twentieth century.[9] The first force was made up of traditionalists, or "humanists." This group consisted of scholars from the academic disciplines who fought a heroic battle to preserve the heritage of Western culture in the face of accelerating social change. Academics such as Charles W. Eliot, the president of Harvard University, and the prestigious members of the "Committee of Ten" (1893) established the "mental disciplines" (traditional academic subjects) and "college entrance requirements" as the core of the American curriculum. The humanists looked backward to the Greek and Roman classics for inspiration. According to them, forward progress in an age of social change would depend on our ability to preserve our classical heritage and transmit it to successive generations of students through the canon of "liberal education." This canon should be available to all students, not just the elite.

The concept of "liberal education" originally came from England. Writing during the mid-nineteenth century, John Henry Newman first defined liberal education. Newman believed that the Judeo-Christian and Graeco-Roman heritage of the West were unquestionably the two greatest religious and intellectual achievements of all time. Through the Bible, Revelation, and the Western canon of literature and science, civilization had acquired the complete body of knowledge necessary for attainment of spiritual and intellectual perfection. For Newman, culture was an end in itself and could be learned only through the canon of liberal education. Matthew Arnold, another Oxbridge Englishman, elaborated on the concept of liberal education. He became the apostle of a new culture, a culture that would pursue perfection through a knowledge and understanding of the "best that has been thought and said in the world." Whereas Newman saw culture as an end in itself, Arnold saw it as having the power to transform society. In his own words, culture would provide "the noble aspiration to leave the world better and happier than we found it." Fearing class warfare and revolution in 19th-century England, Arnold believed that high culture could provide the unifying glue that would bind society together. He believed that the very welfare of the nation was contingent upon inculcating a sense of cultural identity that would stand above class loyalty. Both Newman's and Arnold's concept of liberal education had a profound influence on the humanists and has influenced curriculum theory down to our own time.[10]

Against these stalwart defenders of tradition three Progressive reform groups emerged, all rejecting the "mental disciplines" approach proffered by the humanists, yet all disagreeing with one another on what the ultimate aim of education should be. The first Progressive reform movement to challenge traditional education was called the "child-study" movement, which looked back to Jean Jacques Rousseau for inspiration. Its leaders, such as G. Stanley Hall and John Dewey, theorized that curriculum should be designed around the developmental stages of the child, not around abstract disciplines.[11] The new science of psychology would provide the data needed for understanding the stages of child development. Theoretically, a child-centered curriculum and pedagogy grounded in these developmental stages would release the natural powers within each child. Society would progress as a result.[12]

The second group of progressive reformers, the "social efficiency" educators, was enamored of the scientific management techniques that were making American business and industry the envy of the world. These reformers wanted to apply the principles of factory management, as outlined in Frederick Winslow Taylor's 1911 *Principles of Scientific Management*, to the management of schools. They recommended a differentiated curriculum that would prepare students for adult participation in a technology-based society where specialization and mass production were the rule. In order to prepare students for their adult lives, schools began tracking students by aptitude and ability. With the help of IQ tests, school administrators thought they could predict students' future societal roles, and sort them accordingly into academic and vocational tracks. Waste of any sort was anathema to these reformers. With the publication of Franklin Bobbit's 1912 article "The Elimination of Waste in Education," social efficiency became the predominant pattern for school organization across urban America. Although they considered themselves to be Progressive reformers, social efficiency experts were as much at odds with the child developmentalists as they were with the more traditional humanists.[13]

The last Progressive reform group to appear was the "social meliorist" movement, represented most eloquently by Lester Frank Ward. In his 1882 book, *Dynamic Sociology*, he turned the Social Darwinists' argument of laissez-faire capitalism on its head. Rather than accepting as given the Social Darwinist principle that humans are subject to the same laws of nature as animals (i.e., "survival of the fittest"), the social meliorists argued instead that human beings could intervene and use their intelligence to construct a new social order through the social institutions that they created. The social meliorists believed that schools would be the major force in bringing about this new social order. For them, education was the key to social progress.[14] They dismissed the humanists, the child developmentalists, and the social-efficiency educators alike as too narrow in their vision for transformative social justice reform.

Thus the traditionalist paradigm of the late nineteenth century, when academic disciplines and the canon of Western civilization constituted the core of the American curriculum, was overturned by Progressive reformers as the schools sought to respond to rapid industrialization and mass immigration. No longer could an intellectual canon and pedagogical approach designed for a privileged few serve a society undergoing rapid social change. This battle between those who believe that schools should reproduce the existing social order and those who believe schools should transform it has been refought at intervals. Usually those in power want to preserve the status quo, and those without power want to challenge it. At each stage an uneasy consensus emerges. However, consensus is ephemeral and lasts only as long as the current political tide. For example, during the depths of the Depression, when capitalism itself seemed imperiled, radical curriculum reforms flourished at the center of the curricular debate.[15] However, by 1941, when World War II came along to resuscitate capitalism, the radicals were pushed to the fringe of the Progressive education movement. During the 1940s and 1950s, when economic times were good, a complete reaction set in as America went about its business of doing business. A curriculum based on the twin principles of social efficiency and individual achievement moved to center stage.[16]

Throughout the twentieth century these four reform models would vie for center stage as successive waves of reform advanced and receded. Depending on the economic, political and social climate of a given time or place, policymakers representing one of these four theoretical frameworks would arise proffering the remedy needed to save the American curriculum. However, their success would be ephemeral: conditions changed, and another group then rose to take their place. In the end, curricular change evolved piecemeal as American schools absorbed various aspects of successive reform movements. No reform was ever adopted in toto: rather, ideas were absorbed in myriad ways as schools experimented with them. The result has been an educational tapestry woven of strands from these various reform movements.[17]

These curricular currents and debates play out within a complex educational infrastructure. If one maps this infrastructure, one can better understand the politics of curricular debates and the institutionalized obstacles to democratic reform. Politicians, from the President all the way down to members of local school boards, have specific views on who gets educated and how. In making policy they must respond to their respective political constituencies and to special-interest groups, such as the large foundations, teachers' unions, and corporations. Theoretically, these are democratic forces that should counteract one another and produce an outcome beneficial to all. However, many of these powerful interest groups are not directly accountable to the public: the research funders, the testing industry, and the publishing industry, to name a few.[18] The resulting logjam of competing interests and lobbies makes serious, sustained educational reform a complex and highly contentious affair.

The emergence of the Scholastic Aptitude Test (SAT) as the single most influential college entrance exam reveals how interest groups can set national policy that is essentially private and beyond the control of the electorate. In *The Big Test* Nicholas Lemann offers a provocative account of how the Educational Testing Service, the organization responsible for developing the SAT, was created by "just a handful of quietly influential people, . . . privately, outside the purview of politics and open debate."[19] The Educational Testing Service, a private institution, ultimately gained a near-monopoly over who gets into first-rate universities and who does not, by developing the Scholastic Aptitude Test and the Advanced Placement (AP) tests. The avowed goal was to create a test that would identify a meritocracy in which talent could be recognized and rewarded with access to the best universities. But in practice the SAT and AP scores correlate more with parental income than with the student's subsequent college grades. Thus the tests replicate the class system from generation to generation, rather than overturn it. As Lemann demonstrates, the result has been to create a new quasi-hereditary elite that reproduces itself through the very system that was meant to challenge generational privilege. By the 1990s, high

SAT and AP test scores and access to first-class universities had become a new form of privilege handed down from one generation to the next. However, the establishment of this new hereditary meritocracy was achieved beneath public radar. Indeed, Lemann claims, "standardized testing for college and graduate school admissions was one of the most consequential arrangements put in place without public consensus behind it in the late 20th century."[20]

In fact, Michael Kirst argues that the college admission requirements, the Educational Testing Service, and a few dozen textbook publishers control the high school curriculum.[21] What is notable here is that these private corporations, whose interest is to preserve the existing social order, are not necessarily accountable to the public. They operate outside the system of checks and balances that supposedly forms the basis of our democratic government, and they respond solely to market forces. If we leave policymaking to these institutions and the play of market forces, it raises serious questions about how democratic that policy can be.

In order to understand better how these reform cycles, institutional realities, and competing agendas have affected the curriculum in the past, I will examine two high-profile reforms that preceded the National History Standards Project. One was the "social reconstruction" movement of the 1920s and 1930s; the other was a curriculum developed during the 1960s and 1970s called *Man: A Course of Study*. Both projects were conceived as model "social studies" curricula: Social studies, as I shall explain in Chapter 5, was an amalgam of history, geography, economics, anthropology, sociology, political science, and psychology, which had taken shape during the Progressive era in an effort to update these traditional specializations by combining the elements of them deemed relevant to the modern era. Both projects were initiated by university scholars, both were as unconventional as they were visionary, both were widely acclaimed by the national educational community, and both eventually provoked a storm of controversy among the public and politicians. Although these two curriculum reform efforts were much more radical than the National History Standards Project, their histories present instructive parallels.

THE SOCIAL RECONSTRUCTION MOVEMENT: 1920S AND 1930S

The social reconstruction movement of the 1920s and 1930s challenged the status quo by proposing a radical social justice agenda. Building on the social meliorist tradition of Lester Frank Ward, the social reconstructionists were unequivocal in their belief that the purpose of education is fundamentally social. Indeed, they expounded a visionary role for schools as primary agents of social and economic change. Schools would be in the vanguard of social reform by directly addressing chronic social and economic problems through the curriculum.

Before the stock market crash of 1929 the social reconstructionist movement coexisted uneasily within the Progressive education movement. While the leftist social reconstructionists were tolerated under the Progressive umbrella during the "Roaring Twenties," there was no particular reason for their radical theories to take precedence over the more moderate child-centered or social efficiency theories of the times. In fact, America during the 1920s boasted the highest rate of industrial growth in the world. Superficially, few Americans had reason to question the onward and upward march of capitalism. However, many intellectuals saw through the surface prosperity and suspected that not all was well in "Babbit-land." Beneath the apparent gaiety grew an undercurrent of discontent about the health of the American economic and social system. The work of the Muckrakers, the rise of Eugene Debs, the Russian Revolution, and the rise within the progressive education movement of radicals such as Harold Rugg and George Counts, the founding fathers of the social reconstructionist movement, all represented a growing constituency that questioned the social justice of Hoover's America. With the crash of 1929 and the long unemployment lines of the early 1930s, large numbers of Americans joined this radical group in their critical examination of capitalism and their call for social justice.

The social reconstruction movement envisioned the curriculum as the vehicle by which social injustice would be redressed and the evils of capitalism corrected. Through a radical reform of the social studies curriculum, a new generation of students would be critically attuned to the defects of the capitalist system, and prepared to improve it. Arguing against discipline-based history and geography, Harold Rugg and George Counts proposed that social studies texts should explore enduring social problems and help students engage in critical inquiry and open discussion around contemporary social issues. The new social studies curriculum should be developed around its "social worth."[22]

In the *Twenty-Sixth Yearbook* of the National Society for the Study of Education, Rugg argued that the current curriculum field was biased toward "academic formulae, child interests, or the scientific study of society."[23] In Rugg's view, each reform was too limited and narrow in its goals and failed to grapple with current problems in American life. Rugg's overarching goal was for the curriculum to catch up with modern American life and to lead the way toward the social reconstruction of society. He argued, "It is not refinement of existing 'subjects' that is most sorely needed, it is rather, the radical reconstruction of the entire school curriculum. The content of the current curriculum does not really deal directly and vigorously with the crucial forces, institutions, and problems of American civilization."[24]

Thus the new curriculum should be based on a comprehensive and scientific study of society, conducted by a group of scholarly experts. Indeed, Rugg envisioned a huge collaborative undertaking to remake the curriculum out of whole cloth.

> One of the most needed first steps in reconstruction is a new synthesis of knowledge and a re-departmentalization of the activities and materials of the school curriculum. . . . The tasks of curriculum making are manifold and difficult and can be carried on effectively only by professionally equipped specialists. The day is past in which a single individual—be he professor, teacher, administrator, psychologist, sociologist, or research specialist of whatever brand—can encompass all these tasks single-handed.[25]

Although Rugg never achieved this huge collaborative undertaking, he was one of the few curricular scholars who ever had the opportunity to put their theories directly into practice. In 1922 he created his own social studies textbook series around the fundamental problems faced by American society. By 1939, *Man and His Changing Society* had sold over one million copies, and the accompanying workbook had sold over two million copies.[26] Each volume in the series dealt with a different social issue. Some books attempted to break down stereotypes, and others pointed out the disparity between rich and poor. Many of his ideas were very radical for the time, anticipating the social historians and critical pedagogists of the late twentieth century. For example, in Rugg's discussion of immigrants, he expanded the definition to include the story of involuntary immigrants who were brought to America as slaves. In another book, Rugg used photographs to demonstrate the disparity between rich and poor in American society. He contrasted rich suburban neighborhoods with inner-city slums. Other books stressed the theme that the free enterprise system should be restrained. In spite of their radicalism, Rugg's textbooks found a sympathetic audience during the 1930s. Literally millions of American schoolchildren grew up reading them. However, by 1939, with the approach of war, the heyday of social reconstructionism was over. With an external threat looming, criticism of American society could not be tolerated. Instead, a groundswell of patriotism insured that Rugg and Counts would no longer be in vogue. It is no coincidence that in 1940, Rugg's textbooks, after nearly twenty years of success, were suddenly attacked as unpatriotic, and pulled from the shelves by his publisher. Rugg's texts were accused of debunking heroes, criticizing our Constitution, condemning the American system of private ownership and capitalism, and undermining traditional morality—all accusations that would later be leveled at the *Standards*.[27] With the condemnation of Rugg's textbooks, social justice was taken off the curricular agenda and the educational community moved on to an era of social efficiency and scientific management.[28] For two complacent decades no one dared challenge the status quo. However, Rugg's and Counts's contributions to the theory of social reconstructionism would become part of the rich fabric of American education and would surface again when times were propitious.

MAN: A COURSE OF STUDY: 1960S AND 1970S

Given the more expansive economic and political climate of the 1960s, another social studies curriculum project emerged that would once again challenge the status quo and fall victim, inevitably, to controversy. Funded with $6.5 million from the National Science Foundation (NSF) and developed under the leadership of Harvard psychologist Jerome Bruner and Harvard educationist Peter Dow, an innovative sixth-grade curriculum, *Man: A Course of Study* (MACOS), would eventually go down in history as one of the most dramatic instances of public indignation against the efforts of discipline-based scholars to create progressive curricular reform. The MACOS curriculum, like Harold Rugg's textbooks twenty-five years earlier and the *National Standards for History* twenty years later, would come under fierce conservative criticism.

MACOS began, like the *Standards*, as part of a presidential initiative to create higher academic curricula in the schools. In a special address to Congress in January 1958, President Eisenhower asked for an unprecedented fivefold increase in funding for educational initiatives sponsored by the NSF.[29] Spurred on by the *Sputnik* crisis and the public perception that American students were falling perilously behind their Soviet counterparts in science education, Congress enacted the National Defense Education Act of 1958.[30] This level of federal involvement represented a new chapter in American educational history, and ultimately resulted in a $500 million NSF investment in curriculum projects over the next two decades.

The unlikely leader of this university-based curriculum reform era was physicist Jerrold Zacharias, who, in 1956, took leave from his academic position at MIT to found the Physical Sciences Study Committee (PSSC). Here he spearheaded a curricular reform in the physical sciences. Following his lead, dozens of scholars in other disciplines left their ivory towers to create new K–12 course materials. Not since the "Committee of Ten" convened in 1893 had so many academic scholars taken up the mantle of K–12 reform. Like the Committee of Ten, scholars during the 1960s and 1970s created K–12 curricula based on the structures of their academic disciplines and the methods of academic scholarship.

This new inductive pedagogy was called "discovery" or "inquiry" learning. In these new courses, scholars asked students to form and test their own hypotheses and to conduct experiments mimiking their own. Teams of scholars selected a wide variety of learning materials, including primary sources, manipulatives, games, and film. They believed that classroom lessons should provide opportunities for students to make discoveries, just the way scientists do. According to Bruner,

> What a scientist does at his desk or in his laboratory, what a literary critic does in reading a poem, are of the same order as what anybody else does when he is engaged in like activities—if he is to achieve understanding. The difference is in degree, not in kind. The schoolboy learning physics is a physicist, and it is easier for him to learn physics behaving like a physicist than doing something else . . . [31]

Before long these courses were dubbed the "new math," the "new science," and the "new social studies." The educational community embraced these new experimental curricula wholeheartedly. MACOS would be one of the curriculum projects funded by the NSF and directed by subject matter specialists.

This NSF-sponsored reform movement was one of the few times in the history of American education when university-based research scholars, not professional educationists, led the design of K–12 curricular reform. The National History Standards Project would be another. A brief history of MACOS illustrates just how difficult it is to combine academic idealism with the everyday realities of K–12 education. While research scholars are undoubtedly the best qualified to determine the content of the K–12 curriculum, they often evade public opinion and common sense in their eagerness to bring research knowledge directly into the classroom. By challenging conventional wisdom about course content and teaching methods, the MACOS reformers ultimately succeeded in alienating parents, publishers, and politicians, anticipating the fate of the historians who would lead the National History Standards Project.[32]

Jerome Bruner articulated the philosophy of this scholar-initiated curriculum movement in his classic 1963 book, *The Process of Educa-*

tion: "We begin with the hypothesis that any subject can be taught effectively in some intellectually honest form to any child at any stage of development."[33] Subscribing to the latest principles in developmental psychology, enunciated by Jean Piaget, Bruner believed that if course materials stimulated students' natural curiosity and were presented in a developmentally appropriate manner, there was no limit to what children could learn. He called his approach "the spiral curriculum," meaning that students would revisit central issues and themes at greater levels of complexity as they matured.[34]

Bruner first described his vision for the MACOS curriculum in his 1966 book, *Toward a Theory of Instruction*. Under the influence of structural anthropologists such as Claude Lévi-Strauss, Bruner's overarching goal for MACOS was to help sixth-grade students understand what it means to be human. Bruner posed three questions that would guide the social studies curriculum: What is human about human beings, how did they get that way, and how can they be made more so?[35] Drawing on current work in structural anthropology, Bruner wanted to design opportunities for young students to compare human behavior with that of other species, and to encourage students to consider the distinctive characteristics of human beings that span cultures, such as language, tool-making, social organization, childrearing, and so on.

The MACOS course first examined the uniqueness of being human by contrasting human behavior with animal behavior. By studying the life cycles of salmon, herring gulls, and baboons and comparing them to human life, students would "discover" that only humans possess language, and consequently the ability to change the world around them. After studying animals, students would turn to a study of an indigenous culture very different from their own, the Netsilik Eskimos. (Bruner chose the Netsilik as a subject of study for MACOS because he was able to acquire the rights to extensive film footage taken by a Swedish anthropologist. It is ironic that someone who believed so strongly that disciplinary knowledge and developmental criteria should guide curricular choices ended up choosing the Netsilik subject matter based on the random availability of film footage.) Due to the extreme harshness of their Arctic environment, the Netsilik faced moral dilemmas such as whether to execute first-born females in a hunting culture that depends on males for survival, and the burden of caring for old people beyond their industrious years. Using contrast as a pedagogical technique (i.e., humans vs. higher primates [baboons], modern humans vs. prehistoric humans, contemporary humans vs. aboriginal humans, and adults vs. children), Bruner hoped that sixth-grade students would come to appreciate how different societies come to understand their world and that one kind of worldview is no more human than another.[36]

The course was considered to be a breakthrough both in its content and its pedagogy. In 1969 Bruner received an award from the American Educational Research Association and the American Textbook Publishers Institute for his leadership in the development of MACOS. He was credited with having made "one of the most important efforts of our time to relate research findings and theory in educational psychology to the development of new and better instructional material."[37] By 1974, when approximately 328,000 students in 1,728 schools in 47 states were using MACOS, teachers responding to a National Council for the Social Studies survey rated MACOS second best overall and best of all federally funded curricular projects.[38]

However, by 1975, the course was awash in controversy. Many parents and politicians found the harsh realities of the Netsilik films very disturbing, and many found the course's advocacy of cultural relativism unacceptable, especially for sixth graders. The Netsilik materials, which consisted in large part of graphic documentary films, were designed to illustrate that there is no significant difference between the intellectual and imaginative capacity of Eskimos leading a traditional hunter/gatherer way of life in the Arctic and the intellectual and imaginative capacity of modern-day Americans. Although the Netsilik practiced infanticide and gerontocide, the MACOS course treated cultural differences as a reflection of environmental conditions, not moral character. To judge other cultures by American values, the course suggested, was to deny the Netsilik their humanity. The units examining animal behavior and animal life cycles also raised delicate topics such as sexual promiscuity, parenting, and evolution. By 1975, with the newly dubbed Moral Majority flexing its political muscle, conservative parents in several states began to campaign against the federally funded course by writing stinging opinion pieces in local newspapers. They objected to content dealing with reproduction, aggression, killing, religion, and views of life and death.[39]

In mid-1975 the MACOS controversy reached the halls of Congress. Representative John B. Conlan of Arizona singled it out for a stern rebuke during hearings before the House Committee on Science and Technology, which he chaired, and later in the full House discussion of appropriations for the National Science Foundation for 1976. According to Conlan, the MACOS curriculum challenged American values by exposing children to the customs of another culture at an early, receptive age. He opposed MACOS because he believed that the course encouraged children to question the existing social order and that it made them vulnerable to "foreign values and beliefs."[40]

The MACOS scandal brought the entire NSF sponsored reform movement to an abrupt end. As Peter Dow concluded, the Apollo moon landing in 1969 had erased the memory of *Sputnik* from the American psyche, and the *Sputnik*-inspired academics were sent back to their ivory towers by those who did not share their progressive notions of teaching and learning. Anthropological study by the young was now seen as a threat to traditional American values. In fact, religious conservatives argued that a social studies curriculum that deliberately set out to cultivate an inquiring attitude about human behavior and values was dangerous because it did not deal in absolutes. The mid-1970s brought about a new conservative cycle of reform. Politicians demanded a return to the basics: reading, writing, mathematics, history, and "Judeo-Christian values. The rise of political conservatism, along with renewed concern about federal control of the curriculum, brought the NSF-funded reform to its knees.[41]

The conflict between "traditional" and "progressive" views on education that began at the turn of the twentieth century continues down to the present. However, it never plays out in exactly the same way: Witness the 1990 controversy that broke out in Oakland over the adoption of the new Houghton Mifflin textbook series for social studies, which was assailed by advocates of an Afrocentrist curriculum for its alleged Eurocentrism. This time the liberal center was challenged from the political left, rather than from the right, as Rugg's textbooks and MACOS had been. After vociferous debate, the Oakland school district refused to adopt the textbook series. Ironically, this particular textbook series was perhaps the most fully developed multicultural textbook ever to be published for K–8 education.[42] The series' maverick publisher took a huge economic risk that forced it into near-bankruptcy for several years. What these cases point out, however, is that the curriculum is highly controversial.

The arguments against the *National Standards for History* echoed the attacks on Rugg's textbooks and the MACOS curriculum. The conservatives' attack centered on the *Standards'* assumption that the past was contested terrain, and that the history curriculum could be used for social transformation and redistribution of power. The stakes were high. As the critics well knew, "whoever controls the past controls the future; whoever controls the present, controls the past." As the NHSP controversy played out, all of the constituents weighed in because so much was at stake. Textbook publishers avoided the *Standards* like the plague, the Clinton administration distanced itself from them, the U.S. Senate condemned them, and the press berated them. Finally, the various philanthropic foundations concerned with education joined in to repair the damage, and to fund the building of a new consensus by a blue-ribbon panel. It produced a sanitized version of the *Standards*, but the impetus of reform had been temporarily halted.[43]

2

Mapping an Alternative History

Shifting Historical Paradigms, 1960–1990

D URING THE NINETEENTH CENTURY HISTORIANS were trained
to write historical narratives much as scientists were trained to
write their lab reports, through the voice of an omniscient and
objective narrator. Indeed, historians assumed that primary documents
found in archives were similar to laboratory results: The facts spoke
for themselves and required little interpretation. The historian's function was merely to uncover the documents, read them meticulously,
and narrate the results in order. As with lab reports, the results of historical research were assumed to be replicable. It was assumed that any
other researcher who had seen the same evidence and applied the same
rules of analysis would come up with the same objective historical
interpretation. But by the mid-1960s and 1970s historians had begun
to question their own objectivity and search for new research methodologies and modes of inquiry. A series of paradigm shifts took place
within the discipline over the next thirty years that would challenge
both the theory and practice of conventional scholarship.[1]

TRADITIONAL HISTORICAL PARADIGMS

The work of Thomas Kuhn, a historian of science, had a profound impact on the way historians and other social scientists thought about
their research. At first sight, however, it appears to have little to do
with the work of social scientists. Rather, it applied to how research
was conducted in the hard sciences. In his 1957 book, *The Copernican
Revolution*, Kuhn analyzed the gradual process by which sixteenth- and

seventeenth-century scientists shifted their fundamental thinking about the earth's position in the universe. This shift did not happen overnight. Rather, as Kuhn explains in his case study, the Aristotelian model of the universe (earth-centered) was replaced by the Newtonian (sun-centered) in a long, cumulative process that began with the work of Copernicus 150 years before Newton.[2] In his pioneering 1962 publication, *The Structure of Scientific Revolutions*, Kuhn developed this idea of gradual change into a general theory of how scientific knowledge evolves. He argued that a paradigm shift takes place when an existing orthodoxy is challenged by a community of scholars, and then replaced by a new one. With his model of paradigm shift, Kuhn challenged old theories about the process of scientific discovery, which rested on the romantic assumption that scientific breakthroughs were dramatic, episodic, and conceived by heroic geniuses working in isolation. Rather, Kuhn argued, scientific knowledge is socially constructed over a period of time. He documented how scientific knowledge moves forward, not by the "discoveries" or epiphanies of individual geniuses, but rather by consensus among scientific communities.[3] Thus consensus legitimates both the underlying theoretical framework and everyday scientific practice. When scientists subscribe to an accepted theoretical framework, such as a earth-centered universe in the days before Copernicus, they practice what Kuhn calls "normal science." However, when a proposed new theory fails to achieve consensus among the community of scientists, such as the heliocentric theory advanced by Copernicus, it is relegated to the margins of scientific inquiry. Kuhn labels such peripheral theories "abnormal science." When the scientific community finally agrees to adopt a new theory, a paradigm shift takes place. The new theory then becomes central to the discipline, guiding research and everyday practice and defining "normal science."[4]

Kuhn's model for scientific discovery rested on the belief that the human mind is organized by theories, reinforced by social conventions operating within the community of scientists. Inside this community, scientific revolutions occur when the everyday practice of "normal science" can no longer account for recurrent anomalies that scientific research uncovers. At this point, Kuhn argues, some scientists will find it necessary to break away from the old scientific paradigm and create a new one that offers a better explanation of those anomalies while preserving enough of the previous paradigm to make it acceptable to a majority of their colleagues. Except in cases like the sixteenth-century Copernican Revolution, when religious doctrine was turned upside-down by the new scientific paradigm, paradigm shifts usually occur within a specialized scientific community. Usually the paradigm shift is self-contained, rarely making waves outside the subdiscipline where the particular paradigm is fundamental to the everyday practice of normal science. The outside world remains largely ignorant of these changes.

The pre-Kuhnian, or "Enlightenment," model for scientific discovery portrayed scientists as individual heroes who "peer at nature with eyes that are value-free, neutral and objective."[5] According to this model, Newton discovered eternally true laws of motion and Lavoisier discovered oxygen by "seeing" better than their predecessors, not by rejecting their predecessors' fundamental beliefs and asking fundamentally different questions. Kuhn's model for how cohorts of scientists create new intellectual paradigms in order to accommodate confounding anomalies proposed a far more dynamic and human-centered process of scientific discovery than the Enlightenment model had allowed for. In doing this, Kuhn challenged the then-current belief that scientific truth was absolute, eternal, and waiting to be discovered. He also undermined the commonly believed perception that scientific progress is uninterrupted and linear.

Ironically, Kuhn's own model of paradigm shifts would affect the social sciences far more profoundly than it would ever affect the discipline of science. While scientists continued to go about their business as usual, largely ignoring Kuhn's theories, social scientists adopted Kuhn's theoretical lens as their own. Kuhn's analysis of scientific discovery provided a template for constructing a new social science paradigm. Whereas Kuhn looked at how knowledge was philosophically and socially constructed within relatively limited networks of scientists, social scientists took the argument one step further by placing those social constructions within the context of the larger social and political world. In this way the implications of Kuhn's findings were much more profound than he could ever have imagined. In fact, his theories brought about a seismic paradigm shift in the social sciences, where scholars were trying to derive their basic assumptions about how to conduct research from the heuristics of the hard sciences.

This paradigm shift dramatically altered the way most American historians would conduct their research. No longer would they view themselves as omniscient narrators of historical facts uncovered in the isolation of archives. During the 1960s and 1970s historians searched for a parallel model to Kuhn's for the social construction of historical truth. They began to pose the question: If scientific truth depends on the frame of reference of individual scientists and on consensus within the scientific community, than what does historical truth rest on?

History, they contended, could no longer be viewed from the Enlightenment perspective of cumulative, linear progress, based on the deeds of great men as revealed in the documents, nor could the idea of progress itself be taken for granted any longer.

EUROPEAN BEGINNINGS: THE *ANNALES* SCHOOL

This paradigm shift in American historical scholarship, however, had its roots in Europe after World War II, just as major paradigm shifts in American literary theory, philosophy, anthropology, and countless other disciplines evolved from European scholarship during the same period. This shift would eventually lead to a historiographical revolution, changing the questions historians would ask in all of the field's subdisciplines. Traditionally historians had examined the political and military deeds of great leaders, and the rise and fall of governments. However, in the period following World War II, this canonical approach to history, embedded in the paradigm of "liberal education," began to give way to a new research agenda. Perhaps because scholars had uncovered the hideous anomalies posed by two world wars, Nazi death camps, and Hiroshima, to mention a few major events, historians felt compelled to revisit the story of onward and upward progress, and to turn away from the concept of history as high politics to the study of broadly based social movements.

Beginning with the *Annales* school in France, founded by Lucien Febvre and Marc Bloch in 1929 and carried forward by Fernand Braudel after World War II, many European historians began to criticize the traditional dominance of political and diplomatic history, with its implied teleology. Instead, the *Annalistes* (named for their journal, *Annales d'Histoire, Économique et Sociale*), began to write what they termed "total history," or "history from below." They wanted to uncover the previously-neglected history of the unsung masses of humanity, not the elite. In fact, they believed that the old-fashioned chronicling of kings and battles was superficial. Rather, the *Annalistes* wanted to explain the gradual, long-term transformation of social and economic structures, which they believed determined the course of political events. To do so they used quantitative research methods, focusing particularly on demographic data. They collected statistics on everything quantifiable in their attempt to describe the underlying structures of society. They assembled tables of grain prices; births, marriages, conceptions, and deaths; rents and land values; and financial data. Total history, they believed, was the only way to tell the story of the vast majority of the population, which had left no records in the form of memoirs, diplomatic dispatches, and *belles lettres*. Out of this research would evolve a whole new field of demographic and family history.[6]

By the 1960s the *Annalistes* had not only created a whole new quantitative methodology, but also a whole new set of research questions for historical analysis. Their methodology replaced the traditional historical narrative of rulers' achievements or the rise of the nation-state with long-term demographic patterns and economic cycles. The result was a new historical paradigm, in Kuhn's terminology, that undermined the traditional paradigm. Social history replaced political history as the dominant mode of inquiry in European scholarship. This constituted a historiographical revolution of Kuhnian proportions that would soon affect scholarship in Britain, Italy, Germany, and eventually the United States, in the form of the "new social history," and later, the "new world history."[7]

THE NEW SOCIAL HISTORY

Traditionally, American historiography had always mirrored the dominant European paradigm. Until the impact of the *Annales* school began to be felt, it centered on the deeds of great leaders and the course of great wars. Social history, regarded as peripheral to mainstream research, was relegated to anecdotal accounts of women, children, the poor, and people of color as they went about their daily lives. While colorful, these sidebar social histories did not explain social change. Along these lines, the famous historian Arthur M. Schlesinger Jr. and historian Dixon Ryan Fox edited a thirteen-volume *History of American Life* in the 1930s that lingered on the margins of historical inquiry, strengthening the conventional historical interpretation of national progress at the hands of political elites, rather than challenging it from below.[8]

Historian Eric Foner labels this mainstream model of American historiography the "presidential synthesis," whereby American historians "understood the evolution of American society chiefly via presidential elections and administrations."[9] In a Kuhnian sense, the presidential synthesis was satisfactory as long as historians shared a general consensus about American unity and progress. However, this paradigm would soon be turned on its head as historians absorbed the *Annalistes's* quantitative methodology, and more importantly, as they began to realize that traditional myths about American destiny did not square with contemporary events that were tearing society apart: the civil rights movement, the Vietnam War, and the rise of feminism, to name a few. In a Kuhnian sense, these anomalies could no longer be accounted for by the traditional paradigm of a unified past and progress toward an even better future. "Abnormal" social science was beginning to challenge "normal" social science.

Social historians began to reject the old presidential synthesis and to invent a new problematic to incorporate these anomalies. As Alice Kessler-Harris puts it, the events of the 1960s challenged a new generation of historians

> to explore the dynamic interaction of a multiracial and multiethnic population; to understand how interest groups and classes competed for power; and to develop a sense of how race, sex, and ethnicity served to mold and inhibit conceptions of common national purpose . . . . Beginning with, then, the challenge of a divided society, rather than with the assumption of a unified one, social historians took the poor, the black, and the excluded as their special domain and set out to rewrite the history of the United States.[10]

Gary Nash, who would become co-director of the NHSP, and many of the other historians who would later participate in the NHSP were originally part of this new wave of social historians who adapted *Annales* methodology to the contours of American history. In fact, they were pioneers of the new social history. One of Nash's first publications, *Red, White, and Black*, not only staked out his position as a social historian, but also helped define the new paradigm.[11]

The huge postwar expansion of higher education made possible by the G.I. Bill greatly increased the number of historians available to specialize in the myriad new subfields carved out by the new research agenda. With all these new historians about, and a limitless research agenda, the history of ethnic and racial groups, labor, women, and immigrants could each be studied in its own right, with its own network of scholars and its own professional journals, associations, and discourses. As a result, historians more and more came to identify with their own subdisciplines; the presidential synthesis was "dead and not lamented."[12] Specialization became normal science; teleological synthesis became abnormal. One only needs to consult the program for the annual conference of the Organization of American Historians over the last twenty-five years to confirm this paradigmatic shift.

Perhaps the two subdisciplines of American history that changed most radically during the 1970s and 1980s were African-American history and women's history. According to historian Thomas C. Holt, African-American scholarship before the civil rights movement focused on the oppression of blacks, portraying blacks only through their relationship to white men. The predominantly white historians wrote about black history as "the sum of white oppression."[13] While taking an apologetic stance, historians nevertheless viewed their subject from their own hegemonic position. White historians viewed African Americans as passive, basing their research on the unexamined assumption that blacks lacked agency over their own lives. Whether as slaves, sharecroppers, victims of Jim Crow laws, or urban dwellers, blacks were the subjects of a paternalistic discourse.

In sharp contrast with this earlier historiography, historians during the 1970s and 1980s now switched vantage points and began to research black history as black people had experienced it. Scholars such as Herbert Gutman, John Blassingame, Eugene Genovese, and Lawrence Levine began to frame new research questions as they uncovered new documentary sources such as slave records, diaries, and songs.[14] For the first time in historical research, the "slave *mentalité* became a problematic research question."[15] Historians began to conclude that slaves had created communities outside their masters' control, that family life thrived in spite of forced separations, and that slaves created their own form of Christianity. As Holt puts it, "slaves were actors as well as victims in history."[16] Along with this proliferation of research on black history, historians began to realize that black history could no longer be viewed as peripheral to American history; it would now be placed at the center of the American experience.

By the late 1980s and 1990s African-American history had become not only central to mainstream historiography but also to mainstream popular culture. The 1988 Smithsonian Institution exhibition "Field to Factory," about the great black migration North at the beginning of the twentieth century, drew thousands of visitors. The movie *Glory*, about the heroic deeds of the black 54th Massachusetts Regiment during the Civil War, received both critical acclaim and box office success. By 1999 the *Harvard Guide to Afro-American History* catalogued over a thousand books and several thousand articles about African-American history that had been published since 1965.[17]

Influenced by the rise of the women's movement, women's history underwent changes that paralleled changes taking place in black historiography at the same time. Like African-American historiography before the 1960s, women's lives had been portrayed through the eyes and sources of white males. Feminist historians now began to insist that gender be used as a category of historical analysis, and that scholarship include female sources. Not only did feminist historians analyze power relationships between genders, but also they challenged the assumption that women's history lies on the margins of mainstream history.[18] They claimed that topics such as marriage, birth control, childrearing, prostitution, women's clubs, sexual activity, and house-work were as much a part of the nation's past as were political and military topics. But domestic and family life were not the only domains where women influenced history. One of the most surprising find-ings of this new research was that the majority of women had always worked outside the home and that the myth of the non-laboring woman should be put to rest. "Women who combined house-work, child care, and income-producing work, putting in eighteen-hour days, were as much the characteristic laborers of industrial society as were miners, construction workers, and factory hands. Women's his-tory thus requires a redefinition of who the working class was."[19] Particularly in the case of black women, where much higher percent-ages of African-American mothers have customarily worked outside their homes, in the lowest-paying and most unpleasant jobs, as well as in the professions of teaching and social work, the fable of non-laboring women was unsustainable.[20]

The new social historians centered their research on broad social movements and the contributions of those formerly excluded from the grand historical narrative. This naturally began to alter the familiar contours of American history. Once uncovered, the lives of the excluded could not easily be folded into the comfortable traditional narrative of a shared and glorious past. As Joyce Appleby said in her 1998 presi-dential address to the American Historical Association:

> Their lives couldn't be folded into old stories, because the old story line was too simple in its linear development, too naive in its celebration of individual achievement, too complacent in its insistence upon common national values. . . . The nation depended on and expected a tale of social advance, but there wasn't enough success in the fresh stories to merge them seamlessly into this established narrative.[21]

However, the new social history did not achieve total consensus around its new vision. The deconstruction of the old presidential syn-thesis had its detractors both inside and outside the profession, and still does. Many felt that the new generation of American historians had failed to create a new "synthesis" to replace the old presidential one. Tradi-tionalists themselves, they sought a new synthesis in which social his-torians would recreate a single national story that could weave together black history, women's history, labor history, and various ethnic histo-ries into a seamless, cohesive, yet more inclusive whole. They feared that the very explosion of new histories had fragmented historical scholar-ship into a series of competing voices, overlooking the fundamental beliefs and enduring themes that unite us as a nation.[22]

THE NEW WORLD HISTORY

The pioneering work of the *Annales* school not only gave birth to the new social history of the 1960s and 1970s, but with its emphasis on long-term economic and demographic cycles over vast geographic regions, it also gave birth to the "new world history" at about the same time. World history as a discipline was hardly new. One could argue that the disci-pline of world history dates back to the time of Herodotus, or at least to the eighteenth-century authors of "universal histories," or to Lord Acton, who in 1898 called for a world history "distinct from the combined his-tory of all nations and concentrated only upon 'the common fortunes of mankind.'"[23] However, what passed for "world history" never em-braced such a truly global perspective as Acton's. Even in the hands of Arnold Toynbee,[24] the practice of world history ended up as the study of isolated civilizations, focusing on distinct and self-contained geo-graphic areas, rather than on the larger interregional expanses over which cross-cultural and global developments take place.[25] Until the 1960s his-torians conceptualized world history as the sum of separate national histories, or at best, separate civilizations. It took a new breed of world historians such as Marshall Hodgson, William McNeill, and Leften Stavrianos to write histories that boldly crossed these geographical, tem-poral, and civilizational boundaries. Their goal was to write histories that would unite all of human experience rather than divide it. The focus of their research became cultural interaction and cultural diffusion, rather than cultural isolation and cultural uniqueness.

Furthermore, the new world historians believed that the traditional emphasis on separate national and civilizational histories had created a pecking order among civilizations, with the top ranking reserved for the West. To be fair, there were reasons why the West had gained such promi-nence. During World War I the term "Western civilization" was coined to provide American soldiers with a historical lineage to Europe, and a reason for fighting there.[26] With the invention of the Western Civiliza-tion course in America (a concept largely unknown in Europe, and never taught there), American scholars created a telos in which America be-came the culmination of a democratic tradition born in Periclean Athens and nurtured in Augustinian Rome, Medicean Florence, Tudor England, and Enlightenment France over the centuries. Some have described this historical construction as "American history pushed back through time."[27] Nevertheless, the irresistible appeal of Western civilization meant that other great civilizations would be neglected. For example, historians depicted Chinese, Egyptian, Islamic, and Indian civilizations as immobile, exhausted, and left behind in the onward march of progress. Most non-Western nations and "peoples without history" were not even dignified by the term "civilization." Rather, they were labeled "societies" or "cultures," subject matter better left to anthropologists than historians.[28] According to this civilizational hierarchy, Europeans possessed the one great historical tradition that has stood the test of time. Europe alone could show "progress" over time.

In his 1954 ground-breaking article, "Hemispheric Interregional History as an Approach to World History," Marshall Hodgson described the subtle mechanism by which historians had gradually dropped non-Western civilizations from their research agenda.

> We ceased tracing civilization in those countries almost as soon as Greece and Rome came to have a literate history, concentrating on each of them, in turn; ignoring each time any further history in the lands father east (except when forced to pay attention, by their role in a more westerly story). So as soon as northwestern Europe came to have an independent story, all lands east of the Adriatic dropped from sight, and the very words we used suggested that henceforth the West was the world.[29]

The new world history was a self-conscious attempt to turn this sort of thinking around. It was also an attempt to provide the postcolonial world with a unifying vision of the entire human past. With decolonization, the rise in immigration to the United States from Asia and Central and South America, and the advent of multiculturalism during the 1960s and 1970s, many historians thought that the history of Africans, Asians, Muslims, and indigenous Americans should be allotted at least some space in the history curriculum. However, the new world historians were not satisfied with simply adding these cultures as sidebars to the current canon of Western civilization. They believed that world history had to be redefined. According to Ross Dunn, one of the leaders in the field, new epistemological and methodological approaches would have to be created to integrate non-Western histories into a truly global history with cross-national themes that span the centuries and continents. "What new spatial and chronological architecture would have to be invented" he asked "to properly situate the study of such phenomena as disease pandemics, trade diasporas, transoceanic migrations, or social transformations linked to worldwide deforestation."[30]

However, in spite of efforts to create a cohesive framework for world history, most world historians would agree that they have not been able to define a satisfying world historical synthesis such as the "rise of democracy" in Western Civilization. Historian William McNeill has argued that the study of world history needs "a simple, all encompassing elegant idea with the power to order all human experience."[31] He has offered theories of his own to achieve this, such as his theory of "ecumenical cosmopolitanism." "Ecumenical cosmopolitanism emerged in ancient times along the string of agrarian lands running from China into Africa and Mediterranean Europe—the so-called Eurasian ecumene. In about A.D. 1000 trade routes here developed into a sophisticated world market where east and west came together."[32]

More recently, in "What We Mean by the West," McNeill updated his theory.

> The main story line [for world history] is the accumulation of human skills, organization, and knowledge across the millennia, which permitted human beings to exercise power and to acquire wealth through concerted action among larger and larger groups of people across greater and greater distances until we reach our present era of global interaction.[33]

While such theories are useful organizational tools for scholarly research and teaching, McNeill admits that neither of these conceptual frameworks have the same narrative appeal as the rise of democracy in the West.

In the end, the new world history shared a fundamental problem with the new social history: Both subdisciplines were in search of a grand synthesis. World historians had not come up with a storyline as compelling as Western civilization's story of democracy and industrial progress, and social historians could not come up with a replacement for the presidential synthesis. Social historians were unable to create a cohesive narrative weaving together the many new stories they had discovered into a seamless, unified, yet more inclusive whole. This quest for a compelling narrative has not been resolved to this day.

NARRATIVE AND POSTMODERNISM

Before the historical profession had come to terms with the new social history or the new world history, it was confronted by a still more radical challenge to its established modes of thought: historians began to discover "postmodernism." This forced some historians to change not only the subjects of their research and the types of questions they would ask, but their underlying beliefs about objectivity and historical narrative. During the 1970s, intellectual historians such as Hayden White began to question whether objectivity was possible when writing historical narratives. In his article "The Question of Narrative in Contemporary Historical Theory," White developed a model to describe the fictional qualities of historical narrative. He argued that at the heart of historical narration is a process of emplotment, and it is in the creative act of developing plot structures that the parts find their relation to the whole. As White puts it, "What distinguishes "*historical*" from "*fictional*" stories is first and foremost their content, rather than their form. The content of historical stories is real events, events that really happened, rather than imaginary events, events invented by the narrator."[34] White suggests that narrative histories are always allegorical, that it is impossible to recreate the past without the use of the imagination. He asks, "How else can the past, which consists of events no longer perceivable, be represented in either consciousness or discourse except in an 'imaginary' way?"[35] White asks only that historians should recognize the "constituted" rather than the "found" nature of their referents.

White's contention that writing historical narratives is a creative and subjective process led to a seismic paradigm shift that has rocked the historical profession for nearly three decades. After White, historians could no longer consider themselves as mere chroniclers of events, but had to come to terms with their new role as interpreters. According to the old historiographical paradigm, historical truth would be achieved to the extent that the historian's narrative could be correlated with the facts. Few had dreamed of questioning the narrative form itself, or the creative powers of the narrator.

After Hayden White, historians would question the legitimacy of "meta-" or "master" narratives such as positivism, Marxism, modernization theory, and even the empiricism typical of the *Annales* school and social history. They began to argue that master narratives, whether of the right or the left, imposed on the rest of the world the presumption that Western "progress" toward modernity was universally applicable, that it was in essence the normative historical discourse. Karl Marx, Max Weber, Emile Durkheim, and Fernand Braudel all took narrative history to new heights, the meta-narrative. Marx's narrative centered on the class struggle; Weber's on markets, states, and bureaucracies; Durkheim's on the breakdown of the community; and Braudel's on the enduring tides of history. (Braudel, in fact, created a meta-narrative in spite of his clear rejection of traditional narrative history.) Their "totalizing" narratives swallowed up everything in sight. "The social history of workers, slaves, immigrants and the histories of Third

World peoples could all be incorporated into the dominant western models of historical development, whether in the form of Marxism, the *Annales* school, or modernization theory. These models were all imperialist in their aim to encompass everyone."[36]

While I doubt that White completely rejected Marxism, the *Annales* School, or even narrative history, he apparently was trying to sensitize historians to the constructed nature of historical inquiry and exposition, just as Kuhn had tried to sensitize scientists to the constructed nature of scientific inquiry. In any case, like Kuhn, White had launched another paradigm shift in social-scientific inquiry.

CULTURAL HISTORY AND MICROHISTORY

During the late 1980s other new schools of historiography emerged, unconnected with White and Kuhn, and in some ways opposed to them, accelerating the demise of positivism as the accepted paradigm for the social sciences. The methodologies of "cultural history" and "microhistory" emerged, in part as a challenge to the new social history, positivism, and Marxism, just as the new social history had challenged its predecessors, political and diplomatic history. Indeed, a century after Marx, Durkheim, and Weber had constructed their theories of social change, no better explanations had been developed to replace their theories, in spite of the wealth of new knowledge that had accumulated. This unease with grand theory was reinforced by the fall of the Berlin Wall in 1989 and the retreat from Marxism at American universities.

Cultural history, and its close cousin *microstoria*,[37] borrows from the methodologies of cultural anthropology, particularly ethnography. With an ethnographer's lens, the new cultural historians searched the archives for evidence of how history was experienced, rather than for evidence of the material conditions of everyday life as the social historians had done. But like the latter, their choice of subject matter shifted from the powerful to the powerless. In her 1989 book, *The New Cultural History*, Lynn Hunt explains that, "Cultural history begins from the premise that individual expression takes place within a general idiom. . . . The deciphering of meaning, then, rather than the inference of causal laws of explanation, is taken to be the central task of cultural history, just as it was posed by Clifford Geertz to be the central task of cultural anthropology." Cultural and microhistorians rely on situated local information for their historical analysis, and they hesitate to create sweeping meta-narratives such as those constructed by the *Annales* school historians or the social historians and the world historians who followed them. Rather, cultural historians share with Hayden White an uneasiness with large-scale generalizations based on theories of causation.

Let us consider an example of the microhistorical approach, Natalie Zemon Davis's 1983 *Return of Martin Guerre*, which was turned into a film and a musical. In this work Davis used the narrative written by the judge in a dramatic trial in sixteenth-century France to tell a story about the lives of ordinary people. A specific event—in this case a trial—became a window through which we can watch (at the author's prompting) how people went about the business of living their everyday lives, making the vital choices of love and marriage, acquiring property, and then quarreling over how it was to be shared.[38]

Davis explains her technique in a later book, *Fiction in the Archives*.[39] Here she put the "fictional" aspect of the documents at the center of her historical analysis. Rather than reading requests for letters of pardon addressed to the king as factual sources to help describe sixteenth-century social norms,[40] Davis concentrated on "how people told stories, what they thought a good story was, how they accounted for motive, and how, through narrative, they made sense of the unexpected and built coherence into immediate experience."[41] Thus, according to Davis's account, the documents themselves are fictional. She is more interested in analyzing her subjects' representations of their own world than in trying to find out the "facts" of the case.

As cultural historians shifted the focus of their analysis from the facts to how the facts were construed, interpreted, and represented by contemporaries, they began to question their own research practices as well. They began, like White, to recognize the constituted nature of their own choices as historians, and to be more self-conscious about them. As Hunt puts it, "The master narratives, or codes of unity and difference; the choice of allegories, analogies, or tropes; the structures of narrative—these have weighty consequences for the writing of history."[42]

The methodological challenges of postmodernism and anthropologically based microhistory, coming on top of the profound changes in historical thinking provoked by the new social history and the new world history, left the profession in deep disarray. Surveying the American historical profession in 1989, Peter Novick concluded: "As a broad community of discourse, as a community of scholars united by common aims, common standards, and common purposes, the discipline of history had ceased to exist. Convergence on anything, let alone a subject as highly charged as 'the objectivity question' was out of the question."[43]

But Novick failed to recognize that a sort of broad overarching paradigmatic consensus had gained acceptance through most of the historical profession by the time he wrote. Over the past thirty years historians had invented and legitimized a liberal discourse in ontological opposition to the traditional discourse of "liberal education." Matthew Arnold's canon based on the "best that has been thought and said in the world" had been replaced by a fragmented series of competing counternarratives based on positionality and subjectivity. It was this new fragmented discourse that provided the intellectual underpinnings of the National History Standards Project as it began in 1992, and that would ultimately determine its course. However, while most historians in the academy had undergone this metamorphosis over the past thirty years, many conservative private intellectuals and public policy makers had not. In fact, during the 1980s the conservatives were establishing an intellectual and political framework of their own, centered on traditional values and the canon of liberal education. These two oppositional discourses would collide in a series of culture wars: One of them was fought over the NHSP.

3

A Conservative Restoration, 1981–Present

A society is possible in the last analysis because the individuals in it carry around in their head some sort of picture of that society. Our society, however, in this period of minute division of labour, of extreme heterogeneity and profound conflict of interest, has come to a pass where these pictures are blurred and incongruous.

—Louis Wirth, 1936[1]

THE REAGAN REVOLUTION: BULLY PULPIT REFORM

WHEN RONALD REAGAN RAN for President in 1980 he saw no reason to campaign as an "education president," as George H. W. Bush, Bill Clinton, and George W. Bush would do in each successive election. If anything, he wanted to keep the spotlight off education. His policy goal was to disband the U.S. Department of Education and to fund voucher plans to encourage the privatization of America's schools.[2] This was consistent with his overall campaign to strengthen corporate America by removing government regulations, by privatizing public services, and by devolving power to the states as part of his doctrine of "New Federalism." After a decade characterized by beleaguered presidents (Nixon, Ford, and Carter), the Vietnam War, Watergate, oil crises, soaring interest rates, rampant inflation, unemployment, a ballooning national deficit, and a seemingly irresistible tide of Japanese competition, Reagan found a receptive national audience for his ambitious plans to strengthen the American economy at the expense of government regulation and public services. Only unbridled capitalism could prevent Japan from capturing America's economic hegemony. Armed with the rhetoric of "trickle down" economics and celebrated by a press unwilling to challenge his enormous popularity, Reagan found it easy to sell his program. As far as the Reagan administration was concerned, educational policy would have to take a back seat to a comprehensive policy of corporate welfare.

Ironically, Reagan's retreat from educational policy would not last for long. First of all, the Democratically-held House of Representatives would not dream of letting him dismantle the recently established (1979) U.S. Department of Education, with all of its new entitlements. Second, the very people whom he appointed to key positions inside the National Endowment for the Humanities (NEH) and the U.S. Department of Education (DOE) shared Reagan's conservative ideology and sought to use their posts to revive traditional values in our nation's schools. Their efforts would keep the spotlight on education.

During the 1980s, President Reagan's administration used the power of the "bully pulpit," with all its capacity of moral and rhetorical suasion, to influence public opinion and educational policy in a way unprecedented in the nation's history.[3] In fact William Bennett, upon being appointed to his position as Secretary of Education in 1985, announced publicly that he would "use his office as a bully pulpit to influence educational policy through rhetoric and pronouncements."[4] In his speech "Completing the Reagan Revolution," Bennett argued that he would use this pulpit to promote traditional values.

> National greatness, in the end, depends on—is embodied in—the character of our people. This in turn depends on three things: first, on our sense of who we as a nation are and what we believe in; second, on the well-being of the institutions we create to express those beliefs; and third, on the values according to which we shape the next generation of Americans. And it is here, in the somewhat amorphous but nonetheless palpable realm of beliefs and attitudes and values, that an effort of national recovery must be mounted if we are to realize our potential as a people.[5]

In 1986 policy analysts Richard Jung and Michael Kirst observed that the Reagan administration had chosen this bully pulpit tactic of using speeches, commission reports, and advocacy by the secretary and President as their chief educational strategy. "Although a relatively inexpensive strategy," they argued, "significant personnel and financial resources have been targeted toward influencing public opinion and thereby affecting policy."[6] This bully pulpit strategy would profoundly influence the production of public knowledge about education during the 1980s. Government officials worked in tandem with their colleagues at private foundations to create discursive practices that would define educational policy. In fact, the Reagan and Bush administrations' use of government posts and private advocacy to set the curricular agenda for the nation provides a classic case of Foucault's knowledge/power nexus.[7]

Predictably enough for an administration practicing fiscal conservatism alongside social conservatism, this increased emphasis on rhetoric was matched by a decrease in the amount the Department of Education was willing to pay for public education. "Relative to state and local levels, the U.S. Department of Education's share of elementary and secondary school expenditures dipped to 6.1% by the 1984–1985 school year, its lowest share in almost twenty years."[8] Yet in spite of—or perhaps to compensate for—its unwillingness to fund education, the Reagan administration was very aggressive in pushing forward its intellectual agenda for K–12 education.

Reagan's and Bush's appointees to key positions in the U.S. Department of Education and the National Endowment for the Humanities would labor ceaselessly throughout the 1980s and early 1990s to propagate the notion that our country was a "nation at risk," because our schools were failing to educate our children. How else could we as a country explain the decline of American economic power in the face of Japan's seemingly inexorable rise? Working sometimes as government officials and other times as private intellectuals under the aegis of conservative think tanks such as the Hudson, Olin, Heritage, and American Enterprise institutes, they propagated the idea that the nation's schools were in deep crisis, and proposed remedies they believed were needed to resolve it.

A NATION AT RISK: FROM RHETORIC TO REALITY

When Terrel Bell first assumed his post as Reagan's Secretary of Education in 1981, he recommended that the President convoke a National Commission on Excellence in Education to study the state of American education. However, his proposal met strong opposition from the White House. President Reagan rejected his proposal "on the grounds that such action would highlight the federal role in education at a time when the Administration was committed to abolishing the U.S. Department of Education and to dramatically reducing federal involvement in and financial support of education."[9] So Bell, who was determined to conduct his study, took it upon himself in August 1981 to set up a commission and put it to work. Two years later, on April 26, 1983, the National Commission on Excellence in Education (NCEE) released its 36-page report, *A Nation at Risk: The Imperative for Educational Reform.*[10]

According to Bell, "the Commission's report burst upon the country like a summer storm."[11] Its dramatic rhetoric, which proclaimed a national educational crisis in hyperbolic prose, was quoted on the front pages of nearly every newspaper in the country, and on the evening news. Within two weeks *Newsweek* rushed a sensational cover story to press. In the best tradition of yellow journalism, this cover story, "Can the Schools Be Saved?," proclaimed that education in this country had so deteriorated that "progress from one generation to the next . . . has been nearly shattered."[12] The tree of knowledge had been destroyed, and the schools were blamed for the loss of the American dream.

Bell, who could not have imagined that the national media would disseminate his report with so much fanfare, had arranged for his own blitzkrieg dissemination at no less than twelve regional conferences throughout the year. Governors, mayors, state and district superintendents, and various other high-profile policymakers were invited to attend town hall meetings across the nation. Since 1984 was an election year, they grabbed the opportunity to grandstand their newfound commitment to education reform.[13] Good press coverage about bad schools, combined with political opportunism, thus gave birth to a new reform cycle.

President Reagan, now changed course, deciding to jump on the "at-risk" bandwagon. He showed up at several of the town hall meetings, and served as the keynote speaker at one. He even wrote an article published in the *Phi Delta Kappan* adopting the report's vital message as his own.[14] The "at-risk" report provided Reagan with an educational agenda that turned out to be a handsome political windfall, particularly valuable as his second presidential campaign was about to begin. It appears that Reagan decided to become an education president after all.

But despite the president's endorsement, *A Nation at Risk* would not have gripped the American psyche if its message had not resonated with the public. It provided a compelling explanation for perceived national decline. The real enemy was no longer the Soviet Union, or even Japan: it was ourselves. We had lost the art of educating our children. If we could only cure our current educational malaise, we could once again rise up, phoenix-like, to reclaim our economic preeminence. In its report, the National Commission on Excellence in Education had sent a clarion call to the nation, couched in rhetoric charged with nationalistic fervor and conjuring up images of war:

Our Nation is at risk. Our once unchallenged preeminence in commerce, industry, science, and technological innovation is being overtaken by competitors throughout the world. . . . the educational foundations of our society are presently being eroded by a rising tide of mediocrity that threatens our very future as a Nation and a people. What was unimaginable a generation ago has begun to occur—others are matching and surpassing our attainments.

If an unfriendly foreign power had attempted to impose on America the mediocre educational performance that exists today, we might well have viewed it as an act of war. As it stands, we have allowed this to happen to ourselves. We have even squandered the gains in student achievement made in the wake of the Sputnik challenge. Moreover, we have dismantled essential support systems which helped make those gains possible. We have, in effect, been committing an act of unthinking, unilateral, educational disarmament.[15]

The report brought the issue of education to the forefront of political debate with an urgency not felt since *Sputnik* shook American confidence in its public schools in 1957.

In spite of its hyperbole, and the political opportunism that it unleashed, *A Nation* was the result of a well-intentioned effort by a distinguished panel to assess the condition of American education and to recommend a cure. In order to make its case that American education was in serious decline, the report listed a series of "risk indicators," derived from a variety of national and international studies on student performance. Here are a few:

- Some 23 million American adults are functionally illiterate by the simplest tests of everyday reading, writing, and comprehension.
- Average achievement of high school students on most standardized tests is now lower than 26 years ago when Sputnik was launched.
- The College Board's Scholastic Aptitude Tests (SATs) demonstrate a virtually unbroken decline from 1963 to 1980. Average verbal scores fell over 50 points and average mathematics scores dropped nearly 40 points.
- Between 1975 and 1980, remedial mathematics courses in public 4-year colleges increased by 72 percent and now constitute one-quarter of all mathematics courses taught in those institutions.
- Business and military leaders complain that they are required to spend millions of dollars on costly remedial education and training programs in such basic skills as reading, writing, spelling, and computation. . . .[16]

However, the "evidence" that the commission invoked as indicators of risk is highly suspect. Not only did the panelists make highly inflammatory statements without providing a single footnote, but they also misinterpreted the statistics behind many of those statements. For example, the claim that there had been "a virtually unbroken decline in Scholastic Aptitude Test (SAT) scores from 1963 to 1980" is misleading. Close analysis of the data leads to a very different conclusion. David Berliner and Bruce Biddle have shown that while it is true that the *aggregated* SAT scores have declined ever so slightly since 1963, if one analyzes the SAT data *disaggregated* by race, one draws a very different conclusion. During this period white students were maintaining their average scores, and minority students were earning increasingly higher average scores. The overall decline in SAT scores derives from the fact that during the 1960s and 1970s more and more people from disadvantaged groups were taking the SAT than ever before. Naturally, one would expect that minority and immigrant students would not score as high as the cohort of more privileged students who had taken the tests in earlier times with better preparation. *Disaggregated* SAT scores suggest that student achievement had either been steady or had been climbing over the seventeen years cited in the report. Thus Berliner and Biddle concluded, "Although critics have trumpeted the 'alarming' news that aggregate national SAT scores fell during the late 1960s and early 1970s, this decline indicates nothing about the performance of American schools. Rather, it signals that students from a broader range of backgrounds were then getting interested in college, which should have been cause for celebration, not alarm."[17]

Unfortunately, the press never questioned or analyzed the SAT statistics. Instead, aggregated SAT scores, and the dismal story of decline that they seemed to reveal, would serve as a rallying point for conservative pundits, policymakers, and journalists alike, eager to attach themselves to a newsworthy cause. It was equally unfortunate that the press chose to ignore the good news that could be extrapolated from SAT scores disaggregated by ethnicity: that more Americans now had access to SAT exams and consequently to public and private universities then ever before. Good news rarely makes good press.

Illiteracy too was exaggerated in the commission's report. And yet, ironically the 1981 National Assessment for Educational Progress (NAEP) showed dramatic gains in reading scores for disadvantaged students over the previous ten years. Most notable were the gains made by black elementary students, which reduced the gap between black and white students by 40%. Reading experts argued that federal aid for specialized reading programs had contributed significantly to these gains.

However, in 1981 Congress passed the Education Consolidation and Improvement Act withdrawing significant levels of federal aid from reading instruction, precisely at the time when the success of these federal reading programs was documented in the NAEP tests, and precisely at the time when the NCEE was beginning its work.[18] Yet in its report, the NCEE commission ignored these improvements. Another irony is that the September 1983 Bureau of Labor Statistics report predicted that most jobs available to students by 1993 would be in low-level service positions requiring few academic skills, and not in the relatively small number of high-tech jobs that the NCEE report claimed.[19] Neither prediction proved correct.

Although it grabbed the headlines, *A Nation at Risk* was by no means the only commission report to be released in 1983. A wave of other prestigious commission reports, with similar bleak messages, came out at about the same time, and more than 300 task forces nationwide launched new programs for school reform.[20] The fifty governors put out their own report under the aegis of the Education Commission of the States (ECS): *Action for Excellence*.[21] This report was second only to *A Nation at Risk* in its hyperbole and its political impact. *Action for Excellence* brought the national educational agenda to the states.[22] Similarly, the College Board released *Academic Preparation for College*, the Carnegie Foundation for the Advancement of Teaching published *Education and Economic Progress*, the National Science Board (NSB) released *Educating Americans for the 21st Century*, and the Twentieth Century Fund Task Force issued *Making the Grade*.[23] All of these reports equated economic success with academic achievement: business was the common denominator.

A neo-conservative consensus now began to coalesce around these reports. It held that the permissiveness associated with the liberal school reforms implemented during the 1960s and 1970s had led to our current state of educational and economic decline. According to Jeannie Oakes, the neo-conservatives had concluded that the cost of extending educational opportunity had been a decline in educational quality.[24] The report *Making the Grade* was clear on this point: "Its [the federal government's] emphasis on promoting equality of opportunity in the public schools has meant a slighting of its commitment to educational quality."[25] This avalanche of official and semi-official reports thus created a narrative in which students and teachers, who had allegedly been pandered to by Great Society programs, were now held responsible for the current educational and economic downturn.[26]

Unfortunately, *A Nation at Risk* contributed to this discourse of blame, however unintentionally, leading many Americans to believe that the schools were failing the nation, rather than the other way around. It blamed progressive educational policy of the past twenty-five years for the current decline in education, and recommended that the schools should get out of the social reform business in order to return to their mission of providing quality education. *A Nation* claimed that curriculum was "routinely called upon to provide solutions to personal, social, and political problems that the home and other institutions either will not or cannot resolve."[27] It warned that the "gains inspired by the challenge of Sputnik a quarter of a century ago have been squandered, leaving a generation of young people ill prepared for the new era of technology and global competition. Even the level of shared education essential to a free, democratic society may be threatened if the decline is not reversed." "At risk," the commission's report concluded, "is our very future as a Nation and a people."[28]

This deluge of reports demonstrates the power of national commissions to create a climate of crisis and to mold an emerging discourse. In this case, through the cumulative work of one panel after another, a conservative consensus about the failure of liberal reform coalesced into official knowledge. Through the dramatic use of rhetoric and selective use of "evidence," these reports legitimized the belief in a national educational crisis. Remedies, however, were harder to articulate.

Indeed, all of the reports proposed remedies such as creating rigorous academic standards, emphasizing skills in the curriculum, recruiting better-qualified teachers, and providing better teacher training. Similarly, all the reports called for additional homework and longer school days to help realize some of these goals.[29] These reports used a strategy of repetition, innuendo, and exaggeration to fuel the crisis mentality. But the solutions they recommended were too costly to have any practical application, particularly in an era of fiscal conservatism.[30]

By contrast with the commission reports, university-based liberals such as Theodore Sizer, Ernest Boyer, John Goodlad, and others responded to the perceived crisis by proposing a very different, progressive kind of reform, aimed at increasing academic achievement by creating caring environments for students, teachers, and families. Sizer's *Horace's Compromise*, Boyer's *High School*, and Goodlad's *A Place Called School*, all published in 1983, were noteworthy dissents from the commission reports, which called for "teacher-proof standards, teacher-centered instruction, and authoritarian attitudes towards students." Sizer advised those who wanted excellent schools to "trust teachers and principals—and believe that the more trust one places in them, the more the response will justify that trust."[31] Although these liberal/progressive discourses resonated throughout the educational community and informed local reforms such as the Coalition of Essential Schools and the Los Angeles LEARN project, the neo-conservative discourse had gained ascendancy among national policymakers and, consequently, the general public. The ability of university professors in schools of education to affect national policy all but disappeared. The era of liberal reform begun in the 1960s was officially over.

In fact, the year 1983 marks a watershed in American educational policy. The publication of these highly sensational reports would launch the country on a course of conservative educational reform that has dominated federal policy since that time. This shift in educational policy mirrors the shift in the national political climate nurtured by the so-called Reagan Revolution. Now that the neo-conservatives had established a causal relationship between the alleged educational crisis and the nation's economic decline, "excellence" replaced "equity" as the mantra for reform. If there is any doubt that the "excellence" movement in education was inspired by the recent economic decline, one only has to look at how it borrowed its rhetoric from the gurus of business success. The rhetoric of excellence was lifted directly from Thomas Peters and Robert Waterman's best-selling 1982 book, *In Search of Excellence: Lessons from America's Best-Run Companies*, a study of the most successful companies in America. This book was written to lift the sagging spirits of businessmen after a decade of sluggish economic performance.[32]

Thus "excellence" now became the catchphrase for educational policymakers, and business competitiveness the model for reform. Excellence in education became the *sine qua non* of national economic recovery. Certainly the governors felt so, or why else would they have appointed executives from fourteen major corporations to help them write their report for educational reform? Thus began a new educational discourse defining a new relationship between schools and the economic sector. John Casteen, Secretary of Education in Virginia at the time, argued this point with no holds barred: "Let's bring together the corporate sector and the schools to define common goals, articulate statements of standards for schools, and to pool resources to achieve the goals."[33] According to this philosophy, a coalition should be formed between the business community and schools to keep America competitive in world markets.

Michael Apple concluded that this alliance between education and the marketplace transformed our traditional understanding of the relationship between democracy and education in America. For Apple, the shift to a market philosophy of education meant that instead of teaching students how to discharge their duties as democratic citizens, schools would now teach students how to discharge their duties as producers and consumers in a global economy. Democracy and social justice all but disappeared from the rhetoric of educational reform.[34]

CONSERVATIVE THINK TANKS: RHETORIC IS POLICY, WORDS ARE ACTION

Just as the liberal consensus of the last thirty years developed within the protective environment of the university, the neo-conservative consensus developed within the protective environment provided by the many private foundations, or "think tanks," that sprang up during the late 1970s and 1980s. These organizations were founded in response to a growing perception on the part of conservatives that the liberal elite controlled universities and government bureaucracies, stifling conservative thought and free markets. William Simon, head of the conservative John F. Olin Foundation, led the charge. In his 1976 book, *A Time for Truth*, Simon argued that it was time for a "counter-intelligentsia" to disseminate free-market economic ideas, and to challenge the monopoly of public schools and bureaucracies over education.[35] Support for this counter-intelligentsia would come from privately financed think tanks such as the John F. Olin Foundation, the Hudson Institute, and the Heritage Foundation. Simon's goal was that these foundations would channel funds to scholars, writers, and journalists who "understand the relationship between political and economic liberty."[36]

Since the beginning of the Reagan administration, think tanks such as the Olin Foundation, the Heritage Foundation, the Hudson Institute, the American Enterprise Institute, the Hoover Institute, and the Free Congress Foundation have had a remarkable impact on American educational policy. This is in part because the foundations have provided an institutional base and alternative public platform for conservative public intellectuals, many of whom would later serve terms in key federal positions. For example, the Heritage Foundation was responsible for setting much of Reagan's policy agenda in 1981. With the publication of its one-thousand-page volume *Mandate for Leadership: Policy Management in a Conservative Administration*, the Heritage Foundation delineated policy positions for all thirteen cabinet departments and the regulatory agencies, creating a blueprint for the Reagan administration on all fronts.[37] Not surprisingly, one of their recommendations was to abolish or reduce the size and budget of the U.S. Department of Education because of its alleged interference with state and local decision-making and its promulgation of programs they found abhorrent, such as *Man: A Course of Study* (MACOS). In fact, *Mandate* called into question the entire post-*Sputnik* federal reform movement that had been under way for fifteen years. A major focus of concern was the Education Directorate of the National Science Foundation, the organization that was responsible for overseeing *Man: A Course of Study*.

> During the past 15 years, there has been a concerted effort by professional educationists to turn elementary and secondary school classrooms into vehicles for liberal-left social and political change in the U.S. . . . The replacement of traditional elementary and secondary courses in history, geography, civics, and science with new multi-media interdisciplinary curriculum packages has also been made possible by hundreds of millions of dollars in Federal grants. A major objective of this effort, according to reports and education journal articles resulting from educator conferences held in the late 1960s and early 1970s, is to implement social planning and social change to build a new world social and political order.[38]

Mandate called for a return to moral authority in the schools, and it singled out MACOS as the type of program that should be eliminated from the curriculum. It recommended that the Reagan administration should "draft and propose legislation to terminate federal support for the development and marketing of school course (curriculum) materials, so that full responsibility and control over this area can be returned to state and local education agencies and private schools, in conjunction with private sector commercial firms."[39]

The Heritage Foundation's 1984 sequel, *Mandate for Leadership II: Continuing the Conservative Revolution*, set a similar agenda for Reagan's second administration, and its *Mandate for Leadership III: Policy Strategies for the 1990s* set the agenda for George H. W. Bush's administration in 1989.[40] In 1985 the Heritage Foundation expanded its conservative vision for privatizing education with *A New Agenda for Education*.[41] In 1986, honoring the Heritage Foundation at a gala event, Reagan acknowledged the role the foundation had played in shaping public opinion. Quoting from Richard Weaver's 1948 book, *Ideas Have Consequences*, Reagan summed up Heritage's influence with these words: "It goes back to what Richard Weaver had said and what Heritage is all about. Ideas do have consequences, rhetoric is policy, and words are action."[42]

Thus knowledge and power were inextricably linked through the interconnecting relationships among conservative think tanks, elected officials, political appointees, and bully pulpit rhetoric. Circumventing the universities altogether, neo-conservative politicians could now rely on the think tanks to provide them with well-articulated policy, articles, books, research studies, and opinion pieces to influence public opinion, and a constant supply of scholars and public intellectuals such as William Bennett, Lynne Cheney, Diane Ravitch, and Chester Finn, Jr. to implement policies through appointed positions in the U.S. Department of Education and the National Endowments.[43]

One of the arenas in which the conservative think tanks were the most successful was in formulating policy on cultural conservatism. In 1987 Paul Weyrich commissioned a study by the Free Congress Research and Education Foundation, *Cultural Conservatism: Toward a New National Agenda*, which delineated the advantages of waging a "culture war." The report found that social and cultural conservatism was a far more compelling message than was economic conservatism for the purposes of advancing conservative policies and capitalist thinking.[44] Joel Spring points out the inherent contradiction between the conservatives' expressed belief in laissez-faire capitalism and their hands-on attempts to control and manage their intellectual agenda. "Although conservatives talk about the invisible hand of the free market, the trickle-down distribution of ideas is very well planned."[45] Indeed, these trickle-down ideas were articulated through the think tanks, granted legitimacy by the White House and Congress, and given prominence by the press.

Perhaps the most prolific of the think tanks articulating neo-conservative thought has been the American Enterprise Institute (AEI), established in 1943 in Washington, D.C. to promote free-market ideas in opposition to New Deal policies. In the 1970s AEI began to recruit formerly liberal scholars who had turned conservative during the Stalinist era. Through their publications this counter-intelligentsia sought to challenge the liberal public discourse promulgated at the universities. The two most significant neo-conservative publications, *Public Interest*, a journal about social and public policy, and *Commentary*, a journal about culture and politics, contributed to the cause by criticizing policies associated with the liberal reforms of the 1960s and by criticizing Cold War foreign policy.[46]

In *Soldiers of Misfortune* Valerie Scatamburlo observes that the American Enterprise Institute was one of the first of the conservative think tanks to figure out how to gain access to the mainstream media to market their ideas. For example, according to Scatamburlo, AEI systematically hired ghostwriters to write opinion pieces in the names of well-known scholars and distributed them to newspapers such as the *Wall Street Journal* and the *Washington Times*. Although AEI began as little more than a mailing address in 1943, Scatamburlo claims that by

1985 it had a budget of $12.6 million, a staff of 176, and an entourage of 90 adjunct scholars.[47] In 1994 AEI was instrumental in marketing Charles Murray and Richard Herrnstein's best-selling book *The Bell Curve: Intelligence and Class Structure in American Life*, released amidst a media hoopla just before the election of the 104th Congress.[48] By sponsoring *The Bell Curve*, AEI could help formulate a new racist discourse that would provide the intellectual foundations for its conservative political agenda. AEI sponsorship lent legitimacy to the authors' racist claim that African Americans inherit lower IQs than European Americans, and this in turn lent legitimacy to the authors' policy recommendations: Disband social programs such as Head Start, compensatory education, and affirmative action because programs that attempt to close opportunity gaps are based on the false premise that all men are indeed created equal.[49] The American Enterprise Institute would serve as the launching pad for Lynne Cheney's preemptive strike against the *National Standards for History*, published in the *Wall Street Journal* just in time for the election of the 104th Congress.

A "CRISIS" IN THE HUMANITIES, 1984–1994

Just as the Soviet launching of *Sputnik* in 1957 unleashed a wave of reform targeted at math and science education, the publication of *A Nation at Risk* in 1983 also focused on math and science reform. After all, most people see the logical relationship between high math and science scores and national superiority in military and economic performance. They understand that we cannot afford to lose a whole generation of talented mathematicians and scientists if we are to maintain our status as a military and economic superpower. However, what was different this time around was that through their use of the bully pulpit, public officials and think-tank intellectuals were able to manufacture a new crisis for the *humanities*, at first sight by no means as critical a field of study. Using flamboyant rhetoric, they were able to portray this crisis as even more serious than the math/science crisis delineated in *A Nation at Risk*. The crisis in the humanities was not simply a crisis in technical knowledge and expertise: it was no less than a crisis of the American soul.

Starting from this assumption, in 1983 a group of conservative intellectuals initiated the discourse that would legitimize a full-fledged humanities crisis. From their positions in private foundations and the public sector during the Reagan administration, they joined together to direct educational policy. The books, articles, and policy statements

published by this tightly knit group of intellectuals served as founding documents for this period of conservative educational reform, including the subsequent standards movement. Their works are cited in
this context throughout the educational journals and the media.

Diane Ravitch, adjunct professor of education at Teachers College,
Columbia University, and Assistant Secretary of Education during the
second half of the George H. W. Bush administration, was one of the
major forces behind the humanities reform movement. In fact, Ravitch
has been a consistent critic of American education since 1984, both as
a public intellectual and policymaker.[50] However, Ravitch was not always in this particular camp. In 1983 she published a major work, *The
Troubled Crusade*, in which she chronicled the heroic efforts of educational reformers in the post–World War II period to expand educational
opportunities to all Americans, regardless of creed, class, or race. This
1983 book is characterized by optimism: It recognizes defeats and
missteps along the way and yet it celebrates the considerable triumphs
of the educational reformers. In her epilogue, Ravitch credits reformers from the postwar period with no less than the following achievements: 1) ". . . the attack against racial segregation, characteristically,
was fought out in the schools, and the dismantling of the racial caste
system began in the schools and spread to other areas of American life";
2) ". . . the goal of access to higher education was realized far beyond
the most optimistic predictions of President Truman's Commission on
Higher Education"; and 3) "higher levels of participation in the colleges and universities reflected the rising level of educational attainment for the population as a whole."[51] Ravitch sums up these hard-won
successes in the following words:

> American education had succeeded in so many ways that were real, tan-
> gible and important—in providing modern buildings, larger enrollment,
> better materials, better-trained teachers, more courses, more departments,
> and more graduates—that it sometimes seemed difficult for educators to
> remember what they had accomplished or why they had struggled so
> hard, or not to wonder whether they had gone wrong somewhere or why
> so many people criticized the nation's schools, colleges, and universities.[52]

Although Ravitch acknowledged that critics habitually anathema-
tize educators and educational reformers, she herself sang the reformers'
praises in *The Troubled Crusade*. While she critiqued various educational
reforms, especially the Progressive education movement and the educational experiments of the 1960s, which she blamed for many ills, one
could argue that Ravitch's 1983 book tells a liberal story about the tri-

umph of equity in education. Using Hayden White's categories of analysis, that historical narratives always take a literary form, one could argue that Ravitch presents us with a romantic interpretation of educational reform: a story about continual progress, albeit progress achieved at great cost. One could also argue that *The Troubled Crusade* marks the end of an era of liberal educational reform: this book would be Ravitch's last effort to paint a rosy picture of American education. This was perhaps because, at the very moment of its publication, the paradigm shift in educational policy toward excellence, which I outlined above, was taking place. Ravitch's next book would be decidedly different in tone. The new paradigm made it unfashionable to talk about equity for all students: In tune with the emerging discourse she now directed her attention to the perceived decline and fall of American education.

In 1983, the same year that she published *The Troubled Crusade*, Diane Ravitch and Chester Finn, professor of education at Vanderbilt University, and later Assistant Secretary of Education during the senior Bush administration, were funded by William Bennett, NEH Chair, and by the Vanderbilt-based Education Excellence Network to convene a series of conferences for high school teachers in the humanities.[53] As a result of those conversations, Finn, Ravitch, and Robert T. Francher co-authored a book, *Against Mediocrity*, in which they lambasted the sorry state of humanities education in this country. With this 1984 book, Ravitch et al. launched a brand-new discourse of crisis in humanities education. According to the authors, the social and political cost that would be paid for the "humanities crisis" far exceeded the dangers inherent in the "math and science crisis."

> The problems that beset high school humanities are in ways more serious than even the Commission's [NCEE] apocalyptic language would suggest. They have not yet seized the nation's attention as has the "crisis in mathematics and science." They are not widely understood to be intimately related to the economic vitality, technical prowess, or strategic defense of the United States. They do not tap the veins of utilitarianism that constitute the circulatory system of much educational policymaking. . . . But if the sciences teach one what it is to understand and follow certain rules by which the universe is governed and by which some knowledge is ordered, the humanities teach one about freedom and wisdom.[54]

If the public were to take this crisis in the humanities seriously, however, it would need more than anecdotal evidence. What the cause needed was some hard statistics to prove that students were no longer familiar with our nation's history, or with the canon of great literary works that had supposedly inspired previous generations of Americans.

In fact, a national test in history and literature might reveal whether students were in danger of losing their identities as Americans and of losing the privileged legacy of Western civilization inherited from their European ancestors. In 1986, Lynne V. Cheney, now chair of the NEH, funded an assessment of 8,000 eleventh-grade students in the subjects of history and literature.[55] The National Assessment of Educational Progress (NAEP) administered this assessment in partnership with Ravitch, Finn, E.D. Hirsch, and other intellectuals who were concerned with cultural literacy and the so-called decline in the humanities.

With the 1987 publication of the now-classic book *What Do Our 17-Year-Olds Know?*, Ravitch and Finn, who by now was serving as Assistant Secretary of Education for the Office of Educational Research and Improvement, analyzed the NAEP test scores. Like *A Nation at Risk*, this book captured the country's attention through the national press. Apparently a whole generation of Americans could not answer the most basic questions about American history or literature. According to the NAEP assessment, 80% of the students could answer only a handful of history questions correctly: 15 out of the 141 questions. The average student taking the history test answered 54.5% of the questions they attempted correctly, a failing grade according to Ravitch and Finn's analysis.[56] In fact, for many years journalists seized upon one single question from the NEAP history exam to symbolize everything that was wrong with humanities education: only 32.2% of the 8,000 students taking the test could place the Civil War in the proper half-century, 1850–1900.[57] The press had a field day with Finn and Ravitch's statistical analysis, and so did the newly formed cohort of humanities crusaders led by Ravitch, Finn, Bennett, and Cheney, among others. Finally, with the NAEP assessment, the rhetoric of crisis could be legitimated for the humanities.

Ravitch and Finn now had a firm platform from which to wage their battle for humanities reform, even though they had not really established that this generation of students knew any less history or literature than its predecessors. In fact, as David Berliner and Bruce Biddle have pointed out, throughout history students have never known as much history as the test developers wanted them to know. In an effort to examine whether or not students' knowledge of history had actually declined since 1915, researcher Dale Whittington isolated forty-three items on the 1986 NAEP test that corresponded to items given on earlier tests. He concluded that today's students scored lower than yesterday's students on one-third of the items, equally on another third of the questions, and better than past generations on the remaining third.[58] Christopher Hitchens citing a *New*

York Times survey conducted in 1943 stated that a quarter of enter-
ing college freshmen could not name Abraham Lincoln as President
during the Civil War, and this was during the golden era when history was taught as the "presidential synthesis."[59] Thus Ravitch and
Finn's nostalgic notions of less troubling days when a highly literate
American public had emerged from our nation's schools seem to be
unjustified. While I agree with Ravitch and Finn that there is much
room for improvement in humanities education, and that any retreat
from teaching academic subject matter is deplorable, I would argue that
traditionally most Americans have lacked a deep knowledge of their
nation's literature and history. Intellectual historians such as Richard
Hofstadter and Arthur Bestor argued as early as the 1950s and 1960s
that anti-intellectualism is one of the defining features of American
education: They lamented the historic lack of rigor in the curriculum.[60] In light of this argument, Finn's and Ravitch's conclusions of
recent decline seem less compelling.

By 1987 the battle lines in the culture wars had been clearly drawn.
Working in concert, conservative reformers used the bully pulpit, the
media, and their pens to define and nurture a "crisis in the humanities,"
and once defined, to propose solutions. Their assault on the humanities
was a thinly veiled attempt to reconstitute traditional American culture
in a society that seemed to have lost its bearings through excesses of what
they termed "political correctness." They believed that no less than
America's future was at stake. According to this argument, during the
1960s and 1970s liberal scholars at the universities had introduced postmodernism and its implicit cultural relativism to a generation of students; this cultural relativism had then trickled down to K–12 education
through progressive educational policies.

In the meantime, conservative intellectuals felt, with reason, that
they had been denied a platform for expressing their points of view. With
the election of Ronald Reagan, these conservative intellectuals, working
outside academia and funded in large part by conservative think tanks,
could now rally to put traditional American values back onto the education agenda. Under Reagan, public institutions were also enrolled in the
struggle, battling alongside the counter-intelligentsia and the think tanks.
The National Endowment for the Humanities, under the leadership first
of William J. Bennett and then Lynne V. Cheney, would be one of several public sector bully pulpits from which this new conservative agenda
would be launched. The U.S. Department of Education, the National
Governors' Association, and the 104th Congress would be others. Even
the American Federation of Teachers (AFT), under its conservative president, Albert Shanker, was drawn to the cause.

Secretary of Education William Bennett and Assistant Secretary Chester Finn Jr. openly used their government positions to advocate for a traditional canon. In their 1986 Department of Education report, *What Works: Research About Teaching and Learning*, Bennett and Finn wrote, "A shared knowledge of these elements of our past helps foster social cohesion and a sense of national community and pride."[61] They, of course, were referring to the canon of "liberal education" described in Chapter 1. In the government publication *To Reclaim a Legacy*, Bennett wrote:

> The humanities can contribute to an informed sense of community by enabling us to learn about and become participants in a common culture, shareholders in our civilization. But our goal should be more than just a common culture. . . . we should instead want all students to know a common culture rooted in civilization's lasting visions, its highest shared ideals and aspirations, and its heritage.[62]

However, whose unified vision of our past would be enshrined in this common culture? A critic suggested that Bennett's purpose in *To Reclaim a Legacy* was not only to make the case for transmission of cultural heritage, but also "the cultivation of a one-dimensional view of western and world-historical development in which the United States is seen to be both the heir of Western civilization and the final fruition of its development."[63]

In retrospect, 1987 became a watershed year in the crusade for the humanities because several important advocacy books came out that year that attracted considerable public attention. It was clear that the tide of public opinion was now running strongly in the conservative theorists' favor, and that the humanities crisis had now taken root in the American consciousness. While Ravitch and Finn were writing *What Do Our 17-Year Olds Know?* to establish statistical evidence for a "crisis" in the humanities, E. D. Hirsch was making much the same point in his now-famous book *Cultural Literacy*. At the same time, Allan Bloom's best-selling *The Closing of the American Mind* identified the source of the problem: the universities' obsession with postmodernism and runaway multiculturalism. Humanities education in America was mortally ill, they intoned, and dire remedies were required.

Although they would exercise enormous influence on public policy, few of these public intellectuals held elected office: few of them could be held accountable by the electorate. One is reminded of the reflection by de Tocqueville (one of their chief cultural icons) on the influence of private intellectuals on public policy in the decades leading up to the French Revolution. De Tocqueville asked, "Why was it that men of letters, men without wealth, social eminence, responsibilities, or official status, became in practice the leading politicians of the age, since despite the fact that others held the reins of government, they alone spoke with accents of authority?"[64] Indeed, just as the *philosophes* set the intellectual agenda in eighteenth-century France without holding public office, so these unelected pundits dictated national educational policy, acting in the public space vacated by the Reagan administration.

E. D. Hirsch was a close associate of Ravitch and Finn. A professor of English at the University of Virginia, Hirsch made a compelling case for the importance of a culturally literate citizenry in his now-classic book, *Cultural Literacy: What Every American Needs to Know*. His argument is simple: Cultural literacy is a precondition for democratic citizenship, but American society has lost its cultural bearings. Interestingly enough, in the preface to *Cultural Literacy* Hirsch claims,

> the single greatest impetus to writing this book came from Diane Ravitch, who said simply that I ought to write a book, that I ought to call it *Cultural Literacy*, and that I ought to get it out as soon as possible. . . . These suggestions, coming from someone whose work I deeply admire, proved irresistible. Without Professor Ravitch's original suggestions and continuing support, I might not have undertaken the book at all.[65]

By examining this network of relationships, one can see this group coalescing around a common cause.

Hirsch relied on anecdotal evidence to back up his claim that cultural literacy had declined steadily since his own father's time: He cited his father's use of Shakespeare in personal business letters to prove his point.[66] However, he never provided any hard statistical evidence, other than a rehashing of the risk indicators outlined in *A Nation*, and a repetition of the figures and analysis provided by Ravitch and Finn in *What Do Our 17-Year-Olds Know?* But, as others and I have argued, neither of these documents successfully established a decline in cultural literacy, other than by implication. Nevertheless, repetition of the same studies in book after book gave them a sense of legitimacy.

Like Ravitch and Finn, Hirsch blamed Progressive educational theory for the lamentable state of the humanities.

> The theories that have dominated American education for the past fifty years stem ultimately from Jean-Jacques Rousseau, who believed that we should encourage the natural development of young children and not impose adult ideas upon them before they can truly understand them. . . . His content-neutral conception of educational development has long been

triumphant in American schools of education and has long dominated the "developmental," content-neutral curricula of our elementary schools.[67]

According to Hirsch, John Dewey was responsible for imposing Rousseau's child-centered educational theories on the American educational establishment. "Believing that a few direct experiences would suffice to develop the skills that children require, Dewey assumed that early education need not be tied to specific content."[68] This claim that Dewey's child-centered pedagogy undermined subject-matter competency distorts Dewey's complex educational philosophy. However, all of the humanities reformers employed Dewey's philosophy of progressive education as their touchstone for all that is wrong in education today. Having dismissed Dewey as anti-intellectual, Hirsch went on to establish his reasons why "content-neutral" education posed a danger to democratic society. Hirsch claimed that from "an anthropological perspective, the basic goal of education in a human community is acculturation, the transmission to children of specific information shared by the adults of the group or polis."[69] He argued that Dewey had it all wrong. "Only by accumulating shared symbols, and the shared information that the symbols represent, can we learn to communicate effectively with one another in our national community."[70] Hirsch's argument, simply put, is that today, society no longer communicates to its young the common cultural glue that is necessary to hold it together. "What they [students] know is ephemeral and narrowly confined to their own generation. . . . Our children's lack of intergenerational knowledge is a serious problem for the nation."[71]

Perhaps Hirsch's most compelling case for core knowledge and cultural literacy was derived from a 1985 research report on reading comprehension. The study suggested that the art of reading is far more than decoding words on a page and transferring those skills to new configurations of words. The reader Hirsch argued,

is now discovered to be not only a decoder of what is written down but also a supplier of much essential information that is not written down. The reader's mind is constantly inferring meanings that are not directly stated by the words of a text but are nonetheless part of its essential content. The explicit meanings of a piece of writing are the tip of an iceberg of meaning; the larger part lies beneath the surface of the text and is composed of the reader's own relevant knowledge.[72]

To comprehend the words on a page the reader must have appropriate contextual knowledge that is never explicitly written down on the page.

Studies have shown that readers who lack such contextual knowledge plod through texts sentence by sentence, overloading their short-term memories while losing the thrust of the argument being made.[73] According to Hirsch, only core knowledge programs will provide students with adequate contextual knowledge. "Cultural illiteracy, if allowed to persist, will disenfranchise future generations because they will not be able to comprehend newspapers and other news media that they need as voting citizens."[74]

Hirsch proposes a solution to the problem. While he believes that multiculturalism is a valuable tool for creating tolerance in students, he nevertheless feels that the primary focus of national education should be mastery of American literate culture. He argues that "the acculturative responsibility of the schools is primary and fundamental. To teach the ways of one's own community has always been and still remains the essence of the education of our children, who enter neither a narrow tribal culture nor a transcendent world culture but a national literate culture."[75] Hirsch then takes it upon himself to itemize a detailed list of what literate Americans should know.

However, Hirsch's list of cultural literacy terms fails to provide the deep contextual knowledge that he himself believes in. Rather, it reads like a laundry list of disconnected facts, plucked from the context in which they should be taught. Presented alphabetically, with little rationale for selection or annotation, the idiosyncratic list of terms becomes almost surreal: a postmodern jumble of random tropes that mock Hirsch's own arguments about the integral relationship between contextual understanding and reading comprehension. Here is an example taken from the letter "K" in his alphabetical appendix to *Cultural Literacy*.

Kabul
Kafka, Franz
kamikaze
kangaroo court
Kansas
Kansas City, Missouri
Kant, Immanuel
Kapital, Das (title)
Karachi
Keats, John
keep the wolf from the door
Keller, Helen
Kelvin, Lord
Kennedy, Edward
Kennedy, John F. (JFK)

Kennedy, Robert F. (RFK)
Kent State University
Kentucky
Kentucky Derby
Kepler, Johannes
kettledrum
Key, Francis Scott
Keynes, John Maynard
Keynesian economics
KGB
Khomeini, Ayatollah
Khrushchev, Nikita
kibbutz
Kidd, Captain
kidney

Kiev	Kissinger, Henry
Kilimanjaro	Kitty Hawk
kill with kindness	kleptomania
kilometer	Klondike gold rush
kilowatt-hour (kwh)	knee-jerk reflex
kinetic energy	Knesset
King, Jr., Martin Luther	Knights of the Round Table
King Arthur stories	Knock on wood.
King James Version (Bible)	Knowledge is power.
King Kong	Know-Nothing
King Lear (title)	Koran
kingdom come	Korea
kingdom was lost, For want of	Korean War
a nail the	kosher
King's English, speak the	Kremlin
Kinsey, Alfred	Ku Klux Klan (KKK)
Kipling, Rudyard	Kuwait[76]

Perhaps those who purchase Hirsch's books can research the names, phrases, facts, titles, and places that he recommends. Or perhaps his lists of "what literate Americans know" can serve as a touchstone for teachers and parents. However, how can his lists provide the deep cultural meaning that he ascribes to them? Without the highly trained teachers and educated parents who can provide the deep contextual and interpretive knowledge implied in the lists, they have little value. However, Hirsch's lists do serve another purpose: They reify American culture as an established, unchanging canon of knowledge, in effect a commodity available for purchase.[77] In fact, E. D. Hirsh has become a master at marketing knowledge with his best-selling Core Knowledge Series of books delineating cultural literacy for every elementary grade level (e.g., *What Your Kindergartner Needs to Know: Preparing Your Child for a Lifetime of Learning*). For more than a decade parents have flocked to bookstores to buy these grade-level dictionaries of cultural literacy. However, I believe that Hirsch would be the first to agree that these lists of code words mean little unless parents and schools can teach the critical thinking, analytical skills, and deep historical and cultural knowledge in which each term is embedded.[78]

FORMATION OF NATIONAL IDENTITY

Coincidentally, around the time that *A Nation at Risk* was published, several academic texts about the teaching of national history also appeared, initially outside the United States. But this line of argument converged in certain respects with the arguments being put forward by the conservative educational reformers. Renewed interest in the question of how national identity is formed and develops seems to have been sparked by the publication of Benedict Anderson's *Imagined Communities* in 1983.[79] It launched an international debate over the construction of national identity and what role the state should play in this process. In parallel with E. D. Hirsch and the conservative policymakers in the U.S.—this literature was concerned primarily with Europe and the developing world—a number of scholars argued that a nation's survival depended on its ability to create and maintain a common culture. As the sociologist Ernest Gellner, a major theorist in this debate, put it: "Two men are of the same nation if and only if they share the same culture, where culture in turn means a system of ideas and signs and associations and ways of behaving and communicating."[80] Gellner's advocacy of a common culture and core curriculum as the foundation for nationhood was based on the economic and bureaucratic demand for a mobile, literate, culturally standardized, and interchangeable population in a global capitalist economy. Thus for Gellner, the central role of education should be to safeguard the common cultural/linguistic medium of the nation.

> The state, above all, is the protector, not of faith, but of a culture, and the maintainer of the inescapably homogeneous and standardizing educational system, which alone can turn out the kind of personnel capable of switching from one job to another within a growing economy and a mobile society, and indeed of performing jobs which involve manipulating meanings and people rather than things. . . . populations are anonymous, fluid and mobile, and they are unmediated; the individual belongs to them directly, in virtue of his cultural style, and not in virtue of membership in nested sub groups.[81]

Gellner argued, therefore, that a centralized and standardized educational system is fundamental to the modern social and economic order. At the foundation of the modern state stands "not the executioner, but the professor. Not the guillotine, but the *doctorat d'état* is the main tool and symbol of state power. The monopoly of legitimate education is now more important, more central than is the monopoly of legitimate violence."[82] For Gellner, the educational system therefore becomes a critical component of the social infrastructure. "If some part of the educational system, by default or from surreptitious design, actually produces internal cultural differences and thereby permits or encourages discrimination, this is counted as something of a scandal."[83]

Although uttered in a different context, these words would certainly have struck a responsive chord with the conservative educational reformers in the United States. Although the American reformers seem not to have been particularly conscious of this debate, its conclusions meshed, in many respects, with their own.

BESTSELLERS, CANONS, AND CULTURE WARS

By 1987 the conservatives had consolidated their victory in this round of culture wars by publishing best-selling books. Many, such as Ravitch, Finn, Hirsch, and Bennett, looked back nostalgically to an era when Americans ruled the world both economically and politically, and when Americans adhered to a common culture, at least in theory. Allan Bloom now seconded E. D. Hirsch's criticism, but shifted the blame onto the university curriculum, rather than the schools, for undermining this traditional sense of a unified culture. For example, in *The Closing of the American Mind*, Bloom lamented the passing of a bygone age when, Bloom believed, American undergraduates had aspired toward a liberal education.[84] According to Bloom, during the 1960s, student revolutionaries (e.g., black power activists), had chipped away at the canon of liberal education by forcing professors to drop the classics from the curriculum and replace them with fuzzy, feel-good, politically correct, self-referential texts. Not only had liberal education all but disappeared, but, according to Bloom's subtitle, "higher education [had] failed democracy and impoverished the souls of today's students."

Bloom's book took the nation by storm, triggering a full-fledged culture war in the popular press. On the *New York Times* bestseller list for eighteen weeks, Bloom's polemic spilled over to pundits on talk radio and in the press. As an indication of the scale of the controversy that eventually surrounded higher education, let me point to the 1990 cover story, "The Thought Police," of an issue of *Newsweek* devoted to "political correctness."[85] By then, "P.C." had become a household word, and a key term in the escalating cultural debate. Many argue that Bloom's book was the opening round in a concerted campaign to undermine the public's faith in higher education. However, Bloom apparently did not achieve this market success entirely alone: According to Paul Gottfried, he received more than $3 million in grants and donations from various funding agencies between 1986 and 1989 to write and promote his books.[86]

Riding the anti-P.C. wave, in 1991 the Olin Foundation gave generous research grants to two public intellectuals: Dinesh D'Souza, former editor of the conservative *Dartmouth Review*, and Roger Kimball, managing editor of the *New Criterion*. D'Souza researched how multiculturalism had affected various institutions of higher education around the country. His book *Illiberal Education: The Politics of Race and Sex on Campus* became another bestseller. Roger Kimball assembled an edited book of articles on political correctness that had previously been published in the conservative journal *New Criterion*. Called *Tenured Radicals: How Politics Has Corrupted Our Higher Education*, the book also had a large public following.

Illiberal Education made its impact by anatomizing the perceived political correctness of the academic establishment.[87] It is a provocative, blow-by-blow account of how certain multicultural activists allegedly forced university leaders to dismantle liberal education at institutions of higher learning throughout the country. According to D'Souza, policies driven by political correctness—preferential admission policies, victim-driven curricula, and identity politics based on race and gender—are the real culprits. As an example, he describes Berkeley's policy of preferential admissions: Standards are lowered for African Americans and Latinos and raised for Asians, who are overrepresented in the student population. Although D'Souza believes that extending opportunity is a worthy goal, he attempts to convince the reader that the consequences of preferential admissions are disastrous: Instead of bringing the races together in a mutually informing intellectual and social discussion, the inequalities in ability that result from preferential admissions policies ultimately lead to mutual distrust and separatism on campus.

D'Souza's case against P.C. was greatly exaggerated. In fact, if one consults university catalogues across the country one will discover that even today the vast majority of courses taught are still traditional. However, the fact that most university courses remained traditional did not stop Roger Kimball from claiming that political correctness was not only thriving in university classrooms, but was institutionalized though the hiring and tenure system. In his introduction to *Tenured Radicals* he argued that the very professors who were "paid to introduce students to the great works and ideas of our civilization have by and large remained true to the ideology of the sixties. . . . The university is now supplying many of those erstwhile radicals with handsome paychecks, a pleasant working environment, and lifetime job security."[88]

In *Dogmatic Wisdom*, historian Russell Jacoby joins Allan Bloom, Dinesh D'Souza, Roger Kimball, and a chorus of conservatives in their lament for the passing of liberal education in America.[89] However, he diverges from them when he comes to consider the causes. He disagrees with the conservative argument that preferential admissions, identity politics, and victim-driven curricula are the culprits. Rather, he argues that the forces of American consumerism and capitalism have led to the steady dismantling of liberal education throughout this century, and that the current decline of liberal education is really a continuation of "business as usual" in American education.[90] According to Jacoby, the decline of basic books, core studies, and the Western canon predates the radicalism of the 1960s, feminism, and postmodernism. Today's students, more often than not, are far more likely to take professional courses such as "Business Psychology and Management Economics" than courses such as "Gender or Peace Studies." In 1991, he notes, 250,000 business degrees were conferred compared to 7,300 in philosophy. Even if humanities courses have fallen prey to feminist theory, identity politics, and postmodern neologisms, the fact is that very few students ever take them. According to Jacoby the real crisis in the humanities has been caused by the anti-intellectualism and pragmatism practiced by the American elite, who, more and more, have taken over the leading public universities.

Jacoby attempts to historicize the debate over what constitutes the canon. He cites the case of Charles W. Eliot, president of Harvard University at the turn of the century and distinguished member of the Committee of Ten, who did more than anyone to foster the elective system at the expense of the classics. Jacoby argues that a coherent liberal curriculum has not existed for ages, just a "smorgasbord approach" to curriculum that originated during the Progressive era, long predating the 1960s. What postdates the 1960s, however, is what he calls the increasing gentrification of the university. As evidence, he points to the proliferation of campus coffeehouses and shopping opportunities and the similar proliferation of elective courses catering to utilitarian interests. Jacoby therefore argues that in order for liberal education to survive, the universities must cast out the philistines and recapture its non-utilitarian dimension.[91]

In *The Opening of the American Mind*, historian Lawrence Levine also takes issue with Bloom's, D'Souza's, and Kimball's central argument: that there once was a fixed canon that shaped and guided every American's way of thinking, and that in recent years this canon has been subverted by groups of aggressive and self-interested multiculturalists. Levine asserts instead that there never was such a canon and that the efforts of multiculturalists to broaden the base of America's self-image are part of a process that has been going on throughout American history, and is something to be celebrated.

Levine backs up his argument with historical documentation of the major educational trends since the nineteenth century. Prophets of doom such as Bloom and D'Souza rest their arguments largely on recent anecdotal evidence, hearsay, and personal experience. Their perspective is presentist, he claims: It feeds their nostalgia for a historic canon whose existence they cannot establish, but merely assert. "Much of this nostalgia is fueled by a faulty sense of the history of the American university. . . . In fact, Great Books and Western Civilization courses enjoyed only a brief ascendancy: they emerged largely after World War I and declined in the decades after World War II."[92] In this way Levine uses a longer-term historical perspective to establish a fluid and dynamic concept of an evolving canon. According to Levine, the canon has historically served a transformative purpose: Its very fluidity has guaranteed that the debate over national identity would remain open to successive waves of immigrants. The canon shifted to reflect those historical and political realities.

Levine looks to the history of the university itself to develop his argument for an evolving canon. It was not until 1885 that Charles Eliot, president of Harvard University, campaigned for an expansion of the classical canon to include foreign languages, science, and history, through an elective system. Slowly, and only after much debate, did Ivy League campuses extend the canon to include subjects such as modern languages.

Levine could thus argue that the president of Harvard at the turn of the century had done more to undermine the academic foundations of Western civilization than any 1960s radical, 1970s feminist, or 1980s multiculturalist. The Western civilization canon was never as firmly in place as Bloom, Hirsch, Kimball, and D'Souza would have us believe. Nor was the literary canon, in which American literature was long considered derivative and second-class. Only with the American victory in World War II, Cold War leadership, and the expansion of higher education under the G.I. Bill were Emerson, Whitman, and Dickinson allowed to join the European pantheon and legitimized as literary greats. Once American authors had made it onto the Great Books list, it was only a matter of time before the university would respond to globalizing forces by further expanding the curriculum.[93] Thus Levine argues, "Canons do not reside in some protracted galaxy of universal truths beyond the reach of merely temporal events."[94] The flexibility of the canon is to be celebrated as part of the democratic process, not lamented.

Todd Gitlin's contribution to the cultural debate, *The Twilight of Common Dreams*, although written from the left, supports Bloom's,

D'Souza's, and Kimball's arguments. Gitlin claims, "The squandering of energy on identity politics, the hardening of the boundaries between groups, the insistence that individuals are no more than their labels, is an American tragedy."[95] He explains how this tragedy came about. During the 1960s, the New Left coalition was ecumenical in spirit and politically engaged. However, with the murder of Martin Luther King Jr., African Americans lost all hope for a redemptive struggle across racial lines, severed ties with their former white liberal allies, and espoused separatism, which became the "template for ethnic multiplication."[96] Feminists, gays, Jews, Chicanos, Asian Americans, and other single-identity groups decided to "go it alone,"[97] and the left became fragmented. Instead of marching on Washington *en masse*, special-interest groups marched on English departments demanding symbolic representation. Meanwhile, the right took over the White House.

However, Gitlin parts company with the conservatives when it comes to solutions. Bloom, D'Souza, Hirsch, and Kimball propose that we return to a traditional canon, which they believe has the power to unite all Americans under a single set of ideals. Gitlin, on the other hand, wants to return to a traditional leftist movement. He believes that in the past the left had the power to unite Americans under a common dream of political, social, and economic equality, deriving from American history.

Others on the left agree with Gitlin's analysis. Aijaz Ahmad argues that the cult of theory that gained currency at the university after the 1960s movements had the effect of domesticating the "very forms of political dissent which those movements had sought to foreground, to displace an activist culture with a textual culture . . . with a new mystique of leftish professionalism and to reformulate in a postmodernist direction questions which had previously been associated with a broadly Marxist politics."[98]

From this array of key texts one can get a sense of the crosscurrents of the culture wars during the late 1980s and early 1990s. Battle lines were beginning to be drawn, positions staked out. The advocates of a supposedly traditional canon were articulating their ideal in a series of best-selling books that captured the popular imagination and gained widespread political adherence. Jacoby's and Gitlin's divergent perspectives, on the other hand, show that the liberal left did not speak with a single voice. Nor did their views command the degree of public attention and political support that the cultural conservatives were now mobilizing. This fragmentation and relative lack of public exposure helps to explain why the liberal left took so long to respond to Bloom's, D'Souza's, and Kimball's polemics. By 1987 the intellectual initiative had passed to the cultural conservatives, who were better organized and also enjoyed the backing of the government and private money. Having laid the groundwork intellectually for a return to their ideal of a traditional historical canon, they were now prepared to implement educational policy.

4

Genesis of the National Center for History in the Schools and the National History Standards Project, 1987–1992

I N 1987, JUST AS RAVITCH AND FINN, Hirsch, and others were publishing their jeremiads about educational decline, the state of California came to the rescue with the publication of its bold new *History–Social Science Framework*.[1] This *Framework* is important for two reasons. First, it became a model and rallying point for history-centered curricula nationwide, especially among conservative policymakers. Second, it is closely linked to the genesis of the National History Standards Project through its co-authors, Charlotte Crabtree, professor of Education at UCLA, and Diane Ravitch.

CALIFORNIA DREAMIN':
THE *CALIFORNIA HISTORY–SOCIAL SCIENCE FRAMEWORK*

The *History–Social Science Framework* was the pet project of Bill Honig, then Superintendent of Education for California. Honig, a visionary leader and consummate politician who pried an unprecedented $950 million from the state legislature to pay for an extensive program of systemic reform, sponsored the development of new state frameworks in all content areas as the first stage of this process. Since Honig was an advocate of traditional, discipline-based liberal education, he solicited the advice of academic specialists in math, science, history, and English as to what curriculum should be taught in each subject area. With the input of disciplinary scholars, the State Department of Education began the process of revising the curricular frameworks for these content areas. In California these frameworks served as the guiding state documents shaping classroom instruction, the content of textbooks, professional development, and statewide performance tests.[2] Today standards also serve as curricular guidelines.

Of all the subject matter frameworks that were under development, Honig claims to have taken a particular interest in the *History–Social Science Framework* because he was once a social studies teacher himself and loves history. However, he recalled that it was difficult to find engaging history materials for his students. Like Hirsch, Finn, and Ravitch, Honig blamed progressive education and the social studies movement for banishing historical content from the curriculum and for substituting current events and cultural relativism. Honig was determined that the new state framework would restore historical content, narrative, and drama to the bland social studies curriculum that he believed was in place. History, he believed, should be inspirational for students, providing them with enchanting stories and heroes to emulate.[3] In *Last Chance for Our Children*, Honig articulated his views on the subject: He contrasted the vacuity of social studies education with the profundity of history.

> Modern social studies guides like to rearrange the world for scholarly consumption according to grand, overarching themes, for example, "human conflict," "cultural interaction," and "global understanding," whose loftiness is rivaled only by their ambiguity. The traditional approach is much more down to earth. . . . History is about the risk and daring of real people—Hannibal crossing the Alps, Galileo facing the ecclesiastical courts, Eleanor Roosevelt confronting the bonus marchers—it has a unique ability to engage students in the dramatic unfolding of events.[4]

Inspired by this vision of "heroic" history, Honig commissioned a blue ribbon advisory committee in 1986 to devise a new history-centered History–Social Science Framework. The workings of this advisory committee reveal how the *Framework* evolved under Honig's leadership, and how a long-term professional collaboration began between Crabtree and Ravitch. Honig made a passionate case for restoring traditional history to the state curriculum. He argued that the Western tradition, liberal education, and democratic values should permeate the history curriculum. Inviting historian Paul Gagnon from Boston University and Diane Ravitch from Teachers College, Columbia, to join the committee, Honig sought to shore up his position against an anticipated challenge from the California social studies establishment.[5] The challenge soon came as the Framework and Criteria Committee prepared to do its work. Fearing that the social studies curriculum would be radically altered by a new framework, the California Council for the Social Studies (CCSS) lobbied the Department of Education to reissue the 1981 *Framework*, which had been their own handiwork. As part of this effort to shore up social studies education, Jean Claugus, chair of the framework committee, asked Charlotte Crabtree, professor of education at UCLA's Graduate School of Education, to speak to the framework committee. Crabtree, a social studies professor who had spent many years working in the subfield of geography education, spoke eloquently about how young children acquire geography skills, and how both geography and history should be integrated throughout the curriculum. Claugus hoped that Crabtree might persuade the framework committee to incorporate geography into the social studies curriculum, and thereby break history's monopoly. In fact, Crabtree's presentation was so persuasive that geography became central to the *Framework*, and she was invited to join the committee. Claugus assumed that she had secured a social studies ally in the process.[6]

However, fate would dictate otherwise. Working in three separate writing groups, one each for elementary, middle, and high school, the committee drew up a first draft of the *Framework*. Ironically, Ravitch, a well-known advocate for traditional history, and Crabtree, the acknowledged social studies expert, were now partnered with a group of teachers to write the elementary section. Although they incorporated social studies skills, geography, and literature in their draft, they used history as the central organizing discipline, rejecting the old "expanding environments" approach advocated by the social studies establishment. Ravitch and Honig felt that the "expanding environments" model, in which young students study themselves in kindergarten, their family in first grade, their neighborhood in second, and their community in third, only to discover the historical past in grades four or five, forced young children into mindless presentism.[7]

Ravitch claims that she had developed an antipathy toward social studies when she did her research for *The Troubled Crusade*. According to Ravitch,

> My research ... introduced me to the ideology of the founders of the social studies field, who seemed to care more about socializing students than about encouraging intellectual growth and independent thinking. I came to realize that the social studies field was created in order to shift curricular attention to the present, away from the past; the founders saw social studies as a way of shaping the attitudes and values of students, a means of benevolent social control. History, in their view, was elitist, aristocratic, individualistic, and too difficult for the masses, and they could not see why any student would want to know about remote times and places.[8]

Ravitch believed that engaging stories about remote times and places should form the basis of history instruction, especially for young children. Citing passages from Bruno Bettelheim's *The Uses of Enchantment*, which challenged the psychological premises of the expanding environments approach, Ravitch pushed the committee to encourage the use of myths and legends in the K–4 curriculum because she believed, with Bettelheim, that young children had a psychological need to confront life's basic human predicaments through fairy tales and fiction.[9] Her emphasis on myths and legends converged with Honig's passion for inspirational narratives about heroes and heroic tales. Ravitch also believed that myths and legends made for engaging reading, rather than the current vacuous texts describing neighborhood helpers and family roles. Through her work on the drafting committee, Crabtree too came to support the Honig-Ravitch approach to a history-geography–centered curriculum.[10]

When the full committee reconvened, the task force members deputized Berkeley historian Matthew Downey, who was associated with the social studies establishment, to compile the various grade-level drafts into a coherent framework. Downey produced a draft based on the original materials, but Honig then asked Crabtree and Ravitch to write the final version, based on the history-centered approach.[11]

By March 1987 drafts of the *Framework* were circulating for review throughout the state. Charlotte Crabtree, appointed to conduct the consensus phase of the project, shepherded the drafts through a complex review process including 1,700 field reviews, several public hearings, and numerous meetings of the curriculum commission. All the while Crabtree made the required modifications to the draft as each group gave input. On July 10, 1987, the State Department of Education adopted the new *Framework*.

RETROSPECTIVE: THE HISTORY OF SOCIAL STUDIES REFORM

Ravitch's and Crabtree's emphasis on chronological history in the *Framework* was intended to provide an alternative to social studies education, which they, like Honig, blamed for lack of rigor and multicultural excess. The *Framework* was a decisive victory for Honig, whose vision for traditional education thus helped shape the national trend back to the core academic disciplines that persists down to today. But the battle over the role of history in K–12 education goes back to the beginnings of the social studies movement during the Progressive era. Understanding this historic battle is fundamental to understanding the dynamics of the National History Standards Project.

Hazel Hertzberg's 1981 book, *Social Studies Reform: 1880–1980*, is perhaps the only comprehensive history of the social studies movement ever written. Hertzberg explains why this is so.

> The past of the social studies lives not as written history but as a kind of academic folklore; people acquire a sense of development from their own experience and from hearing the tales of their elders. It is thus possible for major movements to run their course and disappear from current consciousness, continuing to affect present behavior while the records and artifacts of such movements are largely forgotten.[12]

Therefore, Hertzberg explains, in order to understand the development of the social studies curriculum, one must piece together snippets of information from the various proceedings, bulletins, and articles commissioned by the National Council for the Social Studies and other affiliated groups.[13]

Hertzberg's own historical account is invaluable if one is to understand the history of the social studies up until 1980. The concept of the "social studies" was first formalized in 1916, when the Committee on Social Studies of the Commission on the Reorganization of Secondary Education published a report called *The Social Studies in Secondary Education*.[14] Since the 1890s history had been the centerpiece of the pre-collegiate and collegiate curriculum, and the social sciences were only just beginning to be recognized as disciplines in their own right at the university level, let alone in K–12 education. The 1916 Commission report launched the social studies movement in K–12 education, a movement aligned to Deweyan ideals of progressive education and Rugg's ideal of social reconstruction.[15] It is difficult to separate the development of the social studies field from the Progressive movement, especially because many members of the Committee on Social Studies worked with charity organizations and settlement houses.[16] With this Progressive spirit in mind, the Committee proposed that social studies topics should be selected based on two criteria: Topics should correspond to the present life and interests of pupils, or topics should assist them in preparing for the future. Members of the panel, most not academics, recommended the study of utility-minded subjects. Thus they recommended vocational civics and community civics for seventh and eighth grades; a high school course in "Problems of American Democracy"; and high school courses in modern European and American history. They used the umbrella term "social studies" to refer collectively to economics, history, political science, sociology, and civics. Social studies was defined as those courses "whose subject matter relates directly to the organization and development of human society, and to man as a member of social groups."[17]

While the social scientists were lobbying for the inclusion of their disciplines in the K–12 curriculum to help students deal with the complexity of modern life, historians such as Charles A. Beard were revamping academic historiography along parallel lines at the universities, calling for a "new history" that "speaks to the present."[18] All forces were converging to dislodge traditional history from the core of the curriculum. Thus began the long-standing struggle over the K–12 curriculum between advocates of the social sciences and advocates of traditional history that persists down to this day, and that permeated the development of the history standards.

One of the most enduring aspects of the social studies field has been the ongoing debate to define it. The social studies curriculum has been difficult to define because it is organized as a loose confederation of social science disciplines, rather than as a single discipline with a coherent intellectual framework and methodology.[19] Within the social studies, proponents of the individual academic disciplines have vied for a place within the curriculum. One such individual was historian Arthur Bestor, who fought hard to reinstate history at the core.

Bestor was perhaps the most widely read critic of American education during the 1950s. In *Educational Wastelands: A Retreat from Learning in Our Public Schools*, Bestor blamed schools of education for watering down the curriculum with concepts such as "social studies." Reacting to the postwar "Life Adjustment Movement," with its emphasis on vocational education, Bestor criticized the education courses currently offered to teachers, characterizing them as "warping the great intellectual disciplines to serve the narrow purposes of indoctrination and vocationalism."[20] Instead, Bestor advised that learning should draw upon the structures of the academic disciplines and their underlying principles. Like his contemporary Jerome Bruner, Bestor believed that understanding ideas, not assimilating facts, was the prime objective of learning. Therefore he argued that specific social studies skills and topics should never be taught in isolation. Rather, skills and topics should be taught within the broader structural frameworks of the disciplines so that students will be able to transfer what they had learned when they encounter new information. Bruner called this process "nonspecific transfer": a general idea can be used as a foundation for recognizing subsequent problems as special cases or subsets of the more general idea originally mastered. He argued that this type of transfer is at the heart of the educational process—the continual broadening and deepening of knowledge within the structure of a discipline.[21] In this way, knowledge is usable beyond the context in which it is first learned. Bestor recommended that the "problem-centered" approach, so fashionable in the social studies, should be replaced with an academic curriculum designed to train the mind in disciplinary thinking. Social studies, he asserted, ought to be abolished because often social science courses ended up being taught as history courses anyway. He contended that the term "social studies" led to educational "faddism," not to a systematic understanding of the disciplines.[22]

Bestor claimed that the main obstacle to educational change was the "interlocking directorate of professional educationists," a network of education professors, government officials, teachers' unions, and public school administrators who had successfully created an "iron curtain" between public schools and scholars of academic disciplines. He called for a new alliance between disciplinary scholars and schoolteachers, hoping to bypass the entire education establishment. Jerrold Zacharias and Jerome Bruner were just two of the dozens of eminent scholars who responded to this call during the *Sputnik* era by leading the K–12 curricular reform projects in their respective disciplines.

According to another critic, Kieran Egan, most, if not all, of the problems of contemporary social studies may be traced to Dewey's inadequate pedagogy, psychology, and sense of history. In *Teaching as Story Telling*, Egan recommended that social studies be abolished and that students be taught history.[23] This debate continues. Participants in the California framework committee refought the same battle over the place of history within the social studies curriculum. According to Ravitch, Finn, Honig, and many of the 1980s humanities reformers, the social studies field was largely responsible for the presentism that characterized today's students. They argued, like Bestor, that the social studies, with its emphasis on the present, had destroyed liberal education and a coherent vision of the past. The schools were failing because they had given up the goal of liberal education.

Thus Ravitch and the other humanities reformers hoped to revive liberal education with their call for rigorous content standards during the 1980s. They assumed that if they put disciplinary scholars in charge of the standards setting process, liberal education would be resuscitated. However, they got more than they bargained for because by the 1980s the paradigm of liberal education had been overturned by the very academic historians whom they now needed to head up the discipline-based reform. Disciplinary knowledge no

longer conformed to the canon of liberal education, either intellectually or methodologically.

THE TWO FACES OF MULTICULTURALISM:
ASSIMILATION VS. PLURALISM

Not only did the history crusaders of the 1980s criticize the social studies curriculum for its emphasis on the present, but they also objected to
its curricular fragmentation, which they attributed to the centrifugal
pressures of multiculturalism. The National Council for the Social Studies (NCSS), the professional organization representing social studies
teachers, had endorsed a multicultural approach to teaching the social
studies. Under the leadership of James A. Banks, considered by many to
be the preeminent scholar of multiculturalism in K–12 education, the
NCSS published its *Curriculum Guidelines for Multiethnic Education: Position Statement* in 1976.[24] These guidelines made the case for teaching cultural *pluralism*, as distinct from *assimilation*. These two approaches to
multiculturalism have profound curricular implications: pluralism highlights cultural differences; assimilation highlights cultural similarities.
In 1992, the NCSS reaffirmed its commitment to cultural pluralism in
its revised *NCSS Curriculum Guidelines for Education*, thus staking a position in direct opposition to the humanities reformers.[25]

The writers of the California *Framework*, however, in contrast to the
authors of the NCSS guidelines, sought to create a document advancing
an assimilationist rather than a pluralist perspective for multicultural
education. The critics of pluralism, such as Ravitch and Honig, acknowledged the fact that diverse cultures make up the fabric of American
society, but they feared that the pluralistic multicultural curriculum advanced by the NCSS was a threat to national unity. As Nathan Glazer
observed, their, "gravest fear [was] that 'oppression studies,' as they called
it, would cultivate an active hostility among some minorities to the key
institutions of state and society, making effective government as well as
the economic progress of such groups, more difficult."[26] Ravitch's and
Honig's solution was to create a narrative history that would embrace
differences, yet subsume them within the larger story of a shared national
identity. The following statement, written by Ravitch in her introduction
to the *Framework*, sets the assimilationist tone for the entire curriculum:[27]

> To understand this nation's identity, students must: Recognize that
> American identity is now and has always been pluralistic and multi-
> cultural. From the first encounter between indigenous peoples and ex-

ploring Europeans, the inhabitants of the North American continent have represented a variety of races, religions, languages, and ethnic and cultural groups. With the passage of time, the United States has grown increasingly diverse in its social and cultural composition. Yet, even as our people have become increasingly diverse, there is broad recognition that we are one people. Whatever our origins, we are all Americans.[28]

While Ravitch uses the language of pluralism, her message is decidedly one of assimilation.

Indeed, the *Framework*, under the leadership of Honig, Ravitch, and Crabtree, was an attempt to walk the middle ground between the new multiculturalism and a traditional canon. In contrast to the extreme conservatives who would prefer to frame national identity in terms of Anglo America, these more moderate reformers proposed a model of multiculturalism that, while expanding the canon to include hyphenated Americans, nevertheless took for granted a shared conception of American national identity. As Lawrence Blum has argued, the *Framework* offers ". . . no tension between the cultural plurality of the American polity, and the unity necessary for nationhood and civic loyalty."[29]

The mechanism by which the writers would achieve this apparent harmony was to place a greater emphasis on narrative history, as against the "fuzzy" social studies methodologies found in the 1981 California *Framework*. Not only did they believe that social studies lacked narrative coherence, but they believed it encouraged victimization, divisiveness, and negativism. By writing a synthesizing narrative emphasizing the positive aspects of American history and minimizing the negative ones, they hoped to encourage an upbeat interpretation of the American past. Referring to their narrative approach as a "story well-told," the reformers chose not to problematize the omniscient role of the narrator, as Hayden White and Joyce Appleby had done, and chose not to ask the critical question of *what* history, or *whose* history, should constitute the story-well-told. Nevertheless, the expression "story-well-told" became the hymn for the new *Framework*, and the guiding principle for the textbooks that would follow. While Honig and others used the catchphrase "story-well-told" primarily to describe engaging narrative stories, they also, perhaps inadvertently, used it as a trope substituting for "grand historical narrative." The *Framework* narrative read like this:

We are strong because we are united in a pluralistic society of many races, cultures, and ethnic groups; we have built a great nation because we have learned to live in peace with each other, respecting each other's right to be different, and supporting each other as members of a common community.[30]

However, this rather Polyannesque view of our national past did not command universal approval. Catherine Cornbleth and Dexter Waugh, two leading critics of the *Framework*, attacked the California reform for "[creating] a blend of pluralism and nationalism rooted in a concept of America as a land of immigrants who have historically subscribed to a common set of ideals and values—a civic glue that has kept the nation together despite economic disparities and struggles over unfulfilled rights."[31] History, they argued,

> becomes a continuum of inevitability—of development, of progress, of "destiny"—starting with European arrival and colonization, the inevitable if unfortunate conquest of Native Americans, the inhumane enslavement of Africans to replenish and replace the original Native American slaves, and the development of democratic institutions based on the Judeo-Christian, European tradition. America today thus becomes a pluralistic society built by immigrants who fought and came to subscribe to one commonly held set of democratic values. Looking at American history in this way reduces blacks to just another immigrant group . . . it is a way of generalizing the white ethnic experience to encompass enslaved blacks, Native Americans, and more recent immigrant Koreans, Muslims from India and Pakistan, Nicaraguans, and political refugees from Cambodia, Laos and Vietnam—*everyone*.[32]

Several other critics agreed that this "nation of immigrants" perspective seriously distorts the place of African Americans, Native Americans, and Latinos in our national history. First of all, they argued, not all Americans were descendants of voluntary immigrants. Second, not all immigrants were white. Third, some Americans were indigenous. Fourth, it was difficult for nonwhites to visualize themselves blending into the great melting pot. Thus many critics argued that the model of white ethnicity did not work for nonwhites because it left ethnic conflict out of the framing narrative of American history. This model consigned such hideous injustices as slavery and its legacy of institutional racism, and the extermination of indigenous populations, to the margins as aberrant historical phenomena. The central historical narrative remained that of white European immigrants.

We only have to go back to the 1940s and 1950s to see how recently the history textbooks denied any racial conflict whatsoever. Take, for instance, Oliver Chitwood's 1947 fifth-grade textbook on American history:

> The Negroes were brought from Africa and sold to the people of our country in early times. After a while there came to be thousands and thou-

sands of these Negro slaves. Most of them were found in the southern states. On the southern plantations, where tobacco and cotton and rice were grown, they worked away quite cheerfully. In time many people came to think that it was wrong to own slaves. Some of them said that all the Negro slaves should be freed. Some of the people who owned slaves became angry at this. They said that the black people were better off as slaves in America than they would have been as wild savages in Africa. Perhaps this was true, as many of the slaves had snug cabins to live in, plenty to eat, and work that was not too hard for them to do. Most of the slaves seemed happy and contented.[33]

Although difficult to imagine, a similar tone was struck in Dinesh D'Souza's 1995 article, "We the Slaveowners: In Jefferson's America, Were Some Men Not Created Equal," published in the Heritage Foundation's monthly journal, *Policy Review*. In his article, D'Souza advanced a positive interpretation of the long-term benefits of slavery: "Slavery was an institution that was terrible to endure for slaves, but it left the descendants of slaves better off in America. For this, the American Founders are owed a measure of respect and gratitude."[34]

While the 1987 *Framework* represented a tremendous advance over the textbooks of the 1940s and 1950s, critics argued that it continued to characterize the relations among ethnic groups as harmonious. It did this by means of a strategy that Cornbleth and Waugh refer to as "additive multiculturalism." In this interpretation, *other* heroes (usually indigenous peoples and people of color) and their contributions are added to the conventional stories of American history as sidebars. However, according to Cornbleth and Waugh, these newly inducted members to the American pantheon must qualify for membership in the club. "They must contribute to the white mainstream, sustain rather than challenge the status quo, and most importantly, serve as reliable role models for students."[35] Martin Luther King Jr. qualifies for the pantheon; Malcolm X does not. This analysis may not be entirely true: witness that E. D. Hirsch included Malcolm X in his pantheon; however, the *Framework* did not.

Henry Giroux argues in *Border Crossings* that this bland type of "additive multiculturalism" not only glosses over conflict, but glosses over any attempt to "designate how dominant configurations of power privilege some cultures over others, how power works to secure forms of domination that marginalize and silence the subordinated groups. . . . Absent is any account of how various social movements have struggled historically to transform a Eurocentric curriculum that has functioned to exclude or marginalize the voices of women, blacks, and other groups."[36]

However, Ravitch disagreed publicly with this characterization of the *Framework*. In 1989 she argued before the Manhattan Institute that the *Framework* recognized the "central role that blacks had played in shaping American political institutions. Major units are devoted to slavery in American history; to the abolition movement; to the post–Civil War amendments, and to the way they were undermined by racist political actions and replaced by Jim Crow laws, peonage, and segregation; and to the civil rights movement of the twentieth century."[37] Indeed, as Ravitch argues, the *Framework's* pedagogical strategies work against any single interpretation of the past. The *Framework* recommends that students analyze historical controversies through the use of original sources. By analyzing a variety of original documents representing conflicting viewpoints, students can decide for themselves the strength of various arguments.

In spite of these ongoing debates, the humanities reformers were thrilled with the new *Framework*, and so were many historians and educationists. Its middle-ground approach to multiculturalism seemed to strike a satisfactory balance between national unity and cultural diversity, and its emphasis on chronological history offered an antidote to the atemporality of social studies. At last, their tireless efforts to establish a discipline-based social studies curriculum seemed to have been rewarded.

However, the curriculum delineated in the *Framework* could not be implemented in California classrooms unless bold new textbooks were written. Although several publishers submitted new textbooks for state adoption, Houghton Mifflin submitted the only new textbook series that actually met the new state criteria: three years each of American and world history, sequentially articulated. The reformers knew that the textbook adoption process in California was critical to the success of the new history-centered curriculum. Therefore, they monitored the hotly contested textbook adoption process from the East Coast, and they weighed in from afar. The California textbook adoption was deemed so important that Diane Ravitch, Lynne V. Cheney, and Chester Finn all wrote letters to the California Board of Education in support of the Houghton Mifflin books. Finn wrote, "It is one thing to tell the 'whole story.' It is another to fragment the society into warring tribes. This is going to be the most contentious issue in American education in the 1990s, bar none."[38] Cheney was quoted in *Education Week*, "It is, in my opinion, the best history/social science curriculum in the nation." As for the textbook adoption, she said, "What happens in your state will settle once and for all whether or not we are going to be able to teach our children history as it should be taught."[39] The stakes were obviously high, and the cohort of reformers was mobilized for action.

THE BRADLEY COMMISSION ON HISTORY IN THE SCHOOLS

In 1987, Finn and Ravitch's Education Excellence Network established the Bradley Commission on History in the Schools, the self-proclaimed first national group to devote its attention exclusively to the study of history in K–12 schools.[40] Modeling itself on the Committee of Ten and its successors, the Bradley Commission concerned itself with the central role of history for civic education. Its purpose was to combat the prevailing trend toward social studies. The commission was chaired by historian Kenneth Jackson, with historian Paul Gagnon serving as principal investigator. Among its seventeen members were Charlotte Crabtree and Diane Ravitch, and a range of distinguished K–12 teachers and historians.[41] Supported by the conservative Bradley Foundation, the commission published its small but influential 32-page pamphlet, *Building a History Curriculum,* in 1988.[42]

The "Bradley report," as it came to be called, echoed the *Framework* by urging the extensive study of history. Like the drafters of the *Framework,* the commissioners believed that historical knowledge would foster citizenship and contribute to nation-building. This civic vision rested on the assumption of American exceptionalism. In his introduction to the report, Kenneth Jackson argued, "unlike other peoples, Americans are not bound together by a common religion and a common ethnic identity. Instead, our binding heritage is our democratic vision of liberty, equality, and justice."[43] According to this model of exceptionalism, Americans are bound together by a theoretical citizenship based on shared rights, rather than a tribal citizenship based on shared ethnicity and culture. Jackson concluded that our sense of national identity should be defined by this shared democratic heritage. As the report argued, "History can satisfy young people's longing for a sense of identity, and of their time and place in the human story . . . American history tell[s] us who we are and who we are becoming, the history of Western Civilization reveal[s] our democratic political heritage and its vicissitudes; world history acquaint[s] us with the nations and people with whom we shall share a common global destiny."[44]

Following the pattern of the California *Framework,* the Bradley Commission report explicitly recommended that the conventional social studies curriculum model of "near-to-far, expanding environments" be dropped in favor of a more historical approach, even in the early grades. The report claimed, "Historical studies and historical literature have been widely neglected in the early grades."[45] According to the committee, the expanding environments model forced young children to "remain forever in the present." So the Bradley commission proposed several curricular patterns for each school level, emphasizing historical studies at most grade levels. The commission also recommended that students take a minimum of two years of American history and a minimum of two years of world history in grades 7–12.

About the time that the Bradley Commission was preparing its history-centered report, the conservative William H. Donner Foundation established the American Textbook Council under the leadership of Gilbert Sewall, co-director of the Education Excellence Network. With initial funding of $300,000, the New York-based Council's mission was to "advance the quality of social studies textbooks and all instructional materials."[46] The Council had only one full-time employee, its director, but through this skeleton organization, Sewall became a powerful voice in the debate over multiculturalism. According to American Textbook Council literature, the "Council conducts independent reviews and studies of schoolbooks in history, social studies, and the humanities." It also publishes the *Social Studies Review*,

> a quarterly bulletin that provides reviews of social studies textbooks and commentary on curriculum issues to over 4,000 leading educators, public officials, and citizens across the country. The Council endorses the production of textbooks that embody vivid narrative style [i.e., the story-well-told], stress significant people and events, and promote better understanding of all cultures, including our own . . .[47]

Over the years Sewall and his panel of reviewers have critiqued what they regarded as politically correct textbooks, given testimony at textbook adoptions and national conferences, and written articles for the *Social Studies Review*, *Society*, *American Educator*, *American School Board Journal*, and other publications. Sewall himself serves regularly on national advisory boards. For example, in 1987 he served on the advisory board for Paul Gagnon's *Democracy's Half-Told Story*, a review of U.S. history textbooks sponsored by the American Federation of Teachers, the Education Excellence Network, and Freedom House, and in 1992 he served on the 1994 NAEP framework committee and the NHSP National Council for History Standards. Members of his own 1994 advisory board included Paul Gagnon, Charlotte Crabtree, Kenneth Jackson, and Bill Honig, names that will surface again as we discuss the NHSP. With additional funding from the John F. Olin and Earhart foundations and others, Sewall's Council still exists today.

In the case of Sewall, his title as executive director of the American Textbook Council lends authority to what he has to say. The Council serves to legitimize his public statements, and his ubiquitous presence on national committees and advisory boards. His operation forms part of a larger strategy by conservative foundations to fund a cohort of neo-conservative reformers and pundits who then sit on each other's boards, forming interlocking directorates. This network in a sense mirrors the networks of liberal theorists and policymakers that have long existed in the universities and the liberal foundations. However, this institutional division into two warring alliances has polarized intellectuals in recent years, and was to prove a major factor in the making and remaking of the National Standards for History.

CHARTING A COURSE: SOCIAL STUDIES FOR THE 21ST CENTURY

About the same time that the California framework committee and the Bradley Commission on History in the Schools were preparing their new history-centered curricular framework, the American Historical Association (AHA) began its own initiative to revamp the K–12 social studies curriculum.[48] Partnering with the National Council for Social Studies and the Organization of American Historians (OAH), the AHA called for a National Commission on Social Studies in the Schools to "determine goals and to recommend ways and means to reorder and strengthen the curriculum." This was the first time that the AHA had partnered with the NCSS since the 1940s, when the AHA, the Mississippi Valley Historical Association, and the NCSS established the Committee on American History in the Schools and Colleges. During World War II the AHA was concerned with historical illiteracy during a time of war; during the 1980s, the AHA was concerned with the "lack of synthesis in social studies, the lack of coherence in history and geography education."[49] With funding from the Carnegie Foundation for the Advancement of Teaching, the National Commission on Social Studies began work in November 1987.[50]

The Commission's report, *Charting a Course: Social Studies for the 21st Century*,[51] reveals the bind that the social studies establishment now found itself in. The National Council for Social Studies was drawn into preparing yet another history-centered report. Written in sections by various committee members, the report reveals the contradictions inherent within the uneasy alliance. For instance, in the introduction to *Charting a Course*, the social studies perspective is in evidence: "The human experience cannot be taught and comprehended through a single discipline. . . . students must comprehend the interrelationships among those subjects and their combined power to explain the past and the current human condition, and future possibilities."[52] By page three, however, a compromise position is forged between history and social studies. "Because they offer the perspectives of time and place, history and geography should provide the matrix or framework for social studies, yet concepts and understandings from political science, economics, and other social sciences must be integrated throughout all social studies courses." By page eight this uneasy compromise between historical and social studies curricular patterns reverts to the old social studies formula of expanding environments: "Kindergarten children can examine their own immediate environment through neighborhood walks, as well as environments far away in time and space through pictures and films. . . . First graders readily comprehend the concept of community. They can understand that communities, past and present, local and world wide, were developed to meet human needs . . ."[53]

Yet by the time the report addresses the higher grades, the curriculum is clearly history-centered. It boldly recommends an integrated American and world history curriculum.[54] This integrated curriculum, which embedded American history within the framework of world history, forms a radical departure from the more mainstream model in which American national history is taught separately from world history. This radical idea of subsuming national history within a world history framework would come up again during the National History Standards Project, but it was voted down by the curriculum task forces, who, although intrigued by the idea, felt it was too radical a departure from the current schema of national and patriotic history.

In spite of these innovative approaches to the study of history, the NCSS ultimately rejected *Charting a Course*. Even though the NCSS had partnered in its development, the organization felt that *Charting a Course* was too history-centered. Its publication in 1989, on the heels of the *History Social-Science Framework* and *Building a History Curriculum*, was perceived as yet another defeat for the social studies establishment. It was in this changed ideological climate, with history taking a central place once again in the K–12 curriculum, that the National Center for History in the Schools was established.

ORIGINS OF THE NATIONAL CENTER FOR HISTORY IN THE SCHOOLS

In 1986 President Reagan appointed Lynne V. Cheney chair of the National Endowment for the Humanities. Cheney shared with her predecessor, William Bennett, a conservative political agenda. Like Bennett, Cheney planned to use her position to steer the humanities back from the course they had followed over the last two decades, into safe, traditional waters. She also hoped to improve the quality of K–12 humanities education. That is why Cheney commissioned the NAEP study on the state of humanities and arts education in the nation's public schools. This study formed a sequel to William Bennett's *To Reclaim a Legacy*, an earlier NEH report on the lamentable state of the humanities in higher education. Among Cheney's advisory board members for this study were Charlotte Crabtree, E. D. Hirsch, and Diane Ravitch. Cheney published her analysis of the NAEP findings in 1987 as *American Memory*, while at the same time Ravitch and Finn published their analysis in *What Do Our 17-Year Olds Know?*[55] Cheney rehearsed a litany of by-now familiar arguments, repeating language and key terms from the series of studies of national educational decline starting with *A Nation at Risk*. Citing the NAEP study and the alleged fall in SAT scores as evidence, Cheney asserted that humanities education was in serious decline, and concluded, as Finn and Ravitch had in *17-Year-Olds*, that the "mystic chords of memory" would be severed for all time.[56] In her report, Cheney argued, like Hirsch, and the authors of *A Nation at Risk*, that an educational system failing to nurture memory is tantamount to national suicide. Note her repetition of key words and phrases employed by earlier reformers.

> Indeed, we put our sense of *nationhood at risk* by failing to familiarize our young people with the story of how the society in which they live came to be. Knowledge of the ideas that have molded us and the ideals that have mattered to us functions as a kind of *civic glue*. Our history and literature give us *symbols* to share; they help us all, no matter how diverse our backgrounds . . . By allowing the erosion of historical consciousness, we do to ourselves what an unfriendly nation bent on our destruction might."[57] [Emphasis added]

Advocating liberal education, and quoting from Matthew Arnold (the subject of her 1964 Ph.D. dissertation in English), Cheney's goal was to recapture "the best that has been thought and known in the world." Blaming social studies methodology for the current crisis in K–12 history education, Cheney argued that social studies emphasizes the present over the past, skills over content, and equity over excellence. Like the authors of *A Nation at Risk*, Cheney claimed that the recent equity reform movement had compounded the humanities crisis by diverting attention away from the humanities. She argued that

> One effect of this [equity] approach, however, has been to concentrate reform effort on basic skills, mathematics, and science. While these as-

pects of schooling assuredly deserve close attention, it is now time to
elaborate the argument; to be clear that world competition is not just
about dollars but about ideas. Our students need to know what those ideas
are, need to understand our democratic institutions, to know their origins in Western thought, to be familiar with how and why other cultures
have evolved differently from our own. . . .[58]

Having identified the problem in her study, Cheney would now
devote her energies to finding a solution. If the humanities were to be
returned to their proper place in the K–12 curriculum, then Cheney
would have to create exemplary programs to serve as models for how
this was to be done. In October 1987, Cheney announced plans to
establish a National Center for History in the Schools, calling it the
first such venture ever funded by the Endowment.[59] The new Center
would be "similar to the five 'mini-centers' established by the Education Department to improve instruction in mathematics, science, the
arts, literature, and elementary-school curricula."[60] The Center's mission would be to survey the state of history education nationally and
to develop model programs for teaching history. Through it, Cheney
hoped to "reinvigorate the study of history at all levels of elementary
and secondary education. It was [her] hope that the Center would bring
national visibility to the problems confronting schools, teachers, and
parents, and would provide leadership in the effort to improve the
teaching of history in our schools."[61]

Cheney put out the call for proposals and eleven individuals applied to establish a national history center. Among them were Matthew
Downey, a member of the California Framework committee, and Charlotte Crabtree. Crabtree emerged the winner, on the strength of her
work in the *California History-Social Science Framework*, and her success
in shepherding the *Framework* through the contentious adoption process. In an interview with *Education Week*, Cheney noted that the *Framework* had won national praise for adding an additional year of world
history to the curriculum and for the boost it had given history instruction for the early grades. She also commented that Crabtree had been
a member of the Bradley Commission on History in the Schools, and
she announced that members of the Bradley panel would serve as center scholars[62] to identify "essential historical knowledge students should
acquire."[63] Thus the NEH awarded Crabtree $1.5 million on March 22,
1988, to set up the National Center for History in the Schools at UCLA
for a period of three years. This was the Center that was destined to
become the focus of controversy when it published the history *Standards* in October 1994.

In her proposal to establish the National Center for History in the Schools (NCHS), Crabtree argued the need for such a center. She noted that at its November 1987 Annual Convention the NCSS had allocated only 12 (5%) of its 237 sessions for history-based subjects. Fully 80% of the sessions were unrelated to history in the curriculum, "an extraordinary imbalance, given the national attention currently riveted on problems of history in the nation's schools. SIGHT, the NCSS's special interest group for history teachers, drew only six attendees, none of them members."[64] Crabtree added in her mission statement that many members of the National Commission on Social Studies (the commission that produced *Charting A Course*) had publicly rejected history as the integrating core of the social studies curriculum. She concluded that history not only "suffers from benign neglect" but also from the priorities of curriculum leaders who endorse projects other than history.[65] She cited the successful curriculum she had recently helped to develop in California (the *Framework*), and contrasted it with New York's newly developed Social Studies Program.

> Clearly, the schools have abrogated to a significant degree their historic mission to transmit the heritage from the past and, through core studies in American history and Western civilization, to develop the historical perspective, political vision, and ethical understandings that enlighten and inform the problems of the present and that develop an informed and reasoned allegiance to the ideals of a free society.[66]

The National Center for History in the Schools was structured as a "cooperative UCLA/NEH research program." As such, major decisions were to be taken collaboratively by both institutions. Thus Center scholars and advisory board members would be selected by agreement of both partners. In her proposal, Crabtree selected UCLA historian Gary B. Nash as her associate director. Although Nash had a left-liberal reputation as a highly regarded social historian of Colonial American history, Cheney accepted him as associate director on Crabtree's recommendation. (Nash had proven his credentials as editor of the highly regarded Houghton Mifflin textbook series). The advisory panel and Center Scholars consisted of well-recognized historians and teachers from around the country, including some members of the Bradley Commission.[67] This same process of shared decision-making would apply in 1992 when the National Council for History Standards was constituted.

The NCHS was structured as a balanced collaboration between professional historians and K–12 teachers. Sixty-five Teacher Associ-

ates who taught American and world history were selected to participate in the work of the Center through teacher institutes that they
would attend. Traditionally, most commissions had been dominated
by academics, with teachers serving as token members only. However,
the NCHS was part of a growing collaboration between teachers in the
schools and historians in the universities for developing programs to
improve history teaching. The American Historical Association began
this trend in its History Education Project (1969–74), a movement that
had now become a major force among the professionals in both arenas
of education.

The original NCHS assistant director was Patricia Taylor, assistant
director of UCLA's Center for Academic Inter-Institutional Programs
(CAIP), an outreach program responsible for facilitating collaboration
between academics and K–12 teachers. As NCHS assistant director, Taylor helped Crabtree develop the original NCHS proposal and was largely
responsible for organizing the original teacher institutes. I was chosen to
replace her for largely fortuitous reasons. I met Crabtree in February 1989,
when I was a consultant for the nascent California History-Geography
Project, a program sponsored by CAIP. I was collecting primary source
documents to develop a sixth-grade world history curriculum for the
California project, and I came to the NCHS library looking for primary
source materials. Crabtree, who needed a consultant to conduct a three-
month search for exemplary teaching materials from around the country as one of the proposed NCHS projects, hired me as a consultant to do
the job. My job was to research model programs and to disseminate information about them through Center publications. As I will explain later,
my role grew as I became involved with the teacher institutes and the
core work of the Center. Taylor went on to direct CAIP.

LESSONS FROM HISTORY

The cornerstone of the NCHS project was to be a volume setting forth
the essential understandings and historical perspectives students should
acquire in grades K–12, which would ultimately be titled, *Lessons from
History*. It was aimed at an audience of teachers, curriculum leaders,
parents, school boards, and legislators. Once published, the volume
would provide the criteria against which to judge current curricular
offerings in history, teacher training programs, textbooks, resources,
and student learning. The Center was also charged with analyzing the
1986 NAEP data on history teaching, the same data written up in *What
Do Our 17-Year-Olds Know?* and *American Memory*, and correlating the

national data with the criterion statements that would be developed in *Lessons*. In 1992 the volume appeared. Entitled *Lessons From History: Essential Understandings and Historical Perspectives All Students Should Acquire*, it was the fruit of collaboration between center scholars, advisory panelists, historical consultants, and center teacher associates, over a period of three years.[68]

Lessons argues the case for the primacy of history in the K–12 curriculum, establishes the need for increasing the hours devoted to the study of history in the schools, and sets up guidelines for developing the understandings, perspectives, and "habits of the mind" that should be inculcated through the study of United States and world history. In the preface, the editors claim that the historical interpretation is

> broadly integrative of political and social history, and rich in its inclusion of the many peoples and constituent groups of each society under study. . . . Building the new synthesis in United States and world history is one of the great challenges confronting historians today.[69]

Lessons from History was well received by Cheney, Ravitch, Finn, and Shanker, among others on both sides of the political fence. Cheney was very pleased that she had sponsored a national model for history education comparable to the California *Framework*, a new story-well-told.

THE NCHS CURRICULUM PROJECT

Among the other major projects that the NCHS undertook was a curriculum project that I directed. The NCHS's sixty-five teacher associates attended weekend and summer institutes covering topics in both American and world history. The teachers worked with dozens of historians under the leadership of Gary Nash and Scott Waugh, a UCLA colleague, researching primary source documents in order to develop lively lessons on topics that interested them. The idea behind using primary source documents was to remove the distance that students feel from historical events and to connect them more intimately with the past. By developing lessons around these sources, the teachers could recreate for K–12 students a sense of "being there," a sense of seeing history though the eyes of the very people who were making decisions at the time. Theoretically, this would help students develop historical empathy, to realize that history is not an impersonal process divorced from real people like themselves. At the same time, by analyzing primary sources, students would actually practice the historian's craft, discovering for themselves how to analyze evidence, establish a valid interpretation, and construct a coherent narrative in which all the relevant facts play a part.

Referring to their historical topics as "dramatic moments," the teachers and historians examined crucial turning points in history to bring history alive. Although the institutes were designed primarily to promote intellectual enrichment and to help teachers develop engaging curricula for their own classrooms, and ultimately to disseminate videos of best practice, it occurred to me that we were sitting on a gold mine of lively, innovative teaching materials that we could disseminate, with some additional work, beyond the confines of the Center. It seemed absurd to scour the country for exemplary lesson plans, as we were doing, and yet ignore the potential of the models we were creating ourselves. This was particularly true because my nationwide search had turned up only about fifty outstanding examples of history lessons, which I annotated in *Selected Teaching Materials for United States and World History*.[70] I therefore decided to work with the Center's teachers and historians to develop a series of forty-five in-depth teaching units, and to set up a national dissemination project.

Jim Pearson's *Women in the American Revolution* is a typical example of an NCHS teaching unit. Written for students in grades 5 through 8, it demonstrates how primary documents can be used even for this age cohort. Content and pedagogy are mutually enhancing. The unit incorporates a variety of primary sources to explore the role of women during the Revolution: a poem, a broadside, two engravings, and several excerpts from letters and diaries. Students use these materials in their own way to discover that the struggle for American independence involved extensive participation by women, whose role in these events, until recent decades, had been marginalized. Students learn to understand the implications of the basic historical fact that women comprised half the population of Revolutionary America, and that women's participation was essential in achieving victory. To teach about the role of women during the American Revolution, in an almost "microhistorical" way, the unit offers three separate accounts of a single incident.

On July 24, 1777, one Thomas Boyleston, a Boston shopkeeper, was faced by a crowd of determined women protesting against the high prices he was charging for his British imports and against his refusal to lower prices as ordered by the local boycott committee. Below is an excerpt from one of the accounts, a letter from an eyewitness, John Scollay, dated 25 July 1777.

Yesterday we had a high Scene in this town. In the Morning a Number of Women waited on Mr. Boyleston. They told him that they kept little shops to sell necessarys for poor people, they understood that he had Coffee to sell and if he would sell it at a reasonable price they would take it off him. He gave them a verry short answer and they Left him about 3 oClock in the afternoon. A Number of Women mostly from the North part of the town Assembled under the direction of one Mrs. Colter. They were not your Maggys [lower-class women] but reputable Clean drest Women Some of them with Silk gownes on. They went to Boyleston's Warehouse where they found him. They Insisted on having his Coffee at their Price. He refused. They without Ceremony put him into a Cart having one at hand and drove him some way up the Wharf. He found it Impossible to withstand, gave them his Keys, they took one Cask and Carried it off Intending to pay him for it. Poor Boyleston was never so Swetted since he was born. He was verry roughly handled. I am sorry for the occasion but I cant say I am sorry that he has met with a rebuff. . . .[71]

The other two accounts present further details of the riot and give differing views of its causes and how it unfolded. Students compare and contrast each account word by word, and are drawn to the conclusion that no single account is definitive. (The archaic language does not act as a barrier to understanding, but rather helps to heighten the vividness of the narrative.) But this exercise in the use of primary sources has a further purpose. Students are already familiar with the broad narrative of the struggle for independence. They now discover a new dimension to this well-known story, for when examined from a new viewpoint—an awareness of women's political action—it looks rather different. The reading of primary sources can thus add depth and complexity to accepted narratives, and radically modify them in the process.

The initial success of this publishing project led the NEH officers and the NCHS directors Crabtree and Nash to offer me the Assistant Directorship of the Center. Thus it appeared in 1990 that the NEH officers were not opposed to this type of social history, which was at the heart of many, but not all, of the teaching units.

BUSH PUSHES FOR NATIONAL STANDARDS

Elected president in succession to Reagan in 1988, George Bush was determined to keep the spotlight focused on educational reform, which was evidently a winning gambit. Desiring to establish his own reputation as an "education president," Bush appropriated the crisis mentality spawned by *A Nation at Risk*. In 1989 he ordered the statisticians at the Sandia National Laboratory for Atomic Energy to conduct a study of the state of American education, presumably in the hope that his administration could produce its own set of alarming statistics. But as it turned out the Sandia study contradicted most of the claims made in *A Nation at Risk*. For example, did the nation face a severe shortage of trained scientists and mathematicians, as prophesied in the 1983 report? Survey results from the Sandia study found the opposite to be true: Our educational system was turning out more trained professionals than the job market could possibly absorb, both now and in the foreseeable future. Statistics suggested that it was the service sector of the economy that was indeed growing, not the scientific and engineering sector. Although *A Nation* had proclaimed that illiteracy and lack of technical skills were major problems in the workplace, managers denied this claim when surveyed for the Sandia Report. Rather, managers claimed that habits and attitudes of employees were of greatest concern to them, not academic skills.[72] Since this new evidence would undermine Bush's education initiative, he suppressed the Sandia report. Later, after Bush's defeat in 1992, the original report was published in the *Journal of Educational Research*, but for all practical purposes it remained largely beyond the reach of the American public.[73]

At the same time, Bush was pushing ahead with his bold new educational initiative. In 1989 he summoned the nation's fifty governors to attend an education summit in Charlottesville, Virginia. The goal of this meeting was to find remedies for the perceived national educational crisis. At the summit, the governors developed National Education Goals to set targets for nationwide educational reform. It was through these Goals that support for the development of internationally competitive educational standards was first articulated as official national policy. Goal three, out of the goals adopted by the governors, identified history as one of a total of five school subjects for which challenging new national achievement standards should be established. Thus history education was guaranteed a prominent place in national education reform.[74]

But what would this history look like? In the summer of 1989, the publication and reception of the article "The End of History?," written by Francis Fukuyama prior to his appointment by Bush as deputy director of the State Department's policy planning staff, led to the articulation of a new grand narrative about the triumph of liberal democracy based on a capitalist, market economy. Published in the neo-conservative journal *The National Interest*, the piece sparked a long-running international debate.[75] Fukuyama was part of the neo-conservative network of schol-ars. He had been Allan Bloom's student at the University of Chicago, and his current work was funded and assisted by the John F. Olin Founda-tion. Fukuyama argued that economic and political liberalism had tri-umphed over Communism with the fall of the Berlin Wall. "What we may be witnessing is not just the end of the Cold War, or the passing of a period of postwar history, but the end of history as such: that is, the end point of mankind's ideological evolution and the universalization of Western liberal democracy as the final form of government."[76] Al-though Fukuyama admitted that the victory of liberalism had only been accomplished at the level of "ideas and consciousness," he nevertheless explained that the idea of "liberalism had prevailed and, in time, the material world would be transformed in its image."[77]

Thus, as historian Harvey Kaye points out, the neo-conservatives had created a new grand, synthesizing, self-congratulatory narrative. This narrative would endorse the present order of things by portraying it as the culmination of history, "the finest and final fruition of Western and world development, the best of all possible worlds—beyond which the choice is either more of the same or economic and political retrogres-sion."[78] Unfortunately, many historians found it difficult to accept the idea that history had now attained its transcendent goal and that the process of historical development would now end. Many citizens too dismissed Fukuyama's theory as self-serving ideology tailored to an ephemeral event, the fall of the Berlin Wall, which it elevated to the status of the defining world historical event for all time.

MORE CULTURE WARS IN CALIFORNIA AND NEW YORK

Indeed, the historical dialectic continued, in spite of Fukuyama's be-lief that we had achieved "the best of all possible worlds." By 1992 the culture wars had flared up everywhere. In fact, radical multiculturalists had been largely victorious in two of the most hotly contested battles over the American curriculum that this nation has ever seen. One battle took place in New York. In 1987, just as the California *Framework*, *Cultural Literacy*, *American Memory* and *What Do Our 17-Year-Olds Know?* were hitting the newsstands, the New York Board of Regents appointed a new Commissioner of Education, Thomas Sobol. Many were bank-ing that the next commissioner would be a minority-group member, but Sobol was white. Sobol, in an effort to ease the racial tension over his appointment and gain minority support, created a "Task Force on Minorities" whose job was to assess how well the New York syllabus and instructional materials addressed multicultural content. In their 1989 report, *A Curriculum of Inclusion*, the panel concluded that the New York syllabus did not meet the regents' criteria for "understanding, respect, and acceptance of diverse people and cultures."[79] The panel denounced the existing curriculum for its alleged Eurocentrism, and proposed a much more radical form of multiculturalism.[80] The report launched a new battle in the curriculum wars.

Many of the now-familiar humanities advocates networked quickly to discredit the report. Bill Honig claimed that the report was "nothing but racism," and Gilbert Sewall wrote in his *Social Studies Review* that the report was "an angry, ignorant, polemical document."[81] Critics such as Diane Ravitch were quick to point out that the task force had only one white member and "not a single historian." Ravitch and Arthur Schlesinger Jr. formed their own organization of twenty-eight scholars to critique the report. Next they co-authored an opinion piece in the *New York Times* entitled "Statement of the Committee of Scholars in Defense of History." Here they expressed their concern about "the proposed revision of the State of New York's history curriculum" and announced their plan to "constitute [themselves] as a professional review committee to monitor and assess the work of the Commissioner's panel." They described *A Curriculum of Inclusion* as a polemical document that used racial division as the underlying framework for understanding all of American history. They concluded by condemning the document for reducing history to "ethnic cheerleading on the demand of pressure groups. . . ."[82]

Having led the attack on the proposed curriculum, Ravitch called for an increased emphasis on historical narrative and the positive aspects of American history: she recommended that New York employ the more moderate assimilationist approach to multiculturalism that she and Crabtree had used in writing the 1987 California *Framework*.[83] With the founding of the review committee and access to the mainstream press, Ravitch and Schlesinger established themselves, as Cornbleth and Waugh have argued, as "proper authorities to judge what constitutes appropriate knowledge for inclusion in history. . . . Their discourse delimited historical knowledge to a particular version of history and put alternative interpretations out of bounds."[84] Here is a classic example of how an organized group of self-appointed, non-elected, unaccountable pundits, without any official standing, were able to steer the educational agenda in New York by exercising their intellectual and political clout through informal channels.

In 1990 Sobol established a second committee, hoping to repair the damage created by the first. This time Diane Ravitch, Nathan Glazer,

Arthur Schlesinger Jr., Paul Gagnon, and Kenneth Jackson were among its members. In June, the committee released its final report, *One Nation, Many Peoples: A Declaration of Cultural Interdependence*. This report was adopted by a 12–3 vote and made into policy.[85] However, the committee was far from cohesive. Arthur Schlesinger Jr. and Kenneth Jackson, among others, wrote dissenting reports. For them, the new document was still too divisive, as its title suggests. Not only were the committee members at odds, but a new public controversy broke out, even more tempestuous than the first. The report was attacked in a *Time* magazine cover story and in an editorial in *The New Republic*.

About the same time that the New York battle over the curriculum was taking place, another heated controversy broke out in Oakland, California. This time the battle took place over the school district's adoption of the Houghton Mifflin social studies textbook series, which had already been adopted by the state of California. In order to qualify for state funds to purchase textbooks, school districts in California were required to buy the Houghton Mifflin textbook series. This was because they were the only textbooks that met all the new criteria set out in the *Framework*, such as the requirement of three years each of American and world history. If districts chose to purchase other materials, they would have to forfeit state funds. In spite of this clear incentive to adopt the books, on June 5, 1991, the Oakland school board rejected the series with the strong backing of the community. Afrocentrists on the Oakland school board attacked the series for its alleged Eurocentrism. Liberals such as Gary B. Nash, who was editor of the series, were astonished at this reaction because, as Todd Gitlin has argued, "these books represented the most fully-developed multicultural textbooks ever to be published for K–8 education."[86] The Afrocentric critique of the Houghton Mifflin series that now took place in Oakland echoed the critique of the *Framework* when it was under review. Critics accused the textbooks of conceptualizing history from a European immigrant perspective: the books treated indigenous peoples and enslaved peoples as though their experiences were essentially no different from those of European immigrants.

THE NATIONAL HISTORY STANDARDS PROJECT

At the macro political level, however, things looked relatively serene. In the wake of the 1989 governors' summit, bipartisan support grew for development of "world-class" standards in education.[87] In 1991 Congress passed Bush's America 2000 Act, and in 1992 the National

Council on Education Standards and Testing (NCEST) was established
by Congress to review the issue of standards. A report by this council
noted the following:

> In the absence of well-defined and demanding Standards, education in
> the United States has gravitated toward de facto national minimum ex-
> pectations. Except for students who are planning to attend selective four-
> year colleges, current education Standards focus on low-level reading and
> arithmetic skills and on small amounts of factual material in other con-
> tent areas. Consumers of education in this country have to settle for far
> less than they should and for far less than do their counterparts in other
> developed countries.[88]

Later, in 1994, Congress would sustain support for national Standards
by passing Clinton's Goals 2000: Educate America Act, which was in
essence a continuation of the Bush administration's policies, and the
next in the sequence of reform initiatives touched off by *A Nation at Risk*.

It was in this climate of bipartisan support that the National History Standards Project was born. Lynne Cheney of the NEH and Diane
Ravitch, who was by now serving as Assistant Secretary of Education
for the Office of Educational Research and Improvement at the Department of Education, seized the opportunity to fund the National Center for History in the Schools in 1992 with an additional $1.6 million,
this time to develop a broad consensus for what constitutes excellence
in the teaching and learning of history in the nation's schools. Cheney
and Ravitch were now positioned to translate their ideas into public
policy, and it looked as though they and their fellow humanities reformers had finally achieved their goal: Now there would be one set of
history standards that could unify the nation under a single historical
narrative, a single story-well-told. Excessive multiculturalism and political correctness would soon be purged from the K–12 curriculum, even
if as yet their stranglehold on higher education could not be broken.

5

Forging Unity

The National History Standards Project, 1992–1994

RMED WITH THIS ADDITIONAL funding from the NEH and the
DOE, the NCHS set to work developing comprehensive standards
for American and world history. The process by which the *Standards* were developed represented a vast collaboration among public
school teachers, state social studies specialists, school superintendents,
university historians, and a broad range of professional and scholarly
organizations, public interest groups, parents' and teachers' organizations, and individual citizens nationwide, all with a stake in the teaching of history in the schools. Under development for thirty-two months,
the *Standards* were the product of a national forum in which ultimately
hundreds of educators pored over, disputed, revised, and refined numerous drafts of the documents. First I will sketch out the complex
organizational structure through which consensus was achieved (see
Appendix A).

NHSP ORGANIZATIONAL STRUCTURE[1]

At the top of the NCHS organizational structure was the policy board,
the National Council for History Standards, consisting of K–12 history
teachers, school and district administrators, and academic historians.[2]
Charlotte Crabtree and Gary Nash from the NCHS served as co-chairs
of the Council. Appointed to direct the project, the thirty two-member
Council would ultimately be responsible for guiding the consensus
process. In order to insure balance, members were carefully selected to
represent a broad range of political interests, from liberal to conservative. However, as part of the original 1988 cooperative agreement between the NEH and the NCHS, Cheney, Crabtree, and Nash each had

veto power over who would sit on the Council. Consequently, any potential candidate representing the extreme political left or right would not be included. As a result of this process, the political composition of the Council was more or less representative of the mainstream, perhaps just to the right of center, and it was therefore extremely unlikely that the Council would endorse radical departures from current curricular paradigms of how history should be taught in the schools.

Over the two-and one-half years of the project, the Council met for a total of eleven days, hammering out every detail necessary to build consensus with the various groups involved in the project, which in turn interacted with one another. Nine Focus Groups representing the various professional organizations with a stake in history education—the American Historical Association (AHA), the Association for Supervision and Curriculum Development (ASCD), the Council of Chief State School Officers (CCSSO), the Council of State Social Studies Specialists (CSSSS), the National Council for History Education (NCHE), the National Council for the Social Studies (NCSS), the Organization of American Historians (OAH), the Organization of History Teachers (OHT), and the World History Association (WHA)—met on at least three separate occasions, independent of the Council. At these meetings, which took place over the duration of the project, each group of about twenty evaluated drafts of the *Standards* and provided feedback. As it turned out, these Focus Groups, although advisory in function, wielded enormous power within the consensus process because they represented important stakeholder constituencies that the Council could not ignore. In fact, the periodic input from the Focus Groups ignited major debates within the Council, and several of the Focus Group chairs had enough power to put pressure on the Council to meet their individual demands. It became clear to the Council and the project directors that without approval from the major Focus Groups the project could not move forward. This is where the consensus had to be hammered out.

A National Forum for History Standards, made up of representatives from twenty-four different organizations, met with the Council on two occasions to help set the criteria for developing the *Standards*, and to provide feedback on successive drafts.[3] Members of the Forum, while representing constituencies that were less influential than the Focus Group constituencies, still had enough power to push their personal agendas if they chose. Forum participants represented a much broader political range than the Council, from Afrocentrist on the left to neo-conservative on the right. While the project did not need approval from every Forum member to succeed, concerns raised by high-profile groups, such as the American Federation of Teachers, had to be addressed for consensus to move forward.

Finally, three Curriculum Task Forces were formed (members were selected from candidates submitted by the nine Focus Groups), with direct responsibility for drafting the *Standards*. Consisting of fifty academic historians, curriculum specialists, and schoolteachers, these task forces met together on numerous occasions at UCLA, for intensive one- or two-week sessions, to draft the various sections of the American and world history standards.[4] They, too, pored over literally thousands of pages of comments each time they met, revising earlier sections of the *Standards* as they wrote new ones. Given the conscientiousness of the reviewers, the sheer volume of commentary that needed to be addressed usually exceeded the *Standards* drafts by a ratio of about ten to one. The National Center for History in the Schools coordinated all stages of this iterative consensus process.

CONSENSUS PROBLEMATIC

When the project was launched in the spring of 1992 it was clear to the directors that national consensus would not come easily. Crabtree even acknowledged this potential for conflict in her November 1991 proposal to the NEH and DOE. Referring to such controversies as the current one that was taking place over the Columbian Quincentennial, Crabtree wrote, "At the core of much of this controversy is the question of the relative importance to be placed on ethnic diversity, identity, and plurality in our national history and on the binding values, ideals, and democratic institutions that unify the nation and whose origins lie in the history of Western civilization."[5] However, Crabtree believed that consensus could be achieved, even in a subject as contentious as history, citing recent successes in consensus building such as the development of the 1988 National Assessment of Educational Progress's (NAEP) history assessment, and the adoption of the *California History–Social Science Framework*.[6]

However, historian Kenneth Jackson, a prospective member of the NHSP Council, did not share Crabtree's optimism. Having just issued his widely publicized dissenting opinion in the *One Nation, Many Peoples* report, Jackson expressed concern over the daunting new task of drawing up national standards. "I start with a general philosophical feeling against it. The concept is at least value free, but the danger is that it can be politically influenced by people on any side in the whole matter, and it can be difficult to find a consensus."[7]

Historian Harvey Kaye was more pointed in his remarks. He feared that the "pressure would come from Bush Administration officials who had been critical of efforts to de-emphasize the culture and values of Western civilization in college curricula and academic research."[8]

Before I analyze the NHSP consensus process, it is necessary to problematize the concept itself. Consensus is a very fluid process. It is not achieved through party discipline, nor is it achieved necessarily through majority rule. Rather, consensus tends to be more of an ad hoc convergence of people who agree to settle their differences for the sake of shared goals. While they might agree on one issue, they will often disagree on the next. Participants in a consensus project generally share a desire to proceed toward a common goal, in spite of disagreements along the way. However, consensus is rarely achieved through unanimity, but rather by trading off victories and losses. Unlike an election, consensus is nonbinding, leaving participants the option of changing their minds at any point in the process, or afterwards, for that matter. Given the high status of the individuals who are invited to participate in national consensus projects such as the NHSP, their perspectives generally emanate from positions of power, and their decisions often affirm the status quo. Thus a high-profile consensus project, by its very nature, tends to legitimize the knowledge or viewpoint of those already in positions of power, and denies legitimacy to viewpoints that challenge the status quo. However, participants in the NHSP consensus project represented a wider range of viewpoints than is usual in this type of negotiation. Those in power were often at odds as to what history and whose history should be the legitimate subject of the *Standards*. Official knowledge was up for grabs because the players came from academia as well as from the political sector.

Consensus is all the more ephemeral because it operates on many levels, some visible, some invisible. In the case of the NHSP, formal consensus was achieved through the organizational process that I have just described. The formal process was acted out at public meetings: It created its own documentation, and thus was visible to all. However, an informal process of consensus operated parallel to the formal process, and this equally important component was invisible. Through the myriad individual interactions taking place every day, consensus was forged at the interpersonal level. As directors, we took the opportunity to employ phone conversations, recruitment opportunities, public presentations, letters, dinners, media presentations, and workshops to forge consensus informally. These interactions were, in my opinion, as important as the interactions that took place in the formal setting, and they set the tone for the more public debates. Thus, as a problematic, one must keep in mind the effect of these private exchanges between the directors and the participants, and among participants, upon the overall consensus process.

Perhaps the educational theorist who comes closest to describing what was at stake in this consensus process is Michael Apple. His theory of "cultural reproduction" suggests that a "hidden curriculum" is used to perpetuate social myths and recreate forms of consciousness by diverting attention away from conflict and creating a false consensus. With a conservative political tide flowing their way, the Reagan and Bush administrations sought to use history to legitimate a consensual vision of how society worked. Certainly one could argue, and I do, that the Bennett, Cheney, Finn, Ravitch, Hirsch approach to cultural literacy is a thinly disguised attempt to inculcate students with a relatively conflict-free, consensual view of history. But the project ended up moving in a different direction altogether. In the hands of social and world historians, who actually wrote the *Standards* with the K–12 teachers, the *Standards* became a vehicle for the pluralistic vision the government was trying to combat. In the end, consensus history, or cultural reproduction, as Apple would call it, was challenged by those historians who felt that social justice and the redistribution of power demanded a more complex telling of the past.

Ironically, it was the neo-conservative origins of the project that pushed it toward the left. At the very first meeting of the NHSP Council in February 1992, it became clear that many Council members were highly suspicious of what they considered to be the Bush administration's hegemonic ambitions in regard to history education. However, many of the historians who had explicitly expressed reservations about participating in the project decided to participate because they knew that the entire history profession might be left out of the process of developing national history standards, as it was in 1916 when the Committee on Social Studies first developed the original social studies curriculum. These council members were not alone in their fear of a conservative agenda. As the project progressed, it became painfully clear that many Focus Group members were extremely suspicious of this Cheney-Ravitch–inspired project, and so were many of the teachers who participated in the task forces responsible for drafting the *Standards*. At the same time, many participants on the Council, in the Focus Groups, and in the Forum shared the conservative agenda. Given these divergent points of view, the road to consensus was indeed arduous. Bitter battles were waged over the primacy of Western civilization in the world history standards, and over the relative weight to be given to historical content (factual knowledge) vis-à-vis the development of critical thinking skills (social studies skills).

At the very first Council meeting, many of the liberal panelists expressed fear that national standards would lead to national tests. They worried that unequal access to the *Standards* and, more importantly, unequal access to the good teaching and resources needed to implement them would result in unequal student performance. In other words, they predicted that excellence would be achieved at the expense of equity. The Organization of American Historians Focus Group originally split over this issue, and members would debate this issue each time they met. According to their May 14, 1992, report, two-thirds of the committee was against a formal policy of national standards or assessment. In their statement against standards, the majority argued:

> establishing national Standards and testing will do little good and possibly much harm unless commitments are made on national, state, and local levels to address more significant problems in the American educational system as a whole. It is sheer folly to set Standards without addressing the savage inequities in the nation's school systems, the low quality of much teacher education, the inadequacy of facilities, the difficulties of reducing class size, and the many other problems facing American education.[9]

Their fears were justified. Standards were indeed originally designed with national tests in mind. Both President Bush and Secretary of Education Lamar Alexander called for voluntary national achievement tests in the America 2000 legislation. In her proposal, Crabtree wrote that the purpose of the standards project would be to "provide national leadership for . . . developing, through a national consensus process, 'world class' achievement Standards in history which will serve as the basis for new national assessment programs in history at all levels of schooling, elementary through high school."[10] Lynne Cheney was also a strong advocate for national tests, and she intended the *Standards* to provide the framework for them, as she stated in her 1991 report, *National Tests: What Other Countries Expect Their Students to Know*. She asserted that other industrialized nations "administer national tests to students rating student performance according to agreed-upon criteria of competence in all content areas, including the humanities." She also claimed that students in other countries are not only expected to know their own histories, but they are required to learn more American history than are American students.[11]

This issue of testing had to be resolved before the project could move forward. Because the OAH members were so uncomfortable with the coupling of national standards and national tests, the Council discussions and OAH Focus Group rhetoric moved more and more away from testing and more and more toward the concept of "voluntary" national standards. About the same time that the NCHS dropped the issue of testing, Congress commissioned the National Council on Education, Standards, and Testing (NCEST) to make policy recommendations on standards and testing. In its 1992 report, NCEST came to a similar conclusion in regard to national tests. Although the report endorsed national standards, a national system of assessments, and "school delivery standards," it stipulated that standards should be voluntary. It also recommended that the development of voluntary assessments should be left to the states and commercial publishers. The issue of testing was finally put to rest, and standards-making could begin.[12]

LESSONS FROM HISTORY: **TEMPLATE FOR REFORM**

To begin the consensus-building process, the Center's capstone book, *Lessons from History*, was sent out for review to all participants, including Council, Focus Group, and Forum members. Reviewers were asked to assess *Lessons* critically according to a series of questions posed by the Center. Theoretically, these critiques would be used to guide the task forces as they revised *Lessons*, ultimately leading to a new set of mutually agreed upon national standards building on the work already done in *Lessons*. Crabtree, Cheney, and Nash all had assumed from the start that *Lessons* would serve as a template for national standards around which consensus could be forged. Crabtree expressed this hope in her grant proposal. "The work of Standards-setting will build upon the History Center's 300-page volume, *Lessons From History* . . . a major resource to which three years of work has already been devoted. In addition, the NAEP consensus project establishing the Framework for the 1994 U.S. history assessment also will be available to our working groups."[13] But as things turned out, a deluge of criticism from the Council, Forum, and Focus Group members made it necessary to abandon *Lessons* and start the project from scratch.

In many ways the criticisms of *Lessons* laid the groundwork for the recurring debates that would dominate the consensus process. Members used their critiques to stake out their philosophical and political positions on setting standards. For example, the Association for Supervision and Curriculum Development (ASCD) Focus Group, which represented administrators and curriculum experts from around the country, predictably criticized *Lessons* on the grounds that it emphasized historical content at the expense of historical reasoning skills. As educational policymakers, members of this group wanted to make sure that pedagogy would not take a back seat to content knowledge. The familiar history versus social studies debate played out here.

> Content alone is not enough to prepare students for work, citizenship, and productive lives. The development of history Standards must go beyond the basis of content (what students know) and include Standards by which to measure specific student attitudes and values (what students should be like) and intellectual skills (what students should be able to do).[14]

The American Historical Association and the National Council for the Social Studies agreed with ASCD that *Lessons* was heavily weighted toward content over historical thinking and decision-making skills. Thus a coalition of three Focus Groups formed, advocating that the Standards stress an equal balance between content knowledge and critical thinking skills. This coalition of three Focus Groups would push its agenda throughout the duration of the project, ultimately achieving success through the inclusion of a whole chapter in the *Standards* dedicated to historical thinking skills, and through the decision to attach teaching examples to each content standard, providing pedagogical strategies for developing historical thinking skills. It was here that the pedagogues and the subject matter scholars came together in a broad-based compromise. This blending of content and pedagogy made the *Standards* useful for teachers trying to figure out how to teach the content through discipline-based strategies. Indeed, the *Standards* had squared the pedagogical circle. The NCHS participants had figured out how to foster discipline-based content knowledge and discipline-based critical thinking through student-centered learning opportunities.

However, the pedagogical teaching examples would ultimately trigger the 1994 controversy over the history standards, just as Bruner's Netsilik films had triggered the 1975 controversy over *Man: A Course of Study*. Once one descends from general statements about historical or anthropological content to specific examples, one runs the risk of controversy. The devil is in the details. Everyone agreed that a sixth-grade course grounded in anthropology was a wonderful idea, until they were confronted with the harsh realities of Netsilik daily life in the MACOS films. By the same token, most people could agree on sweeping statements about historical content, until they were confronted with concrete examples taken from social history.

Members of the AHA focus group staked out yet another position in their report. They were concerned that *Lessons* had glossed over social history, giving the impression of an uncontested past. "Women and minority peoples are set apart from the larger narrative and the notion of conflict among various groups in American history is watered down to the point where the history implies a monolithic consensus."[15] This AHA argument against a conflict-free narrative is reminiscent of the criticisms lodged at the *California History-Social Science Framework*, the Houghton Mifflin textbook series, and the New York state *Curriculum of Inclusion*. It echoes Michael Apple's theoretical concerns over the hidden curriculum. Like Apple, AHA Focus Group members rejected, in principle, consensus versions of history: They, too, saw it as a means by which to silence alternative voices from the past. Like the social reconstructionists or the critical theorists today, AHA members envisioned the transformative possibilities inherent in teaching social conflict. According to the AHA, *Lessons* had sanitized conflict out of history.

Many members of the OAH focus group concurred on this very issue. According to their May 1993 Focus Group report:

> Those opposing the Standards worried that the interpretation of American history to be used as the basis of Standards will only benefit those already holding the keys to political, economic, social, and cultural power. The result will be a continued neglect of the needs and just concerns of minorities and those who have been traditionally pushed aside. Many of the objections to *Lessons* are related to significant textual omissions or to allegedly distorted interpretations concerning these matters.[16]

While the OAH was most concerned with the treatment of American history in *Lessons*, the AHA took issue with its treatment of world history, which they argued was tantamount to "the history of Western civilization with occasional side glances at other cultures 'affected' by the West."[17] In particular, the AHA objected to the choice of words in *Lessons* that "have negative connotations, either about those excluded or those being identified such as "dark ages," "third world," or "folk" (as used in reference to Africans)."[18] Focus group members argued, "*Lessons* creates an impression of world history that is too peaceful and tidy."[19] The issues that the AHA raised over how the *Standards* should address the relationship between the West and the rest of the world would become the central bone of contention in the entire consensus process.

The AHA Focus Group also objected to the way in which *Lessons* divided up the major periods of American history. Members argued that the periodization revolved around political, military, and diplomatic events, rather than focusing on alternative periodizations such as turning points in social history. For them the periodization in *Lessons* adhered too closely to the old presidential synthesis. The AHA World History Focus Group had even stronger objections to the periodization used in *Lessons*. According to their report, *Lessons'* periodization was inherently Anglocentric. For example, they wrote, "The terminus for Period I, in 1607, as well as the starting point for Period II, in 1585, come perilously close to implying that the English were the only peoples settling and establishing colonies on the American continent. Why start the colonial period with the failed Roanoke colony, rather than the founding of the more durable St. Augustine, in 1565?"[20] This was a compelling argument for providing alternative periodizations, and it highlighted the potential for controversy even in such seemingly innocuous issues as chronology. Given these fundamental critiques of *Lessons*, the Council ultimately decided to abandon it and to start developing history standards from scratch.

Ironically, all of the critiques of *Lessons* had come from the political left, and this in turn would set the tone for the rest of the project. What we have here is a divergence of practicing historians (e.g. AHA, OAH) from the original idea of the *Standards* as laid down by Cheney et al. Professional historians, with a knowledge of recent developments in historiography and method as outlined in Chapter 2, split from the traditionalists, whose concept was thirty years out of date. It is this split between the way people inside and outside the profession view history that ultimately blew up in October 1994, when the politicians and the public joined the fray.

With hindsight, one can see that when the Council rejected *Lessons*, the conservatives had lost control of the consensus process. In fact, when the Council decided to drop *Lessons*, William McNeill and Gary Nash were deputized to write a series of new organizing questions for American and world history that would guide the task forces in their first summer's work of developing standards. These new questions, which were to be aligned to the major spheres of human activity as outlined in *Lessons*, opened the proverbial Pandora's box. With social historian Gary Nash and world historian William McNeill leading the way, and with predominantly liberal academic historians providing the major content reviews, a new story line would soon emerge.

CRITERION 13: WORLD HISTORY PROBLEMATIC

Lessons was not the only document sent out for consideration by participating groups. The other document that served as grist for the consensus mill was a set of criteria established at the first meeting of the

Forum, on February 21, 1992. At this meeting, Forum members were asked to brainstorm a set of criteria for developing standards in American and world history. The criteria would serve two purposes: They would serve as mission statements for the Council as it directed the project, and they would provide a touchstone for task force members as they drafted the *Standards*. Ironically, as the Council debated and refined the wording of each of fifteen criteria at successive meetings, the criteria took on much more significance than was originally intended. Particularly, during the months after the Council had decided to abandon *Lessons*, and before the new organizing questions and draft *Standards* were available for review, in the absence of any other written documents, these criteria became the focus around which consensus had to be debated and forged. Just as in the legislative process, where the truly substantive debates occur only when committees sit down to craft detailed legislative language, so it was with the NHSP that the parsing of words was where real positions were staked out.

Although the Council spent many hours debating and "wordsmithing" each of the fifteen criteria presented to them by the Forum, and although Focus Groups would respond with countless renditions for each criterion, it was Criterion 13 alone that was so controversial as to place the entire project at risk.[21] The wording of this single twosentence criterion launched a two-year debate. At the bottom of this debate was the relative emphasis to be placed on Western civilization within the context of world history. The Forum's original language of February 1992 read as follows:

> Standards in world history should include both the history and values of western civilization and the history and cultures of other societies, with the greater emphasis on western civilization, and on the interrelationships between western and nonwestern societies.[22]

This language launched a firestorm of criticism, coming from many quarters. Council member William McNeill, by all accounts one of the most influential historians responsible for creating the discipline of world history, objected strongly to the implications behind the original wording. In his written comments (where he also critiqued *Lessons* as unacceptably Eurocentric), McNeill laid out an argument against Criterion 13 based on historical grounds.

> I do not agree that Western civilization deserves greater emphasis than others, at least not for the period before 1500 A.D. Why not: world history should explore the history and values of all ten major civilizations of the world, and study some simpler societies as well. Major attention

should be directed toward the traditions that continue to affect the lives of large numbers of peoples today . . . i.e., the civilizations of Europe, the Middle East, India and China. . . . The west is not privileged: indeed we are a minority in the world and ought to know it. For the past five centuries there is reason of course to make our expansion central to the study of world history because it was. Before that time, however, other civilizations enjoyed primacy and Europeans were comparatively backward.[23]

The ASCD Focus Group had other, more political and pedagogical concerns over the Criterion's language. They worried that adopting Criterion 13 as stated "will open up a multicultural minefield." They argued that the current emphasis among history and social studies teachers was to move away from an "ethnocentric" approach to history, and they believed that emphasizing Western civilization over other societies would contradict the current thinking of many teachers.[24]

Of all the focus groups criticizing Criterion 13, however, the AHA would become the most intractable. In their first Focus Group Report of May 1992, they argued, as did McNeill, the ASCD, and the NCSS, that the "language was too Eurocentric, setting Western civilization apart from its global context. The criterion should be worded in a way that allows all cultures equal billing."[25] William McNeill offered the following language as a solution to the problem:

> Standards in world history should include both the history and values of western civilization and the history and cultures of other societies, and the relations among them.[26]

Although Crabtree recommended that the Council adopt McNeill's wording, and although she responded to many other AHA Focus Group concerns, Jim Gardner, Deputy Director of the AHA, felt that the AHA's objections had been largely ignored in Crabtree's recommendations. Apparently Gardner, who was closely allied with NCSS leadership, mistrusted Crabtree's association with Cheney and Ravitch, and assumed that the NHSP was part of the neo-conservative plan to control the curriculum. In a letter to Crabtree, Gardner claimed that she had glossed over AHA's deep concerns in her written summary of the original focus group reports. Although Crabtree had circulated the full text of the Focus Group reports to Council members (over 1000 pages), she had also prepared a chart summarizing the reports and excerpting comments. Gardner felt that in the excerpting process, Crabtree had trivialized the AHA's objections to *Lessons* and to the criteria, and had distorted the arguments prepared by the Focus Group. Gardner sent Crabtree a written ultimatum, firmly stating the AHA's objection to Criterion 13.

This criterion is unacceptable as written. Students with a "world class" education in history should be prepared to act as world citizens, to function in a multi-cultural society, and to understand the historical forces that have shaped and continue to shape the world. It is necessary, then, to make sure that all students have the opportunity to study both U.S. and world history. It is not enough to put the emphasis on western civilization in a world history course, especially when "other civilizations" is so non-specific as to be meaningless. In addition, the use of the word "other" separates western from non-western countries in ways that are particularly problematic. These "other" countries are clearly not "us" and this separation further exacerbates the problems of a Eurocentric curriculum.[27]

A volley of letters now went back and forth between Jim Gardner and Robert Blackey, head of AHA's teaching division, and Crabtree and Nash. Each AHA letter upped the ante, bringing in new issues for "concrete resolution," and threatening AHA withdrawal if resolution was not achieved. Finally, in two letters dated December 1992, the AHA threatened to pull out of the project unless the excerpting process ended. None of the AHA letters were written by the AHA Focus Group chairs, but rather by AHA staff and one AHA Council member, Robert Blackey. It was not clear that the other AHA elected officials or the Focus Group members either knew about or endorsed the AHA position, although Blackey wrote that the Teaching Division had encouraged him to convey [its] concerns to the funders and threatened to "go public with [its] position."[28] All of these letters, including Crabtree's and Nash's responses, were circulated to NHSP Council members for consideration.

In order to save the project, which could not move forward without the endorsement of the country's largest professional historical association, Crabtree and Nash decided to invite the AHA elected officers to the February 1993 Council meeting to resolve their differences. After an extremely tense exchange between the NHSP Council and the AHA Council, it was agreed that language in Criterion 13 would be amended according to a newly proposed AHA draft.

Standards in world history should include both the history and values of diverse civilizations, including Western civilization, and should especially address the interactions among them.[29]

It was also agreed that the practice of excerpting focus group reports would be abandoned in the future.

The ongoing dispute between NHSP leadership and AHA staff has many implications for this study. First, it reveals how tenuous consensus really is. With the thousands of pages of drafts circulating around the country, and all of the important pedagogical issues at stake, the syntax of a single criterion had the power to derail the whole project. A good deal of time, money, and emotional energy had to be spent discussing and editing Criterion 13. However, the feud over Criterion 13 has even greater implications. Encapsulated within the criterion's language was a debate over the survival of Western civilization as the core of our national identity as Americans. The AHA victory meant no less than a repositioning of Western civilization within the curriculum, a decentering of our European heritage, and a radical departure from curricular tradition at the policy level.

Although the Criterion 13 controversy was now resolved and the AHA was back on board, however reluctantly, many of the more conservative Council members, such as Elizabeth Fox Genovese, Gilbert Sewall, Earl Bell, Bill Honig, and others, felt that the AHA had overplayed its hand and had pushed the project to the left by diminishing the centrality of Western civilization within the curriculum. They had hoped that the world history standards would acclaim the superiority of the West, and that the United States, as the pinnacle of the Western tradition, would retain its place at the core of historical values and institutions. However, this position did not make itself openly felt. Council members who felt that the AHA affair had shortchanged Western civilization kept their criticisms largely to themselves, or revealed them in private phone conversations. They did not go public with their distress. Although Lynne Cheney and Diane Ravitch were monitoring the consensus process through their respective deputies Jeffrey Thomas and Sharron Marshall at the NEH and DOE, neither official intervened in any significant way. Thomas and Marshall attended all Council meetings and pored over every draft document with diligence. However, they confined their involvement to phone conversations with Crabtree and Nash, and perhaps individual Council and Focus Group members. They never interfered with the consensus process itself, at least publicly.

In spite of these difficulties, Lynne Cheney was apparently very pleased with how Crabtree and Nash were handling the consensus process, and presumably with the results so far. On October 6, 1992, she sent a note of congratulations to Crabtree: "What nice work you do! I've been saying lately that the best grant I've ever given is to your Standards-setting project."[30]

In November 1992 Bill Clinton won the presidential election. By then, drafts of several eras of the American history standards were well under way. Bush's defeat however led Cheney to resign from her post as chair of the NEH. Before she left office, in December 1992, she had reviewed several drafts of the American history standards, through her deputy Jeffrey Thomas, who had attended the September 1992 Council meeting where American history draft standards for Era 3, "The Revolution and The New Nation," and Era 4, "Expansion and Reform," were discussed. Cheney was evidently so delighted with the evolving product, and with the consensus process that was in place, that she chose to praise the NCHS publicly in her resignation speech. She claimed that as chair of the NEH, her greatest achievements had been sponsorship of Ken Burns's public television series *The Civil War*, and sponsorship of the work done by the NCHS.[31] Ravitch, too, resigned from her position as Assistant Secretary of Education.

A PARADIGM SHIFT: FROM WESTERN CIVILIZATION TO THE NEW WORLD HISTORY

Presidents changed, but the drafting process continued. Although things had now been patched up at the policy level, the Council still needed to create a working framework to guide the task forces of scholars and teachers engaged in drafting the world history standards. The first set of world history standards drafted by the summer 1992 task forces had to be abandoned, and the Council convoked a subcommittee of area specialists to draft a new, second set of organizing questions to guide future work by the individual task forces that would draft the world history standards during 1993. Headed by historian and NHSP Council member Michael Winston of Howard University, the "Winston Committee" met three times in Washington and hammered out a set of thematic questions that were adopted by the Council.[32] This process went a long way toward healing wounds within the project: A new consensus on world history emerged around the "Winston" report.

The problem now was one of money. The project had become infinitely more complicated then originally conceived, when it was thought that consensus could be achieved around a revised version of *Lessons*. During the autumn of 1992 Charlotte Crabtree and I wrote a proposal to the NEH for additional funding of $1 million to broaden the consensus process and to add teachers and historians to the task force that had begun writing the world history standards the summer before. Because the task of drafting world history standards was much more complex and unwieldy than that of drafting American history standards, I suggested that we organize a series of week-long sessions in which task force members would draft the *Standards* one era per week for a total of eight weeks. However, this would obviously require considerably more money than originally budgeted, when we thought the work could be completed in one or two working sessions. Based on the progress they had seen so far, both Cheney and Ravitch approved this supplemental funding before they left office. Richard Riley, appointed Secretary of Education by Clinton, honored the funding commitment made by the Bush administration, releasing funds periodically throughout the rest of the *Standards* project as goals and deliverables were met. With this financial support, the work went ahead at full speed.

Meanwhile, as the political battles were being sorted out both at the policy level and in the public eye, the NHSP project at UCLA was going about the business of developing standards in American and world history on a separate, parallel course. While the Winston Committee was drafting a new consensus version of organizing questions in the spring of 1993, I began recruiting the task forces of world historians and K–12 teachers who would draft world history standards the following summer and throughout the next year. The *Standards* project was far too complex to synchronize the actual work of drafting standards with each stage of the consensus-building process. Because we had to organize the workshops several months in advance, the writing project continued in spite of stalemates and disagreements at the policy level. Gary Nash continued to oversee the American history task force and Charlotte Crabtree continued to head up the K–4 history effort. Each of these efforts was well ahead of the world history endeavor, mostly because of the delay caused by the controversy over Western civilization, but in large part due to the sheer complexity of the task of creating standards for world history.

During this phase of the project, I was responsible for overseeing the world history effort. I recruited the K–12 teachers for the world history task forces, and I also participated in all of the Council, Forum, and Focus Group debates and subcommittees on world history. In consultation with Nash and Crabtree, I had discretion over which historians would be selected to direct the various workshops, and over how to address the new guiding questions in the working sessions. Because the debates had led the project toward a more global understanding of world history, I recruited several world historians in addition to area specialists to head up the series of workshops.

The world historians who participated in the task forces conceptualized world history from a global rather than a Eurocentric or regional perspective. This is not to say that the world historians and area specialists rejected Western civilization as a conceptual framework, or that they had an aversion to European history (several were, after all, originally European specialists), but rather that they conceptualized world history as something very different from Western civilization. It was their global perspective, nurtured by the Criterion 13 controversy and the Winston Report, that shaped the resulting world history Standards. In fact, task force members used this opportunity to reconceptualize world history into a truly global approach. As they worked together drafting standards and periodizing world history, their ideas crystallized into a new paradigm for K–12 education. Other than the handful of historians who researched and taught world history at universities, no one had pushed global thinking this far. In fact, I believe that this was perhaps one of the few times in American curricular history that scholars working on a K–12 school-level reform project would contribute to the development of a new disciplinary paradigm for scholars at the university level. Usually paradigmatic change starts in the academy and trickles down slowly to the K–12 level. In the case of the NHSP world history standards, the K–12 reform effort percolated up to the academy as well. For example, UCLA introduced its first-ever world history course for undergraduate students as a direct result of the National History Standards Project.

During the summer, fall, and winter of 1993, the Center held a series of week-long workshops, using the Winston Report and Criterion 13 as starting points for what became a free-ranging debate on the problematics of world history. Since we were the individuals responsible for actually drafting the world history standards, it was necessary to forge yet another consensus and to develop the standards according to our own conceptual, pedagogical, and historical criteria. Here is where the less visible consensus process that I described above took place. Drawing on recent scholarship in the new subfield of world history, the task forces developed a reasonably coherent vision of the world's past. Influenced by the work of leading scholars such as Marshall Hodgson, William McNeill, Philip Curtin, Alfred Crosby, Jerry Bentley, and Ross Dunn, the task forces developed a sweeping thematic structure for world history that involved more than the simple combination of national and regional histories. According to Jerry Bentley, this is because world historical events such as mass migration, empire-building, long-distance trade, biological exchange, and technological transfer do not confine themselves to traditional geographical boundaries. Thus world history entails the reconceptualization of the past from very different perspectives than those taken in traditional historical studies that focus on nation-states, civilizations, or cultural regions.[33]

The world history standards drew inspiration from this type of scholarship. For example, the task forces used a global approach for developing the major time periods for world history, which did not favor a Western period scheme over any other. Thus, instead of imposing European categories of ancient, medieval, and modern history onto the whole world, task force members attempted to identify global processes that transcended European culture and to periodize accordingly. The task forces divided the world's past into eight periods:

Era 1: The Beginnings of Human Society
Era 2: Early Civilizations and the Emergence of Pastoral Peoples, 400–1000 BCE
Era 3: Classical Traditions, Major Religions, and Giant Empires, 100 BCE–300 CE
Era 4: Expanding Zones of Exchange and Encounter, 300–1000 CE
Era 5: Intensified Hemispheric Interactions, 1000–1500
Era 6: The Emergence of the First Global Age, 1450–1770
Era 7: The Age of Revolutions, 1750–1914
Era 8: The 20th Century

It was never our intention to diminish the significance of Western civilization by this new periodization, but rather to place the experiences of European and American peoples in a larger, interrelating global context. However, in doing this, task force members created a Kuhnian paradigm shift for teaching world history, at least at the K–12 level.

Indeed, Ross Dunn has argued that the task of periodizing world history should become perhaps the central problematic for students. Students should approach periodization as an analytical issue in historical thinking. They should create their own periodization based on critical themes and processes in world history. For example, he suggests, "eco-minded students could reasonably argue that shifts in the biosphere, disease environments, or planetary climate block out more consequential periods of human experience than do the ups and downs of civilizations."[34] Experimenting with this type of macro historical thinking is one of the many possibilities offered up by a truly global approach to world history.

CRITICAL THINKING VS. RECEIVED IDEAS

The debate over the history curriculum during the 1980s had focused almost exclusively on *what* content students should learn, not on the equally important question of *how* they should learn it. The critics of humanities education had tried to demonstrate that today's students lack a basic knowledge of American and world history and demonstrate minimal interest in those subjects. However, as the debate progressed during the National History Standards Project, its focus broadened. Many stakeholders, particularly the NCSS and the ASCD, proposed a format that would go beyond the issue of what facts students should learn, to the pedagogical issue of how best to advance students' critical thinking skills as they develop historical perspective.

As I have shown, the more liberal-oriented groups such as the AHA, NCSS, and ASCD all argued in their Focus Group reports that critical thinking skills should play a prominent role in the *Standards* document. Here the debate between proponents of history and proponents of social studies entered a new phase. The social studies establishment (and their ally, the AHA) took the position that the *Standards* should provide equal opportunities for development of critical thinking skills and exposure to historical content. In particular, the educational establishment, as represented by the NCSS and ASCD Focus Groups, clung to a skills-oriented agenda. This could be expected given the past wars between scholars and pedagogues over traditional versus progressive education. Not only were the NCSS and ASCD seeking to preserve their turf (the NCSS had not received any federal funding to develop social studies standards), but they feared that a traditional view of historical scholarship would prevail. They understood history as taught in schools to be elitist and racially biased, a parade of great men and their achievements leading teleologically to the present, a canon of facts to be committed to memory. One vice president of NCSS went so far as to dismiss history as "factology."[35]

Traditionally history had been conceived as a finished product to be consumed by K–12 students, rather than as an intellectual process in which students could engage actively and critically. Students would dutifully memorize the names, dates, facts, and places prescribed for them in prepackaged, non-negotiable versions of the past. Selection of evidence, analysis, and interpretation had all been done for them: their job was to absorb a list of received "truths." This, by definition, ruled out any possibility of critical thinking on students' part. Naturally, students were alienated because what they were compelled to learn had little discernible relevance to their own lives. The social studies specialists feared that the historians working on the NHSP were operating on a vision of historical thinking that dated from this earlier time. In addition, they were also reacting to the neo-conservative historiographical agenda that had launched this particular reform. As advocates for multicultural pluralism and social justice education, the NCSS and ASCD feared, like Michael Apple, that the history standards would become a mechanism to shore up current power relationships. What they did not realize, perhaps, was that the majority of historians participating in the NHSP subscribed to current historiography, which was based on the very critical thinking skills that they sought to inculcate, social history and all.

The NCSS and ASCD were deeply concerned with making history relevant to students' own lives, and thus their emphasis on critical thinking skills converged neatly with current historiography. The NHSP Council's solution was to incorporate critical thinking skills into a separate section on historical thinking, using the discipline's own heuristics to teach critical thinking skills. "Thinking historically" asks students to read historical narratives imaginatively and critically, to select evidence for themselves, to conduct their own analyses, and eventually to construct their own historical narratives. Fundamental to this investigative process is the use of primary sources. Good teachers expose students to a wide variety of primary sources such as original documents, speeches, cartoons, artifacts, photos, art, music, architecture, literature, drama, dance, journals, folklore, historical sites, and oral histories.

Students use context to analyze primary sources and use primary sources to create further historical context. This process is recursive. As students dig up individual events or voices from the past, they must look for contextual information in order to evaluate the evidence. In doing so, students learn to appreciate the exceptionality and distinctiveness of the event while simultaneously seeing its broader implications. This is very much what archivists and professional historians do for a living as they sift through documents and construct histories, whether narrative or postmodern. Thus Gerald A. Danzer and Mark Newman argue, "the dynamic between the specific and the general, between the unique location of individual events and their place in the larger schema, forms the essential structure of historical studies. Without specific remains there is no history; without concepts there is no meaning."[36] This argument parallels Jerome Bruner's concept of "non-specific transfer": That historical topics should be taught within the broader structural frameworks of the disciplines so that students can transfer specific information to more general concepts. As Bruner argued, a general idea can be used as a foundation for recognizing subsequent problems as special cases or subsets of the more general idea originally mastered. One of the major pedagogical values of using primary source documents in the K–12 classroom is thus to develop students' capacity to make connections between specific events and larger social and political patterns.

In order to guarantee that these historical thinking skills would share equal billing with historical content, the Council decided that each *Standards* volume would dedicate an entire chapter to the development of historical thinking skills.[37] After many rounds of focus group input, Crabtree came up with a model for the following five types of historical thinking skills that students should master:

1. Chronological Thinking
2. Historical Comprehension
3. Historical Analysis and Interpretation
4. Historical Research Capabilities
5. Historical Issues-Analysis and Decision-Making

Although these skills were presented in five separate standards, they were intended to complement one another. Students would draw upon all five categories of skills as they engage in the historical process.

Linda Levstik, a professor of social studies education and chair of the NCSS Focus Group, who has done a considerable amount of research on how young students learn history, examines the implications of critical thinking versus received ideas.[38] She makes an intriguing distinction between two different types of history education: "a cultural *transmission* model that describes history as something one learns (a chronological narrative or body of information) and a cultural *transformation* model that [tends] to describe history as something one does (historical inquiry)."[39] Indeed, the *Standards'* detractors picked up this distinction between passive learning (the cultural transmission model) and active learning (the cultural transformation model) during the controversy. They feared, perhaps rightly, that the *Standards* would encourage students to play an active role in historical analysis and so to challenge the grand narrative with competing narratives of their own.

EQUITY VS. EXCELLENCE

Another critical issue for the NCSS, OAH, AHA, and most of the academic historians was the issue of educational equity. As outlined earlier, the excellence movement, including the *Standards* projects, was considered by many to be a thinly disguised attempt by neo-conservatives to dismantle the liberal reforms of the 1960s and 1970s. These participants worried that students would not be able to achieve "world-class" standards in history if they did not have full access to the resources and highly trained teachers that such standards would require. As the NCSS Focus Group report of May 1993 put it:

The process of setting world class history Standards cannot stand alone as a solution to the educational problems in U.S. schools. Standards must also address the issue of educational equity. The kind of history instruction and learning that we are advocating cannot take place where the resources for quality instruction are not available, if children live in fear or school buildings are unsafe. It is not enough to argue that students of history should be able to use a rich array of primary source documents, artifacts, field trips and the like. There must also be world class Standards regarding access to these resources and support for quality instruction for all children. This issue is inadequately addressed in the current Standards.[40]

The AHA, too, concurred in this requirement:

Implementation of genuine steps toward the establishment of educational equity should be a condition for the acceptance of any national Standards. . . . Disparities in resources (including textbooks, teacher training, etc.) as well as disparities in language skills and income level cannot but create inequities. Since the Standards project is intended to stimulate reform in the schools, the document must address disparities of resources and the diversity of student populations at the beginning of the document.[41]

THE STANDARDS

The *Standards*, as they were developed, reflected all of these debates and negotiations. First, the Council decided that language in the *Standards* must emphasize their voluntary nature, so that no one could accuse the government of imposing a national curriculum. Second, the front matter of the published *Standards* would address the equity issue as one of three policy statements. Third, it was agreed that the *Standards* should be published in three separate volumes: *National Standards for United States History* and *National Standards for World History* for Grades 5–12, and *National Standards for History for Grades K–4*. In this way, United States and world history would be developed separately but interrelated in content. *Standards* for grades K–4 would not only be published as a separate book, but would be delineated through broad themes, rather than through a chronological framework that young students might find difficult to comprehend. Fourth, it was decided that the history of Western civilization should occupy a central place in the world history volume, but that it should be situated within a global world history framework. Fifth, the *Standards* would emphasize the importance of both historical knowledge and critical thinking skills. Chapter 2 in each volume delineated five standards for "historical thinking." In order to illustrate how teachers might go about integrating critical thinking strategies with historical content knowledge, the content standards themselves, which formed Chapter 3 of each volume, were each followed by accompanying examples of student achievement, or teaching examples, as they came to be called. These teaching examples were intended to show how the standards could be translated into actual classroom practice. While the content standards were intended to provide the body of knowledge and skills students should learn (content), the teaching examples were intended to illustrate a variety of practical classroom strategies for engaging students with historical materials (pedagogy).

To see how this arrangement works, let us take a representative example. *National Standards for United States History* is divided into ten broad chronological categories, or "Eras," which in turn are further broken down into a total of thirty-one standards delineating what students should know. Each of the thirty-one standards is further broken down into substandards and examples of what students should be able to do.

The following standard gives a flavor of what the document as a whole is like. This example is culled from "Era 3: The Revolution and the New Nation (1754–1820s)."[42]

A SAMPLE STANDARD

Students Should Understand: The institutions and practices of government created during the revolution and how they were revised between 1787 and 1815 to create the foundation of the American political system.

(*Standard 3B*) *Students Should Be Able to*: demonstrate understanding of the issues involved in the creation and ratification of the United States Constitution and the new government it established by:

- Analyzing the factors involved in calling the Constitutional Convention, including Shays's Rebellion.
- Analyzing the alternative plans considered by the delegates and the major compromises agreed upon to secure the approval of the Constitution.
- Analyzing the fundamental ideas behind the distribution of powers and the system of checks and balances established by the Constitution.

- Comparing the arguments of Federalists and Anti-Federalists during the ratification debates and assess their relevance to late 20th-century politics.

Selected Examples of Student Achievement:

GRADES 5–6
[Students should] Apply their understanding of the Constitutional separation of powers and system of checks and balances by constructing a flow chart, diagram, or narrative demonstrating the checks each branch of government can exert on the other two.

GRADES 7–8
[Students should] Draw upon their understandings of the great debates and the compromises achieved by the delegates in order to construct a sound historical argument or narrative on questions such as the following: Within the context of the late 18th century, were the compromises reached by the delegates reasonable? Were the slavery compromises necessary in order to obtain approval of the Constitution? What might the consequences have been had the antislavery delegates remained firm in their resolve?

GRADES 9–12
[Students should] Compare and analyze the major arguments for and against the *Constitution* of 1787 in leading Federalist and Anti-Federalist writings and major ratification debates.

SHADES OF THINGS TO COME

May 1994 would be the last formal meeting of the NHSP Council and Forum. At this meeting it appeared that consensus had finally been achieved, at least around the American history standards. *Education Week* described the scene: "One by one, men and women gathered around the conference tables offering final words and praise for the American history documents that were nearly completed. 'Extremely admirable,' enthused the American Federation of Teacher's liaison to the project, Ruth Wattenberg."[43]

Although the general atmosphere was one of consensus and self-congratulations on the part of the Council and the NEH and DOE administrating officers, several Forum members who were attending the meeting began to grumble. Chester Finn Jr., representing the organization he had formed, the Educational Excellence Network, began to speak critically about the American history standards. In his follow-up memo to the Council dated May 19, 1994, Finn made a statement that, in retrospect, foreshadowed the prolonged controversy that would break out a few months later.

> In its valiant efforts to gain the approbation of innumerable constituencies within the education and history communities whose blessings have been thought desirable, I believe the project may have given too short shrift to the need for these Standards also to be accepted by legislators, school board members, business leaders, moms and dads, voters and taxpayers, mayors, newspaper editors and talk show hosts. . . . If these Standards were the subject of the Wichita Rotary Club one noontime, what would be said of them? How will they go down with the Chamber of Commerce? With the American Legion? With the League of Women Voters? . . . By columnists and commentators across the spectrum? By callers to the Rush Limbaugh show?[44]

Finn's words turned out to be prophetic. Within a few months Rotary Club members, members of the Christian Coalition, legislators, newspaper editors, and talk show hosts, including Rush Limbaugh, made it abundantly clear that they would not accept the *Standards*. In his public pronouncements at the Council/Forum meeting Finn claimed that the *Standards* were "relentlessly P.C.," and that "political correctness had reared its head in too many places." He elaborated on this thought in his written statement.

> I assume you expected this from me—what can only be termed "political correctness" and "relativism" rear their unlovable (but increasingly familiar) heads in too many places. Sometimes this takes the form of an unwarranted emphasis on various victim groups, overwrought attention to certain minorities, the inflating of the historical contribution of minor figures who happen to have the proper characteristics, and other such slightly overwrought efforts at after-the-fact egalitarianism. Other times, it takes the form of avoiding—or minimizing—events, groups, people and developments that deserve a fair share of attention.[45]

Ruth Wattenberg, speaking for the American Federation of Teachers Focus Group, objected to the overwhelming number and complexity of the *Standards*, and to what she perceived as their anti-Western bias. At the time, however, these criticisms were completely overshadowed by the general euphoria that enveloped the last Council meeting. With hindsight one can see that these comments were laying the groundwork for what was yet to come.

Although the fate of the American history standards seemed sealed with approbation, there was considerable debate over the unfinished world history standards. Much of the discussion focused on the still-festering Western civilization issue, with conservative Council members finally making public their dissatisfaction with the global approach the NCHS had adopted in drafting the *Standards*. Conservative members who had held back during the extended AHA controversy over Criterion 13 now suddenly voiced their concern. They argued that the central role played by the West in world history had been seriously underrepresented in the draft world history standards.

Now, all of a sudden, the political climate changed dramatically. This time the critique against world history emerged from the political right, not the left. In the past Council meetings the AHA, OAH, NCSS, and ASCD focus groups had joined hands to critique the world history standards from the left. Now several of the more conservative Forum and Council members formed a coalition to critique them from the right. This was a new twist in the consensus process, and was a harbinger of things to come. Nevertheless, the majority verdict on the world history draft was positive, and the Council authorized completion of the project over the summer of 1994. The American history standards were nearing completion, and the world history standards had weathered the worst storms, even if much work still lay ahead. Because the NHSP was running out of funds, the Council directed the Center to press on during the summer months and finish all three *Standards* books by October. There would be no need for another Council meeting, particularly with funds running out. Not only did the project receive the Council's blessing, but also the blessing of Cheney's appointed NEH representative, Jeffrey Thomas. He made an eloquent speech praising the project for its comprehensive consensus process and for the contribution that the history standards would make to history education nationwide.[46] However, storm clouds were gathering even as those involved in the project celebrated what appeared to be the successful conclusion of the consensus process.

Before the meeting ended, the NCHS agreed to send out one more draft of the world history standards for review by Council, Forum, and Focus Group members in June and July. Although the Council had given its official imprimatur to the project, individual members and other participants would still have the opportunity to provide written feedback as the Center developed new standards and teaching activities throughout the summer. As directors of the project, we knew that we still had to nurture the consensus that we had worked so hard to achieve during the formal stages of the process, particularly since the world history standards were far from finished. Working with small teams of teacher-editors, under the leadership of Gary Nash and Ross Dunn (who now officially became the head of the world history standards project), we completed the work and circulated successive drafts of the American and world history standards throughout the summer.

By July, however, a new conservative cohort had mobilized to critique the world history standards. On July 7 the Center received a scathing critique from Paul Gagnon, one of the four editors of *Lessons from History* and chief editor of the Bradley Commission's *Building a History Curriculum*. Gagnon, a champion of Western civilization, wrote of the world history standards:

> This draft is deeply flawed and offers no more help to teachers or to curriculum planners than any massive world history text would do. The document fails to set priorities. Like many recent textbooks, the document tends to be pious and uncritical of non-European/western people and actions, while holding Europeans and Americans to higher standards. . . . Throughout the document works overtime to avoid the charge of "privileging" Western civilization—to the extent that the major shaping influences on the US, and much of the rest of the modern world, for good and ill, are lost in the process. What is lost thereby is any chance for the student to grasp a coherent story of who we are and how the world arrived where we are and what that story might tell us about the alternative choices we may have before us.[47]

On the same day that Gagnon's letter arrived, the Center received a faxed report on behalf of the Education Excellence Network, written by Chester Finn Jr. In his report Finn said that he wished to associate himself with the extensive commentary written by Paul Gagnon. Clearly a cohort was mobilizing against the world history standards. Finn's statement seconded Gagnon's:

> Your document resembles an "encyclopedia of world history." A smorgasbord from which others choose, rather than a well-planned, well-balanced nutritious menu that everyone consumes. This means, I'm afraid, that it fails the first and most important test I expected "national Standards" to meet, namely selecting that which is most important for everyone to learn in such a way that significantly improves the odds that our young people will actually learn it. It was presumably, your push for "inclusiveness" that led to the bulk, and to the non-selectivity. Inclusiveness, today, is fundamentally a political motive, designed to appease political factions and interests (more than a few of them within the history profession). You appear to have succumbed . . . you've included a whole bunch of stuff that everybody knows is there only for purposes of factional appeasement and multicultural correctness.[48]

What is significant here is that Gagnon and Finn were angry that the *Standards*, which they had worked so hard to bring about over a period of years, had, in the hands of the NHSP, failed to restore the traditional historical canon. Apparently Finn and Gagnon feared that the *Standards* would give official sanction to the very political correctness that they believed had already destroyed liberal education in the first place. To make matters worse, from their point of view, P.C. would now be mandated for K–12 education.

In part, they blamed this alleged drift in the reform movement on the Clinton administration. Later that summer, perhaps in response to the NHSP, Finn set up a new "Educational Policy Committee" at his Educational Excellence Network, to bring public awareness to the new directions that he believed educational reform had taken under the Clinton administration. "We've birthed a new entity . . . ," Finn wrote. "It consists of a battalion of about forty tough-minded thinkers about educational reform," including William J. Bennett and Lamar Alexander, to name a few. Finn evidently saw the whole reform movement as slipping through his hands. "It's an intellectual, conceptual and ideological war. It's a war of ideas, and it's not a tea party."[49]

Later in July, the NCHS heard from Gilbert Sewall, a member of the NHSP Council, President of the American Textbook Council, and co-director of Finn's Educational Excellence Network. Sewall claimed in his memorandum that he had remained silent during the Criterion 13 controversy, but that finally he had to speak out. He said that in February 1993, at the time the AHA controversy was at its peak, he had drafted an article for the *Social Studies Review* criticizing the "hostage-holding" stance of the AHA. According to Sewall, he had withheld the article at Crabtree's "impassioned request." Now he claimed to regret his earlier silence. He wrote, "This was probably a mistake. It allowed continued development of world history Standards with flaws evident to some Council members and its program officers to proceed without any attention by the media or concerned scholars."[50] With hindsight, one can see that Sewall had joined the outspoken opposition that summer.

Next, on August 9, the Center heard from Albert Shanker, president of the AFT, who, like Finn, cited Gagnon's concerns that the standards "tend to be enthusiastic and uncritical about non-western civilizations and nations and much more critical of things western." Shanker continued:

> There is a whole range of normative, Marxist, negative vocabulary that seems to be used almost solely in the context of western societies. The word "ethnocentrism" is first used with regard to the Greeks; the first

mention of "bias" in history has to do with Herodotus; "subordination of women" first enters the picture in the context of medieval Europe; the conditions endured by slaves is not raised until the conditions of the Middle Passage are noted; "exploitation" first arises with regard to European treatment of Indians.[51]

While a handful of conservative participants were busy staking out their position against the world history standards in their individual written reports, dozens of other participants were voicing their approbation. Just as they had done during the formal consensus process, these individuals now sent in hundreds of pages of editorial comments, asking the Center to modify this or that standard or teaching activity, according to their version of accuracy or balance. The Center would make editorial changes attempting to balance all of this input from the field. However, by and large, the comments were extremely favorable, and it appeared that both the American and the world history standards were achieving consensus with most constituents.

It is only in retrospect, in the light of the controversy that erupted, that we at the history Center came to understand just how extensive the coordinated effort to condemn the world history standards was during the summer of 1994. At the time, however, in spite of the prominence of the people who were suddenly speaking out, their voices, which appeared to be those of an isolated though well-organized minority, were drowned by the general chorus of approval. The fact is that the overwhelming majority of participants liked the direction the standards had taken.

Nevertheless, Charlotte Crabtree, Ross Dunn, and I made every effort that summer to include some of the suggestions proffered by the conservative critics of world history. We added, where we could, teaching examples that were drawn from the Western tradition. At the same time, Gary Nash and his team edited the American history standards, taking into account critiques from conservative participants, particularly claims that the *Standards* had trivialized the Cold War. Yet the lion's share of the editorial input coming in over the summer directed Nash to revise the drafts to include more and more social history.

It is not clear why the conservative participants waited until the final months of the project to raise such vocal objections. Given the controversy over Criterion 13, they had had ample opportunity for more than two years to make their objections known in the public forum. Three possible explanations may be offered for the timing of their assault. One is that they had not really seen enough of the world history standards prior to this time to know just how "bad" they really

were. However, this explanation does not apply to the American history standards, which they had already seen in their near-final form
early on in the project. (Remember Cheney's and Ravitch's resounding endorsement with an additional $1 million in December 1992).
Another plausible possibility is that Council members did not feel
comfortable speaking out in the chilly atmosphere surrounding the
AHA controversy. Everyone participating in the project knew that if
the AHA had pulled out, this would have constituted a lethal blow to
the legitimacy of the entire standards setting effort in history. Even
conservative members of the Council and Forum wanted the project
to succeed at that time, and therefore they remained quiet, perhaps
hoping that their concerns would be addressed later, after the storm
was over. A third possibility is that by summer 1994 critics saw which
way the political winds were blowing in the country at large, and they
wanted to enhance their conservative credentials by registering their
disapproval of the project. Clinton's health reform was in grave difficulties by the summer of 1994, discrediting his entire administration.
Perhaps people closer to Washington, with more political savvy, sensed
that a conservative victory was likely in the upcoming November elections, and perhaps this put wind into their political sails.

However, as far as the directors of the project were concerned, by
October 1994 we thought we had achieved a balance between the views
of the left and the right, crafting a consensus document that all but
the extremists at either end of the political spectrum could accept. Thus
by October 1994, when the three *Standards* volumes went to press, we
thought we had successfully carried out our mandate to produce a
document that would materially advance the teaching of history in the
nation's schools. Even the educational press reported that national
consensus had been achieved.

6

The Consensus Unravels

The National History Standards in the Culture Wars, 1994–1996

C ONSENSUS WAS EPHEMERAL, to say the least. On October 20, 1994, Lynne Cheney wrote an opinion piece in the *Wall Street Journal* entitled "The End of History," denouncing the soon-to-be-released *National Standards for United States History*.[1] In her piece, Cheney charged the authors of the *Standards* with political correctness, excessive multiculturalism, and neglecting America's many triumphs and heroes. Not only were the NHSP directors stunned by this sudden attack, but it sent shock waves throughout the entire national educational community. With this single article, Cheney launched a controversy over our nation's past that would rage for the next eighteen months in the national press, over the airwaves, and in the halls of Congress. During this protracted battle in the ongoing culture wars, Charles Krauthammer of the *Washington Post* would accuse historians of "hijacking" history, right-wing radio and TV talk show host Rush Limbaugh would demand that the *Standards* be "flushed down the toilet," and Senator Slade Gorton from Washington state would propose a Senate resolution to censure the *Standards*. Chester Finn's prophecy had come true, chapter and verse.

Since Cheney had sponsored the *Standards* project in the first place, and since she had remained silent about it since her 1992 resignation speech in which she sang its praises, it seemed strange that such a public assault would come from her. Just as surprising was the fact that she focused her comments on the American history standards rather than on the world history standards which had been the recurring locus of controversy throughout the entire project. One can only surmise that her motives were political, and that a critique of the world history standards would not have resonated with the American public. Perhaps what

Cheney needed politically was to sponsor a wedge issue: a debate over who owns our national past. It was highly unlikely that the public would have become engaged in a debate over who owns the world's past.

THE END OF HISTORY

Historian Jon Wiener has laid out a chronology of how the controversy first developed in late 1994.[2] Just a few days after Cheney's article appeared, Rush Limbaugh jumped on the "end-of-history" bandwagon. While hosting his evening television show, he dramatically tore up a textbook, claiming that if the *Standards* were adopted, none of the topics covered on those pages would be taught anymore. As he ripped pages out of the text, he blamed a secret cabal of UCLA radicals for creating a set of politically correct standards that should be "flushed down the toilet." Mainstream journalists soon rushed to pick up the story. On October 26, the very day that the *Standards* were released, the *New York Times* ran an article entitled, "Plan to Teach U.S. History Is Said to Slight White Males."[3] This article, which the *Times* borrowed from the Associated Press, rested on Cheney's characterization of the *Standards*, not on a thorough analysis of the *Standards* themselves. Two days later the *Washington Times* weighed in with an article suggesting that the NHSP had wasted $2.2 million of taxpayers' money, and columnist Joe Urschel wrote an article in *USA Today* criticizing the project for forcing innocent schoolteachers into political correctness. Next the *Washington Post* printed an opinion piece that parroted Cheney's now familiar complaints. On November 4 conservative columnist Charles Krauthammer published an essay in the *Washington Post* entitled "History Hijacked." Like the other commentators, Krauthammer had not done his homework, either: he relied on Cheney's piece as his source.[4] Soon *U.S. News & World Report*, *Time*, and *Newsweek* joined in the fray. It was not until the *Newsweek* article, however, that a reporter actually took the time to look at the *Standards* themselves, and to interview teachers to see how practitioners in the trenches felt about them.[5] The *Newsweek* report was somewhat more balanced, but it didn't really challenge Cheney's characterization of the *Standards* as a "grim and gloomy" version of our national past.

It is clear that during the early days of the controversy, journalists and editors found it more convenient to quote from the Cheney script, rather than to do their own research. For example, on November 8 the *Wall Street Journal* ran a series of letters to the editor under the headline "The History Thieves." The *New York Times* opinion page featured an article by Patrick Diggins, a conservative historian, who once again used Cheney's arguments as his point of departure; he evidently had not bothered to read the *Standards* themselves.[6] On November 11 the *Wall Street Journal* quoted Al Shanker, president of the American Federation of Teachers, who now extended the criticism to the world history standards. According to Wiener, it was not until three weeks after Cheney's initial salvo that a major paper, the *New York Times*, finally featured an article that was based on the actual content of the *Standards*. According to the article, the *Standards* "keep William the conqueror . . . but also give emphasis to non-European hallmarks like China's powerful Sung Dynasty."[7]

The way in which this controversy took hold is a perfect example of how Foucault's knowledge/power nexus operates through the press. Cheney, with her position as ex-chair of the NEH, and with direct access to a mainstream newspaper, the *Wall Street Journal*, not only set the terms of the debate, but dictated the script that others would follow. Her framing discourse focused on the teaching examples, rather than the actual *Standards*, and these consequently became the storm center of the debate. Following her lead, too, the American history standards became the target of the critics and pundits, rather than the (actually more radical) world history standards. In her attacks, Cheney kept the focus off the actual thirty-one overarching standards. It would have been difficult to create the impression of multicultural excess by focusing on the actual standards, which were couched as bland generalizations about broad topics of American history (see Appendix B for a list of the thirty-one standards). Instead, Cheney, and the other critics who followed her strategy, targeted a small handful (perhaps twenty-five) of the 2,600 illustrative classroom activities attached to the *Standards* as strategies for how teachers might bring the historical period alive in the classroom. Here the critics misunderstood (or, in many cases, misrepresented) the purpose of the teaching examples. As I explained in Chapter 5, the examples were never meant to represent an exhaustive list of content (the content was delineated in the actual standards), nor were they in any way mandatory, as some of the critics chose to represent them; rather, they were written by teachers, for teachers, as possible ways to showcase active learning strategies and critical thinking skills.

Cheney's method might be described as "the numbers game": It consisted of counting up the number of times particular names appeared in the books, and then expressing outrage that, for example, Harriet Tubman, the African American who led slaves to freedom before the Civil War, is "mentioned" six times when George Washington "makes only a fleeting appearance and Thomas Edison gets ignored altogether." Cheney argued, "It's hard to get into the books if you're a white male." In fact, as Gary Nash explained at the time, "most of the names referred to in the teaching examples in *National Standards for United States History* are white males only because this group has held political, economic and cultural power throughout most of this nation's history."[8]

If one looks at the sample drawn from the actual *Standards* on pages 119–120, one can see how Cheney went about distorting and manipulating the content of these books. For example, she claimed, "not a single one of the thirty-one Standards mentions the Constitution." Technically she was right. The word "Constitution" does not appear in any of the thirty-one overarching statements about American history. However, it does figure some 177 times in the sub-standards and the teaching examples, and a major section of the book is devoted to a thorough analysis of Constitution-making.[9] To cite one example among many, Standard 3, Era 3 of the United States history book requires that ". . . Students should understand the institutions and practices of government created during the revolution and how they were revised between 1787 and 1815 to create the foundation of the American political system."[10] It is clear from this one small example, pulled from the American history book, that the Constitution and many other such crucial events in American history are not only covered in the *Standards*, but contrary to what Cheney alleged, students are encouraged to analyze them in depth.

Historian Ross Dunn labeled this strategy of misrepresentation as the "sin of omission" approach to condemning the standards. Cheney would use this tactic to suggest that many other traditional topics were neglected in the book. For example, she maintained that the *Standards* had expunged Robert E. Lee from the historical canon.[11] Again, technically, she was correct. Robert E. Lee, the famous Confederate general from the Civil War, was never mentioned by name anywhere in the book. But Cheney's argument bordered on sophistry: would not Lee become a central subject if teachers were to teach the following standard on the Civil War? "Evaluate how political, military, and diplomatic leadership affected the outcome of the war. [Assess the importance of the individual in history]."[12] Similarly, how could one fail to mention George Washington when invoking the following standard? "Analyze the character and roles of the military, political, and diplomatic leaders who helped forge the American victory in the Revolutionary War. [Assess the importance of the individual in history]."[13] Given that Washington sustained his role as the preeminent American leader in military, political, and diplomatic affairs for over fifty years, it would be difficult to ignore him.

However, by writing the script as she did, and through her access to the mainstream press, I believe that Cheney was able to frame a discourse about the *Standards* that was hard to refute. The discourse went like this: by leaning over backwards to be inclusive, the authors of the *Standards* had overplayed the historical impact of such arcane figures as Harriet Tubman and underplayed the impact of such historical giants as George Washington and Robert E. Lee. All of this was based on a simple numerical count of how many times someone was mentioned in the teaching examples, not on the actual wording of the *Standards*.

And yet, ironically, while Cheney et al. were able to create an uproar over the proposed *National Standards for History*, they completely ignored the *U.S. History Framework for the 1994 National Assessment of Educational Progress*, which was released earlier that year. Yet the NAEP assessment framework, developed through consensus by many of the same historians and educators who worked on the *National Standards for History*,[14] made detailed recommendations that were just as politically correct as the *Standards* were portrayed to be. The assessment itself, developed by the Educational Testing Service, contained many items that were similar in tone to the teaching examples given in the *Standards*. For example, one test item from the eighth-grade assessment showed an illustration by Currier and Ives depicting women in a horse-drawn carriage leaving their husbands behind with babies and laundry. The test item asked: "The drawing above is from 1869. Describe the point that the artist is trying to make. How does the point the artist is making relate to social changes during this period?" Presumably this question was intended to prompt students into writing responses about gender role reversals and the women's movement. Another test item from the twelfth-grade assessment showed a magazine cover from 1876 depicting American Indians in full dress. The subtitle read, "What Shall We Do with Our Indians?" The prompt asked students to "Look at the magazine cover. What historical events would have led this question and picture to appear on the cover of a popular magazine in 1876? What attitudes displayed toward American Indians by other Americans are suggested by this magazine cover?" Forgetting the impenetrable syntax, test-makers were apparently prompting students to discuss the debate over Indian removal taking place in 1876. Another item asked fourth graders to study a picture of Phillis Wheatley (1753–1784) and to identify two ways that she was different from most slaves in the American colonies. Apparently students would have to learn a good deal of social history if they were to do well on the NAEP assessment, the so-called "Nation's Report Card." Yet somehow, the NAEP assessment sponsored by the U.S. Department of Education, went undetected during the entire debate over the *Standards*.[15]

One can see why the teachers who had labored for more than two years developing the teaching examples were stunned by Cheney's distortions of their work. Gloria Sesso, a teacher from Long Island, and John Pyne, a social studies coordinator from New Jersey, wrote a letter to the *New York Times* expressing their outrage.

> As two of the history teachers involved in the writing of the National U.S. History Standards, we are appalled that we have become the object of a virulent ideological attack by Lynne Cheney and her cohorts. Scouring the hundred of specific student activities that we helped draft, they have made a national issue out of perhaps half a dozen examples, and in the process have suggested that everyone involved in the project is obsessed with political correctness. All of the classroom teachers who wrote the Standards and developed the activities are mainstream educators with long experience in the classroom and are highly regarded by their colleagues, by students, and by parents. To be labeled as some sort of left-wing radicals by critics such as Ms. Cheney is an injustice to classroom teachers everywhere.[16]

As this protest revealed, not only had Cheney and her fellow critics invented their own "fictional" version of the history Standards, as Ross Dunn has argued, but they had also invented their own imaginary version of the two-and-a-half-year collaborative process by which the *Standards* were developed.[17] According to them, the *Standards* volumes were the result of a secret "conspiracy." Cheney and her fellow critics portrayed the writers of the *Standards* as a tight-knit band of left-leaning professors who gathered in clandestine meetings at UCLA with the aim of perverting the minds of America's youth. Thus John Leo, a conservative pundit and ally of Lynne Cheney, proclaimed that the *Standards* got "to be so bad" because "most of the power and control of the drafting process stayed in the hands of academics with a heavy ideological agenda."[18] Carol Gluck, a professor of Japanese history at Columbia University who sat on the NHSP Council that oversaw the Center's work, felt impelled to refute this allegation. In a *New York Times* opinion piece Gluck described how the *Standards* had emerged "through an admirable process of open debate that could probably only happen in the United States." She also pointed out that consensus does not mean "national unanimity."[19]

Kirk Ankeney, another member of the team of teachers that had worked on the *Standards*, also felt compelled to rebut these criticisms.

Noting that he had been a registered Republican all his life, Ankeney wrote:

> One of the controversial issues, which arose, had to do with questions about the authorship of the *Standards*. The error of their [the critics'] ways lay in their contention that the history Standards were the creation of one historian, one university's history department, and one point of view. The facts are these: A host of prominent historians were involved, and the teacher-writers were selected from virtually every corner of the United States and we were inclusive of the diversity of this country. There was no philosophical or political litmus test or paper screening applied to the educators who came to work on the Standards. On this latter issue, as I have stated elsewhere, the topic of one's political beliefs never came up during the two-and-a-half years I was associated with the project. No one asked, or if they cared they were masterful at hiding it.[20]

At least Ankeney's, Pyne's, and Sesso's letters and opinion pieces were published in the mainstream press. However, most of the K–12 teachers whose lives were most directly affected by this controversy, and who had spent months sending letters to the editors, never appeared in print or on the radio. Their voices were silenced in a debate that was conducted exclusively among well-known academics and prominent politicians who had more ready access to the media. It is extraordinary that this debate took place excluding the very social studies teachers and students who were directly involved in teaching and learning history in the schools. Two educational researchers observed, "The fact that university professors should become the spokespersons for K–12 teachers suggests the higher status accorded to them, their greater accessibility, and their stronger ties to the media."[21] In the case of K–12 teachers, the knowledge/power nexus was closed to non-members.[22] But pundits and politicians, not historians, dominated the airwaves and newsprint. Certainly Lynne Cheney, John Fonte, John Leo, Charles Krauthammer, Patrick Diggins, Phyllis Schlafly, Rush Limbaugh, Gertrude Himmelfarb, Rush Limbaugh, Pat Robertson, Ralph Reed, Newt Gingrich, Bob Dole, Arthur A. Schlesinger Jr., Diane Ravitch, Al Shanker, George Will, and countless other pundits and politicians had access to the op-ed pages and the airwaves throughout the country. Rebuttals such as Ankeney's, Dunn's, Nash's, and those of countless other participants in the project never achieved headline status, and the few that did appear as featured articles were too few and too late to reverse the damage done by Cheney's domination of the debate early on.

But even the editorial endorsement of the *Standards* by many major newspapers such as the *New York Times, Los Angeles Times, San Francisco Chronicle, Christian Science Monitor,* and *Minneapolis Star Tribune* made little difference.[23] By now Cheney's view of the *Standards* had been completely legitimized by repetition in the press, and major politicians soon took notice.

Not all criticism of the *Standards* was mean-spirited, politically motivated, or based on hearsay. Some critics actually read the *Standards*, and wrote honest and heartfelt critiques of the text. At times it was difficult for us at the NCHS to separate hostile from constructive criticism, due to the barrage that came our way by fax, phone, and mail. However, it was fairly easy for us to determine which critics based their analysis on a careful reading of the text, and which critics based their remarks on a resuscitation of the Cheney script. Diane Ravitch fell into the former category. On December 7, 1994, Ravitch wrote a mixed review of the *Standards* in *Education Week*. Titled "Standards in U.S. History: Solid Material Interwoven with Political Bias," the article revealed that Ravitch had read the text carefully. However, her conclusions echoed Cheney's general argument and compounded the perception that the *Standards* were "grim and gloomy."

> Conventional histories present the main theme of American history as the ongoing struggle to extend democratic rights to all Americans. In the Standards document, the implicit theme seems to be the ongoing (and usually unsuccessful) struggle by the oppressed to wrest rights and power from selfish white male Protestants. In this act, democratic ideals seem to be a hollow façade, like storefronts in a Hollywood western, while greed, racism, and corruption appear to be the real commonalities of American history.[24]

Ravitch went on to blame the consensus process itself for what she perceived as a negative version of the American past. She had concluded from this controversy that the process of "negotiating and log-rolling" had forced historical "truth" to be sacrificed at the altar of political correctness. Further, she warned, "we must take care not to make some interpretations of the past 'official knowledge,' while shunning conflicting points of view."[25]

Throughout this controversy, each side of the political spectrum would use the term "official knowledge" to label attempts by the other side to control the direction that the *Standards* ought to take. Both the right and the left believed they held a direct line to "the truth," and that the opposing party was promoting a "political agenda." Thus the AHA and OAH Focus Group members honestly believed that they held a direct line to "the truth" through scholarly research that had pried open the traditional historical canon to include non-Western cultures and ethnic minorities. At the same time, these scholars believed that the neo-conservative critics had a simple "political agenda": to restore a hegemonic view of the past. On the other hand, the neo-conservatives were equally convinced that they held a direct line to "the truth" through the traditional canon of liberal education, all "sweetness and light," to quote Matthew Arnold. Yet they too believed passionately that their opponents had a "political agenda": using history to reconstruct society along leftist principles. In a polarizing discourse such as this one, each side of the political spectrum was able to characterize its opponent's version of truth as politically motivated; neither side had the will or capacity to problematize its own search for truth.

THE CENTER STRIKES BACK

Although the three NCHS directors and three support staff members were completely overwhelmed by the media flurry, with faxes and phone calls flooding in from all over the country and orders for the *Standards* books piling up at a rate that far exceeded the small staff's ability to open them, none of us took this assault lying down. However, Cheney's *Wall Street Journal* article had set the tone for the debate, and the NCHS was put on the defensive from the start. To counteract the negative press, Crabtree, Nash, Appleby, Dunn, I, and countless other NHSP participants mounted a public relations campaign to set the record "straight." However, as Ross Dunn described in a January 25 listserv e-mail about the *Standards* controversy,

> it is of course far easier to make flip accusations about the Standards and to drop bombs on them than to explain in detail their organization and content, the criteria guiding them, the consensus-building process by which they were written, and so on. But it is important that efforts continue to be made to resituate the discussion in a forum of reason and sanity.[26]

In spite of this disadvantage, the NCHS urged members of the various professional organizations to write their local newspapers and congressmen. So did Page Putnam Miller, the AHA lobbyist, who sent weekly *NCC* [National Coordinating Committee for the Promotion of History] *Washington Updates* via e-mail. The NCHS sent out hundreds of letters, news clippings, and e-mails in an attempt to control the damage already done, and to ward off further damage. For example, Gary Nash sent out a list of "talking points" that participants could use in rebutting the Cheney charges. As early as December 6, 1994, Joyce Appleby sent an e-mail over Historynet to alert fellow historians to the possible implications of what was happening in the press. Appleby feared that Krauthammer's comments in the *Washington Post*, in which he used the *Standards* as an example of why "federal culture agencies are beyond redemption," would be used to weaken the NEH and the NEA. In her e-mail Appleby prophetically warned historians that

> since the Standards might be a staging ground for a larger war on the NEH, NEA, NPR and NHPRC [National Endowment for the Humanities, National Endowment for the Arts, National Public Radio, and National Historic Publications and Records Commission], and everything else that involved federal support of education and culture, then let's take our bearing now for the fights ahead.[27]

Galvanized by such efforts, many participants went on local and national radio and television to get the message out; others wrote to their congressmen and the press.

In the meantime, Gary Nash was trying to negotiate directly with the critics. On January 12, 1995, Nash convened a meeting with the "principal" critics at the Brookings Institution in Washington, D.C., hoping to address their concerns by meeting with them.[28] The meeting had been organized and chaired by Charles Quigley, director of the Center for Civic Education in Calabasas, California, who hoped that by salvaging the history standards he could help save the other standards projects as well, which would surely go down with them. (This included the civics standards that Quigley's organization had developed.) At the meeting Nash explained that he intended to address the criticisms in a responsible and timely manner. He proposed that he would organize a team of people to carefully examine each standard, along with its supporting teaching activities, and correct any instances of historical bias. He hoped that this would satisfy the critics without jeopardizing the consensus already forged. At the NCHS, we had already embarked on an editing project of this nature.

In an effort to reassure Council members that the original consensus would not be overturned by this new effort, Nash wrote a letter to participants explaining the purpose of the meeting and what had taken place. Nash wrote that he had discussed the *Standards* with Diane Ravitch, Al Shanker, Ruth Wattenberg, Gilbert Sewall, Elizabeth Fox-Genovese, and Joy Hakim, noted critics who were invited to the Brookings meeting. John Fonte, Cheney's deputy from the American Enterprise Institute, attended as well, although he had not been invited. In his letter Nash reassured the NHSP Council members that any changes would be done in ways that would be welcomed and supported by the same organizations that had supported the original documents.[29] Since three of the six critics (Ruth Wattenberg, Gilbert Sewall, and Elizabeth Fox-Genovese) now at the table had been major participants in forging the original consensus it was difficult to imagine just how Nash could hold together the original consensus.

THE SENATE'S VERSION OF HISTORY

Just as it seemed that the controversy might calm down, things got worse. The debate now entered the political arena. Early in the morning of January 18, 1995, we at the NCHS began to receive a barrage of phone calls from the East Coast announcing that the Senate had just passed a non-binding "Sense of the Senate" resolution, on freshman senator Slade Gorton's motion, condemning the *Standards* by a vote of 99–1.[30] Again we were caught completely by surprise. This resolution passed in spite of the continuous, three-month effort on the part of the NCHS and its associated scholars and teachers to respond to critics with changes and to set the record straight on the actual content of the *Standards*. Gorton's resolution called on the National Education Standards and Improvement Council (NESIC), a body yet to be appointed by President Clinton,

> to disapprove the center's history Standards, forbidding any federal funds to be awarded to, or expended by, the National Center for History in the Schools, after the date of enactment of this Act, for the development of voluntary national content Standards, voluntary national student performance Standards, or criteria for the certification of such content and student performance Standards, on the subject of history, and, mandating that any federal agency providing funds for the development of Standards must require that the recipient of such funds should have a decent respect for the contributions of western civilization, and United States history, ideas, and institutions, to the increase of freedom and prosperity around the world.[31]

The vote of 99 to 1 to condemn the *Standards* (and the history center that oversaw their development) was a stinging rebuke for the *Standards* and the history profession that had produced them. The one holdout, Senator Bennett Johnston of Louisiana, cast his vote against the resolution because he thought that the *Standards* had gotten off too lightly with a non-binding Sense of the Senate resolution. Even the 1964 Gulf of Tonkin Resolution was passed by a less persuasive majority: 98 to 2.[32]

At the time, we could not comprehend how this censure by the Senate could possibly have come about. We were stunned that so many Democrats, including our own senators, Barbara Boxer and Dianne Feinstein from California, voted with the conservatives to condemn the *Standards*. But with the Republican majority, the "Contract with America," and the Christian Coalition in power, it should not have been surprising. Soon, however, we began to understand what had transpired: The *Congressional Record* provides the explanation. Senator Slade Gorton, a freshman senator from the state of Washington and chair of the Senate Appropriations Subcommittee on the Interior and Related Agencies, which was responsible for the funding of the NEH, put the resolution forward with a speech whose wording strongly suggests that it was written by Cheney, or more probably by one of her colleagues at the American Enterprise Institute, the conservative think tank in Washington, D.C., where she was then based.

Gorton's speech recapitulated the by now familiar discourse first enunciated by Lynne Cheney.

> Mr. President, what is a more important part of our Nation's history for our children to study—George Washington or Bart Simpson? Is it more important that they learn about Roseanne Arnold, or how America defeated communism as the leader of the free world? According to this document—the recently-published "National Standards for United States History"—the answers are not what Americans would expect. With this set of Standards, our students will not be expected to know George Washington from the man in the moon. According to this set of Standards, America's democracy rests on the same moral footing as the Soviet Union's totalitarian dictatorship.
>
> Mr. President, this set of Standards must be stopped, abolished, repudiated, repealed. It must be recalled like a shipload of badly contaminated food. Today, before our children are asked to spend their evenings studying Bart Simpson instead of Benjamin Franklin's discovery of electricity, these Standards must be abolished.
>
> My amendment will stop this set of Standards from becoming a guide for teaching history in America's classrooms. In order to stop this perverted idea in its tracks, and to ensure that it does not become, de facto, a guide for our nation's classrooms, it must be publicly and officially repudiated by this Congress.[33]

Gorton was following Cheney's line of attack, which was to concentrate on the teaching examples, wrenched out of context, and not on the *Standards* themselves. But let's look at the actual document to see just how big a threat Bart Simpson is to George Washington, and to discover the context within which he is mentioned in the *Standards*. First of all, the television show *The Simpsons* is indeed mentioned once, in an activity designed for how teachers might flesh out the following standard.

> Explain the influence of the media on contemporary American culture." The teaching example reads: "Analyze the reflection of values in such popular TV shows as "Murphy Brown," "Roseanne," "Married with Children," and "The Simpsons." Compare the depiction of values to those expressed in shows like "Ozzie and Harriet," "The Honeymooners," "Father Knows Best," "My Three Sons," "All in the Family," and "The Bill Cosby Show.[34]

Slade Gorton took this single pedagogical strategy for teaching about the influence of the media on contemporary culture, pulled it completely out of context, and inflated it into a national mandate for the celebration of Bart Simpson at the expense of George Washington. Had he in fact read the *Standards*? His comments suggested he had not. He deliberately ignored the fact that an entire twenty-two-page section of the *Standards* dedicated to the "Revolution and the New Nation" (1754–1820s) covers events and movements in which George Washington was a pivotal figure,[35] and yet the one instance where Bart Simpson's name is invoked to illustrate how a teacher might compare popular culture now and in the 1950s is elevated into a central element of the national curriculum.

In his speech Gorton became passionate about the need for a celebratory official history. Predictably, perhaps, he harked back to William Bennett's *Devaluing of America* and to the Finn/Ravitch study, *What Do Our 17-Year-Olds Know?*, to explain why the nation needed national standards in the first place. After all, according to Bennett, Finn, and Ravitch, our children had not learned many of the founding truths on which our democracy is based by the time they graduated from high school. To make his point on the vital importance of a unified vision of the past, Gorton quoted from Abraham Lincoln's first inaugural address. "Lincoln, on the eve of the Civil War in March 1861 reminded the troubled country of the importance of our shared and common past:

> Though passion may have strained, it must not break our bonds of affection. The mystic chords of memory, stretching from every battlefield and patriot grave, to every living heart and hearthstone, all over this broad land, will yet swell the chorus of the union, when again touched, as surely they will be, by the better angels of our nature.[36]

Gorton concluded by saying that those mystic chords of memory are already perilously frayed. "Study after study demonstrates the wounding absence of a shared knowledge of our nation's history. These Standards would only serve to deepen that wound, and so they must be rejected." He then called for a vote on his amendment, in a resounding peroration: "Like the infamous exploding Pinto, these manuals pose a horrendous threat to the vitality and accuracy of American history education, and they must be recalled."[37]

But just how the senator from Washington proposed to arrange for a recall of the *Standards* was not made clear. It would have been extremely difficult to arrange, since, ironically—thanks to the controversy stirred up by Cheney and her fellow critics—the *Standards* were now selling like proverbial hotcakes.[38] But at this point more moderate voices made themselves heard. Senator Jeffords, a maverick Republican from Vermont, with the support of Senators Bingaham of New Mexico and Pell of Rhode Island, proposed an amendment to water down Gorton's binding resolution into a toothless "Sense of the Senate" resolution. Jeffords pointed out that the *Standards* were soon to be reviewed by a committee that the President would appoint: thus any action by the Senate was premature.[39] He concluded his speech by praising the process by which the *Standards* had been developed, and by praising the Center's efforts to respond to the controversy by meeting with the critics at the Brookings Institution and by proposing editorial changes. It was this watered-down version of the original amendment that passed 99–1. Jeffords argued that the Senate had no place interfering with the standards-setting process at this early stage. The governors had initiated the process, and the National Education Standards and Improvement Council (NESIC) panel had not even been constituted.

> We are prematurely criticizing something which is not even ready to be adopted. . . . Mr. President, I must oppose the amendment offered by my colleague from Washington. The amendment, which has not been subject to any hearings or review by the committee of jurisdiction, prohibits the NESIC panel from certifying any voluntary national content Standards in the subject of history. The history Standards were developed by the UCLA Center for History in Schools with the contribution of hundreds of individual teachers, scholars, and historians. The Standards which have just recently been published, have raised concern among some readers. Criticism has focused not on the Standards themselves but upon the examples of activities for students in each grade level. Of the thousands of examples not more than twenty-five were considered controversial. However, upon receipt of public input and criticism the Center is reviewing and altering its work. This in fact is, and should be, the appropriate process and primary purpose of public commentary.[40]

As Senator Jeffords pointed out, the review process was already under way. Several weeks before Senator Gorton proposed his resolution, the NCHS had already begun revising the *Standards* in response to the controversy. A group of writers at UCLA, including myself, had already revised many of the teaching examples, deleting some of the activities that had been most maligned, changing language in others, and adding examples here and there about traditional figures such as George Washington to create a more balanced overall impression. Standard 3 of Era 3 was revised to include the word "Constitution." Senator Gorton must have known these revisions were in process, and certainly Senator Jeffords knew, as his speech confirmed. In fact, as I indicated earlier, Nash had informed the critics of these changes at the Brookings Institution on January 12, bringing samples of changes with him.

The deal Senator Jeffords proposed looked like this. He would agree to censure the current history standards in a "Sense of the Senate" resolution if the conservative senators would agree to drop their binding prohibition against the yet-to-be-established National Education Standards and Improvement Council (NESIC), the board that would ultimately be responsible for certifying the *Standards*. With the majority in Congress now decidedly conservative in the wake of the November 1994 election, the embryo NESIC might well be stillborn because the conservatives would view it as a symbol of federal authority over the states. The new Congress had little use for federal agencies in general, and in particular one that would certify national standards, particularly if NESIC board members were to be appointed by the Clinton administration. This is why Jeffords's Democratic colleagues were willing to censure the history standards and the NCHS with a non-binding "Sense of the Senate" resolution that would not have the enforceability of law. In this way they could deflect the conservative assault and avoid any language in the bill that would jeopardize the establishment of NESIC. However, Jeffords's strategy would ultimately fail: Due to the controversy over the history standards, NESIC was never constituted.

The next day Sheldon Hackney, chair of the NEH during the Clinton administration, made a public statement that "the way some people have politicized the discussion is a real disservice to the nation; the discussion has become more of a 'drive-by' debate. School reform is much too important to be made a hostage to the culture wars."[41] However, on March 12 Hackney himself was held hostage to the culture wars when he was called upon to testify before the Senate Appropriations Committee and to answer questions regarding the NEH budget. Senator Gorton, chair of the committee, asked Hackney if the NCHS center that had produced the *Standards* had any pending applications, knowing full well the Center had applied for an extension of our grant. Hackney responded that indeed the Center had written a proposal that would be evaluated in May. "Be very careful with that application," Gorton warned.[42] Needless to say, the grant proposal was rejected by the NEH.

The Senate condemnation gave legitimacy to the media blitz against the *Standards*, and provided fresh fuel. Ross Dunn described the effect of the Senate action in *UCLA Magazine*.

> The hostile critics immediately vaunted the Senate action as a triumph for their cause, proclaiming that the Standards would now have to be "junked," and that even the likes of Ted Kennedy, Paul Wellstone and Carol Moseley-Braun were opposed to them. In fact, the Senate action was a Democrat-led tactical move to prevent language undermining the independence of NESIC from entering into law. Congress had conducted no hearings on the history Standards, and the floor debate consisted mainly of three senators making one-sided attacks using scripts undoubtedly supplied by the Cheney forces. At any rate, early in February, the Senate deleted the anti-standards resolution from the [unfunded mandates] bill to which it had been attached. [Thus the final bill that passed the Senate included no mention of the History Standards.] Even so, a cold wind blew through the Center. Clearly, the hostile critics had scored a point, impressing even the club of 100 with their upside-down version of the Standards.[43]

Just five days after the Senate condemned the history Standards, Lynne Cheney launched her next salvo in the history wars. Again, it was the *Wall Street Journal* that published her opinion piece, entitled "Kill My Old Agency, Please." In it, Cheney castigated the *Standards* for their allegedly anti-Western bias. But this time she made clear that the *Standards* were merely a weapon in her arsenal: her real goal was to destroy the agency over which she had once presided, the NEH. In this article she explained how she had come to the NEH hoping to do wonderful things for the humanities, but how she had been sabotaged by projects such as the National History Standards Project. According to Cheney, more often than not, project directors funded by agencies such as the NEH reneged on their original promises. In this case, she claimed that the NCHS directors had promised her a very different set of Standards based on their earlier book, *Lessons from History*. Her conclusion was that the federal government should not be involved in sponsoring the arts and humanities.[44] Never mind that prior to the Standards project, *Lessons* had not been subjected to thoroughgoing public and professional scrutiny. Cheney failed to mention that in the National History Standards Project, she had funded a broad-based consensus project to be conducted with stakeholders, not a project that could promise to deliver the ideal message she wanted.

This opinion piece was evidently part of an orchestrated campaign. The next day, January 24, Cheney would testify before Gorton's House Interior Appropriations Subcommittee against future funding for the NEH and the National Endowment for the Arts (NEA), which was under even more violent attack by the conservatives in Congress. Another key witness invited to speak before the committee was William Bennett, Cheney's predecessor at the NEH. Both Cheney and Bennett cited examples of what they considered to be inappropriate grants awarded by the NEH. Cheney argued, "In a time when we are looking at general cutbacks in funding to many groups, including to welfare mothers and farmers, it is time to cut funding for cultural elites."[45] Presumably the cultural elites she referred to were the university professors who had been funded by the NEH. Cheney testified that the "humanities had become politicized." The state of history in higher education was such, she said, that she did not believe that any national group of historians would be able to produce standards that were acceptable. This was because she believed that "many academics and artists now saw their purpose not as revealing truth or beauty, but as achieving social and political transformation. Government should not be funding those whose main interest is promoting an agenda . . ."[46]

Citing examples from the *Standards*, Cheney blamed the National History Standards Project for playing a type of "intellectual shell-game," promising her one thing and giving her quite another. Her testimony went unchallenged, except by Congressman Skaggs (Democrat-Colorado), who pointed out specific pages in the books that contradicted her claims. In fact, Skaggs had been prepared by the NCHS and the AHA to ask these questions. He commented that Cheney had picked examples out of context and had distorted the *Standards*. For example, he pointed to the numerous occasions when the Constitution was mentioned and to standards that called for the study of military leadership.[47] However, the Republican-controlled Congress wouldn't let Skaggs's evidence get in the way. After all, Cheney, through her scare tactics, had marshaled public opinion on her side. It was no accident, presumably, that she had been able to place her opinion piece in the middle of the *Wall Street Journal* the day before she was due to testify on the "hill."

Now that Cheney's motives were out in the open, some criticism of her began to surface in the press. The day after she testified before Congress, Frank Rich of the *New York Times*, who had been following this story closely, published an opinion piece entitled "Eating Her Offspring," in which he questioned Cheney's motives.

> Did Mrs. Cheney turn against the Standards and the NEH because both have changed so radically since the '92 election—or simply because she will stop at nothing to be a major player in the Gingrich order? The evidence suggests she has deliberately caricatured her own former pet project (the Standards) as P.C. hell-incarnate so it can be wielded as a Mapplethorpe-like[48] symbol to destroy the agency she so recently championed. . . . as Mrs. Cheney distorted the *Standards*, so she also may have distorted the chronology of how her once-beloved project "went wrong." According to three sources who worked on it, a 100-page draft of the opening section was available to Mrs. Cheney when she was still at the NEH and still singing the Standards' praises. The draft contained some of the same elements—the treatment of the Constitution, for instance, that Cheney so strenuously denounces now.[49]

As Rich pointed out, it was precisely at the time when Cheney was about to resign as chair of the NEH that those earlier drafts were disseminated. Nonetheless, Cheney approved $1 million supplementary funding for the project based on her apparent satisfaction with its progress.[50] And it was precisely at that time that she wrote to Charlotte Crabtree praising the consensus process that was producing the *Standards*.[51] Copies of those early drafts can be found in the UCLA Archives, and they can be chronologically linked to the public praise that Cheney made of them. The standards for these early eras of U.S. history were developed in the summer of 1992, reviewed by the Council in September 1992, distributed in public hearings and meetings in Washington, D.C. and Detroit in November 1992, and reported to the NEH in quarterly reports of November 1992 and January 1993.[52] At that time, the standards in Era 3, "The American Revolution and the New Nation," paid more attention to women, blacks, and Native Americans than the final edition, and less attention to leaders such as George Washington. As Crabtree discovered later when comparing the 1992 draft of the standards with the 1994 published version, in the earlier draft George Washington was never identified as first president, the first congress was never mentioned, and no attention was given to Hamilton at that time. Yet Cheney said nothing but good things about those earlier drafts.[53]

Later, Cheney, whose passion for history was well known, admitted that she had never read a version of the standards until someone called it to her attention in late summer or fall of 1994. Cheney claimed that she never kept close tabs on the project while she headed the NEH. "Typically," she said, "the chairman does not see projects until after they are completed." As for letters she wrote in praise of the project's progress, Cheney later said that she did not recall writing any such letters. "People wrote letters for me that I sometimes signed because they were an important part of the grant-giving process." Similarly, Ravitch claimed that she had access to early drafts all along but had never read them. "I was very concerned not to be seen as directing the process, so I stayed at arm's length, she explained."[54]

Frank Rich and Congressman Skaggs could not possibly have worked out this chronology of events by themselves. They were much too busy for that. It was the AHA that provided Skaggs with his script. Indeed, politics makes strange bedfellows. It is ironic that the AHA staff now worked vigorously to save the very project that they had once tried to derail. The day before Cheney was due to testify before Congress, the AHA prepared a list of questions for Skaggs to ask Cheney during the next day's hearings. On January 23 Crabtree and I received a fax from the AHA asking us to correct any factual errors that might have appeared in the AHA's version of events and to add any pertinent details that the AHA had missed. We provided critical information on the timing of events, such as information leading to the following question.

> You claimed a number of problems with the early eras of the U.S. History Standards, particularly the treatment of George Washington, the Constitution, the first congress, and the antebellum period preceding the Civil War. Why did you wait until two weeks before the November election to raise these questions when these particular Standards were all developed and widely disseminated for public review in the fall of 1992, long before you resigned from the NEH, and two full years before you made them an issue?[55]

But small victories like these did not matter, even if they were won in the halls of Congress or on the opinion pages of the *New York Times*. The damage was done. The Senate had lent the weight of its authority against the *Standards*, and this gave continued legitimacy to the campaign against them, and more importantly, to the campaign against the NEH and the U.S. Department of Education. Not only had conservatives across the country, under Cheney's leadership, framed the conservative attack on the *Standards*, but the Senate, without the benefit of a single public hearing, appropriated the conservative attack on the *Standards* and turned it into law. Encouraged by the Senate's condemnation, the critics now redoubled their attacks.

For those of us involved in directing the project, the Senate resolution was the low point in what would be an eighteen-month uphill struggle. With this sweeping resolution, the Senate achieved three goals:

1) it condemned the work of hundreds of dedicated schoolteachers, educational leaders, and academic historians who had devoted countless hours to the project, 2) it jeopardized the future of the National Endowment for the Humanities and the U.S. Department of Education, and 3) it gave its imprimatur to a single official version of American and world history.

A discourse had been formulated, and had gained general currency, because it originated from positions of power. With the help of the conservative media, and aligned with the new majority in Congress, Cheney had seized the commanding heights, imposed her vision of events on the public mind, and dictated the terms of the debate. A Foucauldian power/knowledge nexus had been established, which her opponents could not overcome: Their response came too late and was too fragmented for them to seize the initiative and promote their own version of events.

Fueled by the victory of the 104th Congress, conservative politicians and journalists nationwide were eager to follow Cheney's lead in attacking the alleged multicultural excesses of the *Standards*, because the political gains would be considerable and there was absolutely nothing to lose. By attacking the federally-funded *Standards*, politicians like Senator Gorton could grandstand their conservative credentials without spending any money. At the same time, politicians bent on reducing the role of the federal government could use the *Standards* to demonstrate how government agencies such as the NEH and the U.S. Department of Education habitually misuse tax dollars to fund such "Mapplethorpe-type excesses" as the *Standards*. Few people noticed that Cheney and Ravitch were the very people who, under the Bush administration, were responsible for funding the project they now castigated. Political memories are short. Cheney's contention that liberal historians had sidetracked the project from its original intent went largely unchallenged, and was vehemently repeated in the media. And who would defend the drafters of the *Standards*, who were portrayed as a bunch of careworn K–12 classroom teachers and sixties-generation professors, centered at UCLA, and allied with a national network of radical postmodernists? Any defense would serve to make their case even stronger. Let's face it, this was a "win–win" situation all the way around. Even better, rather than actually reading the *Standards*, conservative pundits could simply follow Cheney's brilliant strategy of caricaturizing the *Standards*. Cheney and her followers would select particular passages from the 271-page document, distort them, and then repeat the distortions *ad nauseam* in the various media. And the media happily went along with this approach. As Nathan Glazer had observed during the 1991 controversy over the New York *Curriculum of Inclusion*, "One of the problems with the press in dealing with such reports is that it doesn't read them. Press reporting tends to consist of who said what about the report, who attacked and who defended it."[56]

Never mind whether or not the *Standards* themselves were as politically correct as alleged in the press, the damage to the NEH and the NEA was severe. The NEH and the U.S. Department of Education were nearly abolished by the 104th Congress, and both agencies faced severe financial cutbacks during the ensuing two years. After the Senate vote, the *Standards* became so radioactive that even Richard Riley, U.S. Secretary of Education for the Clinton administration, and Undersecretary Marshall Smith denounced them in an effort to save their own agency. Smith rejected Cheney's contention that the Clinton administration would adopt the proposed *Standards* as the new official knowledge. "We're really trying to keep hands off," Smith said, stressing that the *Standards* were meant to be voluntary.[57] Secretary of Education Riley's disassociation with the *Standards* was even more pronounced.

> This was not our grant. This is not my idea of good Standards. This is not my view of how history should be taught in America's classrooms. As I have said previously this first effort was a set back and a disappointment. The historians need to go back to the drawing board to produce a positive and well-balanced history of our country. . . . The president does not believe and I do not believe that the UCLA Standards should form the basis of our history curriculum in our schools.[58]

Many were frustrated by the Clinton administration's attempts to distance itself from the *Standards*. David Vigilante, a retired teacher who was one of the major contributors to the American and world history standards, wrote to Secretary Riley criticizing the timing of his words: "You had a forum in which to criticize and to have the corrections made then and there. To hold back and wait until it's published and then attack, to me, is a reflection of a political motive rather than a motive of trying to improve the history education of students in K–12."[59]

THE SENATE AND ACADEMIC FREEDOM

Many historians and K–12 teachers saw this as more than a drive-by debate. They had concluded that the Senate action was a direct threat to academic freedom. A groundswell of historians, academic departments, and K–12 teachers from all over the United States wrote to their senators condemning the censure of the *Standards*. Sandi Cooper, chair of the Faculty Senate at the City University of New York (CUNY), wrote this critique of the Senate resolution in a letter to New York Senator Daniel Moynihan:

> I am afraid you have been hornswaggled, cut off at the pass and taken for a ride, sir. You and your senatorial colleagues, those of you that bother reading and thinking, that is—really have better things to do than collectively threaten academic freedom; imply that there is one politically-correct view of the past; and promise to defund the National Council as well as the NEH because of some alleged left wing cast to modern social science scholarship that the triumphalists require, without the Soviet Union as their favorite demon.
>
> Having just learned of the excellent resolution voted by the University Faculty Senate of the State University of New York, I shall endeavor to persuade the University Faculty Senate of the City University of New York to endorse the initiative of our upstate colleagues. The U.S. Senate vote, instigated by Senator Gorton and the campaign to destroy the Endowments, was a shameful moment in U.S. history. Mrs. Cheney's testimony and allegations will earn her a very long nose.[60]

The City University of New York (CUNY) signed the SUNY resolution. The entire history department at Stanford University sent their own letter to the *New York Times* censuring the Senate action.[61] Ron Mellor, chair of the History Department at UCLA, tried to organize a similar resolution for the University of California Academic Senate, but it failed to go through.[62] All in all, however, the Senate's action caused historians around the country to rally around the cause of academic freedom.

Not only did historians rally around the issue of academic freedom, they also engaged in a vigorous Internet debate over the *Standards* controversy.[63] The majority of historians, most of whom had been weaned on the new social history, characterized the *Standards* as mainstream history, merely the application of their own scholarship. In a Kuhnian sense, the *Standards* represented "normal science" as historians practiced it. If anything, the main concern expressed in the e-mail debates was that the *Standards* were too ambitious: that they were too voluminous and too sophisticated for practical classroom use. Several historians claimed that the *Standards* were so sophisticated that they could not be mastered by their own Ph.D. students, let alone by K–12 students.

However, not all the historians in this e-mail dialogue supported the liberal approach taken in the *Standards*. Some expressed concerns over their alleged political correctness. For example, one historian challenged his colleagues' assumption that their work deserved to be funded and supported by federal agencies.

> The fact is intellectuals in this country, the bulk of them liberal, have
> behaved as if they had some sort of entitlement to federal funding and
> that once funded they had *carte blanche* to proceed as they please. To put
> it another way, intellectuals are somewhat arrogant. Because we search
> for truth we come to believe that we have it and others are excluded from
> it. Unfortunately, those excluded from it are to a degree paying the tab
> for it.[64]

In spite of the ongoing efforts to organize the historical profession
through e-mail, and Page Putnam Miller's efforts to galvanize support
in Congress, the historians' endorsement of the *Standards* did not really get much publicity beyond the narrow confines of their own academic community. Although seventeen past presidents of the AHA and
OAH wrote letters of support to their members of Congress, and although the OAH made small grants to individuals to organize public
conferences on the *Standards* debate, these discussions never entered
the mainstream: they never really altered the public's perception that
the *Standards* were hopelessly tainted.

Perhaps the most eloquent critique of the Senate's action was written neither by a well-known historian, nor by a famous journalist or
policymaker. Rather, it was written by one of the many teachers who
had tried to make public their opinions about the *Standards*, with no
success. Jean Johnson, a high school teacher from New York who
worked as a task force member on the world history standards, sent
the NCHS copies of ten letters she and her husband had written to the
press, none of which was published. She wrote the following statement
in a letter to her senator, dated January 25, 1995.

> After working on these Standards that took more than two years to de-
> velop, and experiencing first-hand the constant give and take, discussions,
> and compromises that went into the consensus on the final product, we
> affirm the democratic process more than ever. Those of us involved in
> the Standards project remain deeply respectful of that process. Somehow
> we assumed that the inclusive and thoughtful deliberations in which we
> were involved would continue and include the way the Senate of the
> United States considered the issue. Yet without any serious debate and
> seemingly relying on a few vocal critics whose criticism, from our view-
> point, were emotionally charged half truths that do not accurately rep-
> resent what is actually in the Standards, you voted overwhelmingly to
> reject the proposed Standards.[65]

Jean Johnson gets to the heart of what was at stake here. It is one
thing for Cheney, Limbaugh, and Bennett to sit in their corporate-
funded think tanks or their radio stations and condemn a set of stan-

dards incorporating some of the new findings of social historians over the last thirty years; it is quite another for the United States Senate, without proper debate or hearings, to attempt to impose an official version of celebratory history on this nation's schools. But it was by no means alone in this endeavor.

THE CHRISTIAN COALITION

One of the groups most responsible for organizing the political campaign against the *Standards* was the Christian Coalition, led by Ralph Reed. The Christian Coalition had been largely responsible for delivering the decisive votes in the Gingrich victory, and consequently its members had tremendous influence in setting the political agenda for the 104th Congress. The "Contract with America" reflected their input. Soon after the Senate took its vote on the *Standards*, the Christian Coalition joined the political attack against them, using the *Standards* as a political weapon to discredit the two agencies that had funded them, and to discredit the entire Goals 2000 legislation. Given their political agenda of limiting federal control and their own educational agenda, the Christian Coalition devoted extensive resources to this cause.

In their "Contract with the American Family" the Christian Coalition set out a legislative agenda for Congress, "intended to strengthen families and to restore common-sense values."[66] One of the ten principles outlined in the "Contract with the American Family" was to return educational control to the local level. They argued that Goals 2000 had moved the country in the opposite direction: establishing several new federal bureaucracies, such as NESIC, which they feared would be the equivalent of a national school board. Citing Cheney's examples of bias in the *National Standards for History*, and the Senate's condemnation, they claimed that the history standards were an example of how the federal government was undermining parental involvement and local control of education. They argued, "The time to return federal educational control to parents and local communities through elimination of the Department of Education is long overdue, and a good first step would include repealing Goals 2000 legislation."

The religious right's agenda to keep the federal government out of the education business and to abolish the Department of Education was hardly new in 1994. Since the formation of the Moral Majority in the 1970s, the Christian conservative movement had conducted a highly organized campaign against public education, mostly through efforts at the local school and district levels. Indeed, it was the Christian right that led the campaign against *Man: A Course of Study* during the mid-1970s, and it was the Christian right that led state and local campaigns against textbook adoptions for many years. Represented by such groups as Citizens for Excellence in Education, the National Association of Christian Educators, the Concerned Women for America, the Eagle Forum, the Educational Research Analysts, the Family Research Council, Focus on the Family, the Institute for Creation Research, the Heritage Foundation, the Rutherford Institute, and the Traditional Values Coalition, the Christian Coalition has worked systematically to attack public education in the press, on television, and at the ballot box. Their goal has been to discredit public schools, shut them down, and thereby direct public funds to home schooling and private schools where they can control the curriculum.

Conservative Christians blame the recent revolution in learning theories for most of what is wrong with public education today. Believing that God-fearing children should never challenge adult authority or the inerrancy of the Bible, evangelical Christians condemn the child-centered teaching methods advocated by educational theorists and psychologists such as John Dewey, Jean Piaget, Jerome Bruner, and Howard Gardner. According to them, contemporary learning theories have led to nontraditional teaching methods such as cooperative learning groups, peer tutoring, discovery or inquiry learning, multicultural curricula, and performance-based assessments. These techniques are anathema to conservative Christians, who advocate traditional instructional methods such as direct instruction, individual seatwork, rote memorization of factual knowledge, and competitive norm-referenced exams.[67]

With hindsight, one can see why members of the Christian Coalition found the *National Standards for History* so objectionable. Designed by the liberal educational establishment of university intellectuals and education experts, the *Standards* embodied many of the elements of "secular humanism" that the Christian right was trying to combat: social history, world history, multiple viewpoints, and inquiry-based learning strategies, to name a few. The *Standards* encouraged students to make decisions based on multiple sources rather than from a single authority such as the Bible. One can understand why this was unacceptable for fundamentalist Christians. What is difficult to understand, however, is that the open-ended and inquiry-based approach to history embodied in the *Standards* was equally unacceptable for neoconservative intellectuals and policymakers such as Lynne Cheney,

E. D. Hirsch, Alan Bloom, Dinesh D'Souza, Chester Finn, William Bennett, and countless others who did not share the fundamentalists' views on religion.

In addition to abolishing the U.S. Department of Education, the "Contract with the American Family" set out to abolish or privatize the federal agencies concerned with culture, including the National Endowment for the Humanities (NEH), the National Endowment for the Arts (NEA), and National Public Radio (NPR). Again the *Standards* served as ammunition against those agencies as well. But traditionally Republicans had supported the NEH and NEA because, as members of an educated elite, Republicans were far more likely to attend the symphonies and museum exhibits and watch the PBS specials funded by those organizations than were Democrats. However, all this changed with the emergence of the Christian Coalition as a major grass roots movement within the Republican Party. With the election of the 104th Congress, wage-earning populism replaced "country club" elitism as the dominant force within the Republican Party. Coming from the less-educated and nonprofessional classes, with little exposure to high culture, many members of the Christian Coalition felt that federal support for the arts and humanities was tantamount to a subsidy for the secular elite. They now claimed victim status for themselves as a wronged minority whose rights had been usurped by a cultural elite that controlled Washington, the media, and the universities. With this shift in the class basis of the Republican Party, considerable resources were now allocated to fighting culture wars against cultural elites.[68]

Gary Bauer, President of the Family Research Council (FRC) and former-Assistant Secretary of Education under the first President Bush, devoted considerable FRC dollars to discrediting the *Standards*. In a full-page advertisement in the *Washington Times*, entitled "National History Standards: Clintonites Miss the Moon," Bauer claimed that the "world class" history standards include references to "Soviet advances in space, and to the *Challenger* disaster, but neglect to mention that the U.S. won the space race."[69] This was not entirely true; the moon landing was mentioned in the K–4 book of history standards. On his Internet site, Bauer accused the federal government of trying to determine "official knowledge with the publication of the *Standards*."[70] Later the FRC would publish its own eighteen-page pamphlet, *Let Freedom Ring*, which was touted as an alternative to the *Standards*. Written by a single schoolteacher from Virginia, the pamphlet amounted to little more than a table of contents, the substance of which could be almost anything.

As the debate escalated, Cheney founded the Committee to Review National Standards, a panel of critics under the direction of John Fonte, her colleague from the American Enterprise Institute. The Reader's Digest Association and the John M. Olin Foundation funded the committee. However, the committee never met formally, and no review of national standards ever took place. Instead, John Fonte and Gilbert Sewall announced that they would publish a *Guide for Developing American and World History Standards* (with a foreword by Lynne V. Cheney). As far as I know, it has never been published: When I tried to order the book in 1999, I was told it was unavailable.

THE FINAL COMPROMISE

Even if it appeared that everyone from pundits in the press to politicians in Congress was out to discredit the *Standards*, the NCHS was not alone in its desire to salvage them. Under the leadership of Charles Quigley, director of the Center for Civic Education; Christopher Cross, President of the Council for Basic Education (CBE); and Robert Schwartz, Education Director of the Pew Charitable Trusts, several liberal foundations joined together during the spring of 1995 to fund a blue-ribbon panel under the aegis of Cross's Council for Basic Education, a nonprofit organization founded by Arthur Bestor in 1956 to ensure the primacy of intellectual and moral development in the schools by strengthening the academic curriculum.[71] This panel would review the *Standards* for their scholarly merits and make recommendations for revisions. The foundations, which tended to take a longer view than the average congressman, were in a position to save the *Standards*, and along with them the whole reform program set out in Bush's America 2000 and Clinton's Goals 2000. The Pew, MacArthur, Ford, and Spencer foundations together set aside a total of $100,000 to fund the two independent review panels, and to fund the NCHS for making the revisions. The establishment of these panels held the promise, finally, of a thoughtful and constructive review of the *Standards*.

This intervention on the part of the foundations was reminiscent of other times in the history of American educational reform when the educational foundations took it upon themselves to fill the leadership vacuum left at the federal policy level. Certainly Richard Riley, Secretary of Education, had shown little inclination to salvage the history standards project; rather, he had worked hard to distance himself from it. In this void, the liberal foundations constructed their own knowledge/power nexus to relegitimize the *Standards*, and perhaps to challenge the neo-conservative framing of issues.

In June 1995, the CBE convened two separate panels, one for world history and one for American history. Each panel included respected public figures, teachers, and academic historians.[72] According to the preface in the final report, members of the panel were selected for their strong commitment to improving history education.[73] One indication of just how prestigious these panels were was that Secretary Riley now came out to publicly endorse them.[74]

To ensure the independence of the review, "no one was invited to participate who was involved in the National Center project."[75] This was not entirely true. Diane Ravitch, the person whose name is most consistently associated with this reform, was invited to participate. Ravitch was responsible for putting history education on the reform agenda since the mid-1980s and for co-funding the project: Now she sat prominently within the group that would determine the ultimate fate of the *Standards*.

On October 11, 1995, the CBE released the panels' report, *History in the Making: An Independent Review of the Voluntary National History Standards*. Both panels endorsed the *Standards* and determined that they were worth salvaging. Their starting point was to draw a distinction between the standards themselves (i.e., the general statements of what all American students are expected to learn) and the accompanying teaching examples. The standards themselves, detached from the teaching examples, won praise from both panels. They particularly liked the emphasis on historical thinking, which they thought would broaden students' conceptual understanding of the discipline. They concluded that the overwhelming majority of criticism had been targeted at the teaching examples. Panelists recommended deleting the teaching examples because they found many of them "tendentious," and said that in "their totality, [the teaching examples] give the mistaken appearance of a curriculum."[76] The panels went on to give a detailed review of the American and world history standards, era by era. In these reviews they found that "the world history Standards, without the teaching examples, make a significant contribution toward strengthening students' knowledge of world history." The panelists found that the history of the West was emphasized in the standards, but that "world history standards should not be confused with Standards that might be developed for the teaching of Western Civilization."[77] Their final verdict was that the standards, minus the teaching examples, should be revised and adopted. The revision and all future work should be guided by the fifteen criteria established during the consensus process.

It is fascinating to observe how the various stakeholders now quickly repositioned themselves on the *Standards*. On October 11 Secretary Riley stated that the

> "panels' recommendations are an important step forward in the resolution of controversy regarding proposed voluntary national history Standards. . . . The recommendations are concrete, specific, and should form the basis for developing a new consensus regarding what our young people need to know regarding America's proud history."[78]

Diane Ravitch, not surprisingly, given her participation as a panelist, told the *Los Angeles Times* that she was "very enthusiastic about the report of the panel. It should help quell attacks on the Standards and end this particular battlefront on the culture wars."[79] John Fonte, executive director of Cheney's Committee to Review the National Standards, however, felt that separating the teaching examples from the *Standards* would do little good. "There are 25,000 or 30,000 copies of the books already in circulation. The problem is the horse is out of the barn, the train has left the station. . . . They [the Standards] are not worth revising, they are flawed throughout."[80] Cheney herself wrote an opinion piece for the *Wall Street Journal* entitled "The National History (Sub) Standards." She argued, like her emissary Fonte, that the *Standards* were irreparably flawed and that parents should now insist on a recall of the thousands of volumes already distributed.[81] However, the framing discourse had shifted toward the political center, and Cheney's could no longer steer the course of events.

With the CBE report in hand, the NCHS constituted a new advisory board and spent the next few months editing the *Standards* according to the CBE recommendations. First, the teaching examples were dropped. Second, several areas that needed strengthening in the original *Standards*, such as the treatment of science, technology, economic history, and intellectual history, were enhanced. The wording of Standard 3 now included the word "Constitution," and Washington, Jefferson, Franklin, and Madison were added by name to the standards. Similar changes were made to the world history standards and to the historical thinking standards, addressing once and for all the most egregious omissions identified by Cheney and her cohort.[82]

On April 3, 1996, the NCHS released the revised edition of the *Standards*, incorporating the two panels' recommendations.[83] This time the Center was in control of when and how news about the *Standards* would be released: It was able to marshal advance support in the press and to release the *Standards* preemptively before the hostile pundits could attack them. By careful planning with UCLA's public relations department, the Center was able to control the initial spin on the revised book. Moreover, the political climate had changed dramatically since November 1994, and the *Standards'* former detractors apparently did not think it opportune to renew their attack. They were in fact lying low because the 104th Congress had completely discredited itself. It had failed to pass its beloved "Contract with America," its leader, Newt Gingrich, had been accused of verbal excesses and financial irregularities, and it had closed down the federal government in January 1996 because it had failed to approve the federal budget in time for the new year. One way to measure the political winds on the day the revised *Standards* were released was to read the opinion section of The *Wall Street Journal*. That very day, timed to coincide with the UCLA press release, critics Diane Ravitch and Arthur Schlesinger Jr. co-authored an opinion piece in which they lauded the new *Standards* and called for continued reform.[84] A symbolic truce had been called in the culture wars.

7

Conclusion

Utopia Postponed

I N 1998 THE HERITAGE FOUNDATION released a revealing education proposal called *A Nation Still at Risk*. Among its authors were William Bennett, Chester Finn Jr., E. D. Hirsch, and Diane Ravitch. The report claimed that since 1983, when *A Nation at Risk* was published, more than 10,000,000 American students had completed high school as ignorant as ever, if not more so. It blamed "the big government monopoly over public education" for this sorry state of affairs, and argued that a "vast transfer of power is needed from producers to consumers."[1] *A Nation Still at Risk* not only trumpeted a clarion call for a new reform based on the familiar demand for rigorous content standards, but broadened the neo-conservative agenda to include school vouchers, charter schools, and high-stakes accountability through testing. In other words, the policy paper outlined a plan for the marketization or privatization of American public schools, combining the arguments of economic conservatism with the agenda of the Christian right. It sought to set the clock back and recenter the debate on reform around the discourse first articulated by the Heritage Foundation and the Reagan administration in 1981 and taken up again in the 1995 *Contract with the American Family*. *A Nation Still at Risk* demonstrates incontrovertibly that the conservative humanities reform project described in this book is part of a larger political agenda.

This study has traced how the reformers manufactured a crisis in the humanities by measuring the schools of today against a utopian past that never really existed. As the publication of *A Nation Still at Risk* shows, the claim for crisis continues to be advanced. This discourse emerged with the publication of *A Nation at Risk* in 1983, and was primarily the work of privately funded intellectuals supported by conservative think tanks. It can be seen as a response to the discourse initiated

by liberal intellectuals at the universities during the 1960s. While neither side was originally monolithic in outlook, a *Crossfire*-style debate
escalated between them, polarizing and solidifying the contenders into
irreconcilable camps. One of the crucial terrains on which the battle
would be fought between these competing discourses was the field of
history education. With the publication of the *National Standards for
History* in October 1994, these two discourses clashed in an all-out
culture war.[2]

In terms of Foucauldian theory, this is a continuing story of discourses competing for hegemony. The problem with Foucault's conception of discourse, however, is that it excludes people from the
analysis and does not explain motive and intentionality. For Foucault,
competing discourses are disembodied processes that move by their
own dynamics. For many scholars, including me, this is not entirely
satisfactory, because the model lacks human agency and temporality.
In this case study on the National History Standards Project I have attempted to modify the Foucauldian notion of discourse by reinstating
human agency and anchoring the analysis of discourse in empirical
evidence. I have traced how a small group of neo-conservatives initiated a discourse of educational crisis in the early 1980s, and with it
captured first the public imagination and then the imagination of those
in power. Between *A Nation at Risk* in 1983 and Goals 2000 in 1994,
the original discourse about the nation's educational—and in a more
profound sense, moral—crisis crystallized into policy. The claim that
this crisis was specifically a crisis in the humanities was first made in
the 1986 NAEP assessment, and then in the ensuing jeremiads by Finn,
Ravitch, Bennett, Hirsch, and Cheney, all deploring the state of humanities education. In response came the call for national standards,
the America 2000 legislation, the creation of the National Center for
History in the Schools, the Goals 2000 legislation, and finally, the
National History Standards Project. A network of real actors, whose
interrelations are clear and demonstrable, initiated and developed the
discourse of educational crisis and the urgent need for reform. Far from
being a Foucauldian abstraction, this discourse was an instrument of
policy initiated and implemented by real people, acting through real
institutions, in real time.

The debate on educational reform took place in a kind of political
vacuum, because in the federal system of education, policymaking is
largely delegated to the states and to the 16,000 local school districts,
leaving a partial void at the top. The federal government's role in educational policymaking is limited: It can suggest (as it tried to do with
the *Standards*), but it cannot compel. By default, therefore, educational

policy is made at least in part by private interests. Much of what passes for national policy is in fact made by such institutions as the Educational Testing Service (college entrance exams), the textbook industry (content and pedagogy), university admissions offices (course and grade point requirements), and self-constituted pressure groups such as the ones I have examined here (policy rhetoric and reform proposals). In the right circumstances the initiatives of these pressure groups may be picked up by the media and become the agenda for a national debate (national standards). Such was the situation with humanities reform during the 1980s.

The debate on educational reform in the 1980s took place in a broader context of cultural conflict in which conservative forces, energized by the Reagan Revolution, reacted against the cultural and moral relativism they saw inundating the nation's educational system. For them, social history, and what I might call the "anthropological turn" in the social sciences, had contributed to cultural relativism: now any culture seemed as good as any other. They believed that cultural relativism had dethroned national supremacy and called into question hallowed, shared beliefs about policy, institutions, and leaders. These beliefs, in their opinion, had held the nation together for more than two centuries and had created the conditions for its political and economic success. This teleological view of history, with the United States as its climactic point (exemplified by Fukuyama in 1989), or, in other terms, the national myth of ever-upward progress and perfect democracy, was threatened by new historical methodologies and visions. The conservatives felt the ground moving under their feet in a Kuhnian paradigm shift: Their "normal" science (traditional history) was in danger of being relegated to the trash heap of history, and relativistic thinking (the "new social history," or worse still, postmodernism) was replacing it.

At this point we should pause to examine the credentials of these would-be humanities reformers. They had set out to redeem the nation from mediocrity, cultural relativism, and economic decline by regenerating the teaching of the humanities in the schools. But what they initiated as a movement to reform the humanities, broadly conceived, became increasingly focused on the teaching of history: History became the core discipline around which their entire program for the humanities was to be structured. Ironically, however, only Ravitch, as far as one can ascertain, had any formal training in the discipline that they now had made the vital center of their program. Since their background was mostly in literature, they could not really grasp how history had evolved as a discipline since the time they were undergraduates, before the tectonic shift that started in the 1960s with the advent of social history. They were not practitioners of the historian's craft as it had re-defined itself, so when they turned over the drafting of the *Standards* to a group of professional historians, they did not fully understand the implications of what they were doing.[3] They called for the reaffirmation of the historical narrative that they had imbibed long ago, and which they now saw being subverted by cultural relativists.

On the other hand, the professional historians they entrusted with the task of drafting the *Standards* did not fully understand what the crusading reformers expected of them. To the historians, "world-class" standards meant bringing the latest advances in historical methodology, social and cultural history into the classroom. It did not mean the rehearsing of what they considered to be an outmoded teleological narrative in an uncritically patriotic mode. This fundamental misunderstanding between the two groups engaged in the project became the contradiction around which it would founder. The collapse of the *Standards* project can be seen as a still unresolved argument over what constitutes state-of-the-art historical thinking, fought out between professional historians and a cohort of reformers whose grounding was in other disciplines. A kind of dialogue of the deaf was conducted— and is still continuing—across a yawning gulf between the practitioners of disciplinary and non-disciplinary knowledge.

The public, too, had difficulty accepting this paradigm shift. Raised on political narratives of heroes and leaders, many Americans were bewildered and angered by a new scholarship based on the lives of ordinary people. As Lawrence Levine explains,

> Certain ideas are so deeply ingrained that they do not seem like ideas at all, but rather part of the natural order of things. To challenge them seems akin to repealing the law of gravity. Thus when someone comes along who both perceives and treats them as ideas, subject to the challenges that all ideas should be exposed to, it is as if reason itself were being challenged. The notion of the melting pot—that great crucible of American environment swallowing, nurturing, transforming—and the notion of American culture as deriving primarily from northern and western Europe came to assume this aura of the natural order. Any challenges, then, no matter how scholarly and carefully rooted in the sources and the normal rules of historical discourse, have been seen by many as assaults on rationality.[4]

To the public the *Standards*, as they were portrayed in the press, seemed an affront to reason itself. So in October 1994, Lynne Cheney's battle cry, "Where's Robert E. Lee?," quickly taken up by a cohort of right-wing pundits, struck a very responsive chord among the public at large.

The professional historians were also perplexed. They had great difficulty understanding why the public failed to embrace their cutting-edge research: After all, was it not their mission to uncover the "best that has been thought and said in the world," even if this meant including the voices of ordinary people and transgressing received ideas about the past? Wasn't it their duty to challenge conventional wisdom? Peter Dow's reflections on the MACOS controversy acknowledged this scholarly puzzlement.

> We saw ourselves engaged in the task of closing the gap between the research laboratory and the classroom, and we assumed that the social value of this enterprise was self evident. . . . How is it that curriculum projects such as *Man: A Course of Study* could generate so much enthusiasm and support among schoolteachers and scholars and yet attract so much political and public opposition? How is it that scholar/reformers can be so sophisticated intellectually and yet completely unaware of the extent to which political considerations shape the content of K–12 instruction?[5]

The answer lies, I believe, in the inherent tension between the the academic and the public use of knowledge. The very nature of scholarly research is to push the limits of current knowledge. Scholars are trained to master the current knowledge base in their field, to identify gaps in current research or theory, and to conduct original research in areas that have not yet been explored. They do this in two ways: They either search for new empirical evidence to support existing paradigms, or they use new evidence to challenge current paradigms both theoretically and empirically. Kuhn described how this process works. However, it can take twenty years or more before this new knowledge finds its way into non-scholarly publications, public discourse, and popular culture. Since the K–12 school curriculum is inherently traditional, the time lag there can be even greater. Thus when university-based scholars such as Rugg, Bruner, Dow, or Nash lead K–12 curriculum reform movements, they run a great risk of encountering misunderstanding and outrage. Unbeknownst to them, by bringing their scholarly knowledge directly into the schoolhouse, they are short-circuiting the slow process by which society absorbs new scholarly knowledge. Given a conservative political climate, as in late 1994, controversy is almost inevitable.

It is rare, however, that scholars are asked to lead K–12 reform projects. In fact, the historians who worked on the National History Standards Project were among the few scholars who were invited to participate in setting national standards for any of the disciplines. This is because the impetus and funding behind the NHSP came from Lynne Cheney and Diane Ravitch, who had been tireless advocates for disciplinary knowledge. By contrast, in several of the other disciplines, such as literature, mathematics, and science, scholars were virtually barred from developing national standards. Instead, educational policymakers and K–12 teachers worked alone to develop the standards in those content areas. As advocates for child-centered teaching methods, most of the standards developers in the other disciplines designed constructivist standards whereby students construct their own meaning based on personal experience and with minimal teacher intervention. Having been excluded from the standards-setting process in their disciplines, some university mathematicians and scientists soon began to speak out against K–12 standards that they believed had been watered down. They argued that the topics for the standards had been generated around social and political factors rather than by the structure of the disciplines; that practical problem-solving approaches had replaced abstract and deductive reasoning; and that direct instruction from the teacher had been sacrificed to small-group collaborations.[6] The predictable clash between proponents of traditional (discipline-based) and progressive (child-centered, social meliorist, or social efficiency) educational theories that we have witnessed throughout the twentieth century played out again in these controversies.

The *National Standards for History* challenged the traditional historical narrative during a period of acute national soul-searching, brought on by a belief that America was losing its economic lead over the rest of the world. In the late 1970s and early 1980s, a perception of wholesale economic decline gripped the nation, and was increasingly ascribed to a supposed decline in educational standards. According to the humanities crusaders, who began to make their voices heard at this time, cultural relativism was not merely subverting the shared truths that held Americans together culturally and politically, but was also threatening America's economic ascendancy. This threat, they felt, had to be countered. History teaching was central to their program to restore the nation's cultural unity and economic ascendance, and so the National Center for History in the Schools and the National History Standards Project were instituted with professional historians playing a leading role in designing the reform.

Building on the work Charlotte Crabtree had done writing and overseeing the adoption of the *California History-Social Science Framework*, the reformers established the NCHS, and based on the work Crabtree and Nash had done on *Lessons from History*, the reformers funded the NHSP. These key documents led the reformers to believe that Crabtree and Nash could come up with the winning formula: that they would hold the middle ground between cultural relativism and the traditional canon of liberal education. Cheney and her fellow reformers believed that in the NCHS they had the perfect instrument for reform. Crabtree and Nash had established their credentials and seemed to be the ideal agents to fulfill the reformers' purpose.

But this they did not do. Once the drafting of the *Standards* began, the historians and teachers called in by Nash and Crabtree to compose them followed their own historical instincts, which lay in the direction of social history and the new world history. At the same time, members of the NHSP Council and focus groups such as the ASCD, AHA, NCSS, and OAH were tugging the project toward the left. Thus, gradually and subtly the whole thrust of the reform project changed, as a consensus was established among the historians and teachers actually drafting the *Standards*, which moved them far from the original intent of Cheney and her allies. A gap opened up between the professional historians and teachers drafting the *Standards*, who were products of the revolution in historical thinking that took place during the 1960s and 1970s, and the conservative reform lobby, whose vision of history was rooted in an earlier era. The rift between them was at once a generation gap and a divergence of thinking on the nature of history itself, a clash between "normal" and "abnormal" science.

With hindsight, one can see why Cheney and her allies lost control of the reform process and then were deeply disappointed with its outcome. They had inadvertently turned the job of crafting the history *Standards* over to a predominantly liberal group of university professors and schoolteachers, the very people they held responsible for cultural relativism in the first place. So when the *Standards* came out in October 1994, Cheney et al. understandably felt cheated. From their point of view, the *Standards* were a Trojan horse that would smuggle back into the curriculum all the multiculturalism they had sought to banish from it. Their reaction was one of deep moral outrage. But the authors of the *Standards* were shocked, too. Caught up in the political firestorm that followed the 1994 elections, they were taken aback by the depth and virulence of the reaction their work provoked. What to them was an innocuous document of mainstream history had suddenly become the very eye of this storm. The conservative leaders of the 104th Congress, riding high after their victory at the polls, joined in the chorus led by Cheney and echoed by their allies in the media. They demonized the *Standards* and capitalized on their notoriety to win support for their own educational program, which was to revert to Reagan's and the Christian Coalition's original strategy of minimizing the role of government in education.

Thus we had come full circle. It was in this highly charged political atmosphere that the *Standards*, the pet project of the conservative humanities warriors, would be repudiated by the very people who had fought so hard to bring them to fruition. The *Standards* became, in the hands of these conservative reformers and the 104th Congress, a convenient pretext for challenging the government's role in education. In the press, on television, and on the radio, a battery of conservative pundits successfully portrayed the newly published *Standards* as documents riddled with multicultural excess and political correctness. With a rhetorical strategy that outbid *A Nation at Risk*, they worked together with the newly elected conservatives in Congress to discredit not only the *Standards*, but also the institutions that had sponsored them, the NEH and the DOE.

The repudiation of the *National Standards for History* by the 104th Congress and the conservative intellectuals who had originally fostered them should not be written off as simple political opportunism, although this undoubtedly played its part. By following the intellectual and political trail that began during the presidency of Ronald Reagan and ended with the 104th Congress, one can see that the rise and fall of the *Standards* forms a logical and coherent sequence of events. The original project resulted from a convergence of purpose between private intellectuals and public policymakers. With the help of the Reagan Revolution's bully pulpit, the reformers of the right were able to set forth an agenda for national *Standards*. Conversely, without their efforts the government would not have taken up the cry for reform, and the *Standards* would never have come into being. But once created, the Standards project escaped the control of its original sponsors, and was taken over by their intellectual adversaries. Then, with the 1994 elections, the tide turned again in the conservatives' favor. The slash-and-burn politics of the 104th Congress allowed them to press home their attack on the *Standards* in 1995. But without the years of ideological preparation by these same reformers, the 104th Congress would not have zeroed in on the target of the *Standards* as it did.

What, then, are the policy implications to be drawn from this episode in the culture wars? In a democracy, curriculum will always be contested terrain, as it should be. As Michael Apple and others have argued, teaching subjects in schools and colleges gives them cultural legitimacy, which explains why the confrontation over the curriculum and the canon is so intense and so public, as the *Standards* episode makes abundantly clear. People will always differ on what they perceive to be the purpose of education and the best way to achieve its goals. Historically, the goals of curricular reform in the United States have constantly shifted as one perspective or the other became dominant politically. For example, earlier in this century, Harold Rugg and George Counts responded to the perennial social problem that periodically forces itself upon the nation's attention: inequality and its political consequences. In the tumultuous 1960s the issue of social inequality again pushed itself into the nation's consciousness and evoked a similar response. The school again moved to center stage as a primary instrument for social change. This time, however, those in power embraced the concept of social engineering and implemented reforms associated with the Great Society.

It is rare, however, that the government takes up the mantle of social reconstructionism in this way. During the 1930s and 1960s, when society seemed to be unraveling at the seams, the government espoused these reform movements as a way to remedy the dramatic social injustices revealed by the Great Depression and the civil rights movement. But the tide then turned. During the 1980s and 1990s, the government turned its back on issues of social justice and instead fought the battles of big business: It confronted the issue of perceived economic decline and the loss of a national sense of purpose. Thus the government set out to restore national cultural unity and economic ascendancy at the expense of democratic pluralism.

The *Standards* controversy demonstrated that the curriculum will always remain a terrain of struggle in a democracy, not a received canon of knowledge that simply has to be transmitted from one generation to the next. The controversy over the *Standards* was a highly democratic process, in which fundamental educational issues were debated by contending conservative and liberal forces competing for moral ascendancy. The debate was thought-provoking and ranged across the entire gamut of issues involved in educational reform. But in the end neither side achieved victory. The conservatives did not succeed in implementing their reform agenda, and the liberal content infused into the *Standards* was discredited and repudiated by Congress and the opinion makers. Finally, after the dust and smoke of battle had cleared, the reform process stalled, and the moral high ground remained, as ever, contested and untenanted.

Appendix A

National History Standards Project Organizational Structure

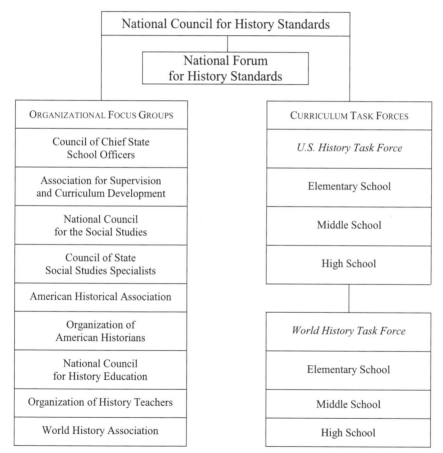

ORGANIZATIONAL FOCUS GROUPS	CURRICULUM TASK FORCES
Council of Chief State School Officers	*U.S. History Task Force*
Association for Supervision and Curriculum Development	Elementary School
National Council for the Social Studies	Middle School
Council of State Social Studies Specialists	High School
American Historical Association	
Organization of American Historians	*World History Task Force*
National Council for History Education	Elementary School
Organization of History Teachers	Middle School
World History Association	High School

Note: Adapted from, National Center for History in the Schools, *National Standards for History: Basic Edition* (Los Angeles: National Center for History in the Schools, 1996): 216.

Appendix B

Overview of the Thirty-One U.S. History Standards

National Standards for United States History: Exploring the American Experience/Grades 5–12 Expanded Edition (Los Angeles: National Center for History in the Schools, 1994): 35–37.

Era 1: Three Worlds Meet (Beginnings to 1620)

1. The characteristics of societies in the Americas, western Europe, and West Africa that increasingly interacted after 1450
2. Early European exploration and colonization; the resulting cultural and ecological interactions

Era 2: Colonization and Settlement (1585–1763)

1. The early arrival of Europeans and Africans in the Americas, and how these people interacted with Native Americans
2. How political institutions and religious freedom emerged in the North American colonies
3. How the values and institutions of European economic life took root in the colonies; how slavery reshaped European and African life in the Americas

Era 3: Revolution and the New Nation (1754–1820s)

1. The causes of the American Revolution, the ideas and interests involved in forging the revolutionary movement, and the reasons for the American victory
2. How the American Revolution involved multiple movements among the new nation's many groups to reform American society

3. The institutions and practices of government created during the revolution and how they were revised between 1787 and 1815 to create the foundation of the American political system

Era 4: Expansion and Reform (1801–1861)

1. United States territorial expansion between 1801 and 1861, and how it affected relations with external powers and Native Americans
2. How the industrial revolution, the rapid expansion of slavery, and the westward movement changed the lives of Americans and led toward regional tensions
3. The extension, restriction, and reorganization of political democracy after 1800
4. The sources and character of reform movements in the antebellum period and what the reforms accomplished or failed to accomplish

Era 5: Civil War and Reconstruction (1850–1877)

1. The causes of the Civil War
2. The course and character of the Civil War and its effects on the American people
3. How various reconstruction plans succeeded or failed

Era 6: The Development of the Industrial United States (1870–1900)

1. How the rise of big business, heavy industry, and mechanized farming transformed the American peoples
2. Massive immigration after 1870 and how new social patterns, conflicts, and ideas of national unity developed amid growing cultural diversity
3. The rise of the American labor movement, and how political issues reflected social and economic changes
4. Federal Indian policy and United States foreign policy after the Civil War

Era 7: The Emergence of Modern America (1890–1930)

1. How Progressives and others addressed problems of industrial capitalism, urbanization, and political corruption
2. The changing role of the United States in world affairs through World War I

3. How the United States changed from the end of World War I to the eve of the Great Depression

Era 8: The Great Depression and World War II (1929–1945)

1. The causes of the Great Depression and how it affected American society
2. How the New Deal addressed the Great Depression, transformed American federalism, and initiated the welfare state
3. The origins and course of World War II, the character of the war at home and abroad, and its reshaping of the U.S. role in world affairs

Era 9: Postwar United States (1945 to early 1970s)

1. The economic boom and social transformation of postwar America
2. The postwar extension of the New Deal
3. The Cold War and the Korean and Vietnam conflicts in domestic and international politics
4. The struggle for racial and gender equality and for the extension of civil liberties

Era 10: Contemporary United States (1968 to the present)

1. Major developments in foreign and domestic policies during the Cold War era
2. Major social and economic developments in contemporary America

Notes

Introduction

1. *Congressional Record* (Jan. 18, 1995), S1080.
2. Ibid.
3. Alec McHoul & Wendy Grace, eds., *A Foucault Primer: Discourse, Power and the Subject* (Melbourne: Melbourne University Press, 1993): 51.

Chapter One

1. National Commission on Excellence in Education, *A Nation at Risk: The Imperative for Educational Reform* (Washington, D.C.: U.S. Department of Education, April 1983).
2. *America 2000, Excellence in Education Act*, H.R. 2460, 102nd Congress, October 24, 1991.
3. *Goals 2000, Educate America Act*, Public Law 103-227, 103rd Congress, March 31, 1994.
4. Christine Sleeter & Carl A. Grant, "Race, Class, Gender, and Disability in Current Textbooks," in *Politics of the Textbook*, eds. Michael W. Apple and Linda K. Christian-Smith (New York: Routledge, 1991): 281.
5. Michel Foucault, *Power/Knowledge, Selected Interviews & Other Writings, 1972–1977*, ed. Colin Gordon (New York: Pantheon Books, 1980); Michael W. Kirst, *Who Controls Our Schools?: American Values in Conflict* (New York: W.H. Freeman and Company, 1984); Michael Apple, *Ideology and Curriculum*, 2nd ed. (New York: Routledge & Kegan Paul, 1990); Apple, *Cultural Politics and Education* (New York: Teachers College Press, 1996); Stanley Aronowitz & Henry Giroux, *Postmodern Education: Politics, Culture and Social Criticism* (Minneapolis, MN: University of Minnesota Press, 1991); Joel Spring, *Conflict of Interests: The Politics of American Education* 2nd ed. (New York: Longman, 1993); Peter McLaren, *Critical Pedagogy and Predatory Culture: Oppositional Politics in a Postmodern Era* (New York: Routledge, 1995).
6. Lester F. Ward, *Dynamic Sociology* (New York: D. Appleton, 1883); George Counts, *Dare the Schools Build a New Social Order?* (New York: John Day Co., 1932); Counts, *The Social Foundations of Education* (New York: Scribner, 1934); Harold Rugg, *The Great Technology: Public Chaos and the Public School*

(New York: John Day, 1933); Paulo Freire, *Pedagogy of the Oppressed*, New Revised 20th Anniversary Ed., trans. M. B. Ramos (New York: Continuum, 1973, 1997); McLaren, *Critical Pedagogy and Predatory Culture*.

7. Elliott Eisner & E. Vallance, eds., *Conflicting Conceptions of Curriculum* (Berkeley: McCutchen, 1974); Herbert Kliebard, *The Struggle for the American Curriculum, 1893–1958* (New York: Routledge, 1995).

8. Kliebard, *Struggle for the American Curriculum*, 1.

9. Ibid., 23.

10. John Henry Newman, *The Idea of the University* (New Haven: Yale University Press, 1869/1996); Matthew Arnold, *Culture and Anarchy* (New Haven: Yale University Press, 1869/1995): 9, 31.

11. John Dewey, *The Child and the Curriculum* (Chicago: University of Chicago Press, 1902).

12. Kliebard, *Struggle for the American Curriuclum*; Phillip Jackson, "Conceptions of Curriculum and Curriculum Specialists," in *Handbook of Research on Curriculum*, ed. Phillip Jackson (New York: Macmillan, 1992): 3–40.

13. Franklin J. Bobbit, "The Elimination of Waste in Education," *The Elementary School Teacher*, 12, 259–271.

14. Ward, *Dynamic Sociology*, 1883.

15. Counts, *Dare the Schools*; Rugg, *The Great Technology*.

16. David Tyack & Larry Cuban, *Tinkering Toward Utopia: A Century of Public School Reform* (Cambridge, MA: Harvard University Press, 1995).

17. Kliebard, *Struggle for the American Curriculum*, 20–25.

18. Michael Kirst, *Who Controls Our Schools?*; Joel Spring, *Conflict of Interests*.

19. Nicholas Lemann, *The Big Test: The Secret History of the American Meritocracy* (New York: Farrar, Straus, and Giroux, 1999): 83.

20. Ibid., 288.

21. Kirst, *Who Controls Our Schools?*

22. Harold Rugg, "Needed Changes in the Committee Procedure of Reconstructing the Social Studies," *The Elementary School Journal*, 21 (1921): 697.

23. National Society for the Study of Education, *The Twenty-Sixth Yearbook*, (Bloomington, IL: Public School Publishing Company, 1926): xi.

24. Ibid., Part II, 148.

25. Ibid., 154.

26. Kliebard, *Struggle for the American Curriculum*, 175.

27. Orlen K. Armstrong, "Treason in Textbooks," *The American Legion Magazine* (September 1940): 70–72.

28. Harold Rugg, *That Men May Understand: An American in the Long Armistice* (New York: Doubleday, Doran, 1941).

29. Sandra Stotsky, ed., *What's at Stake in the K–12 Standards Wars: A Primer for Educational Policy Makers* (New York: Peter Lang Publishers, 2000): 284.

30. National Defense Education Act, Public Law 85-864, 85th Congress, September, 1958.

31. Jerome S. Bruner, *The Process of Education* (Cambridge, MA: Harvard University Press, 1963): 14.

32. Peter B. Dow, *Schoolhouse Politics: Lessons from the Sputnik Era* (Cambridge, MA: Harvard University Press, 1991/1999): 4.

33. Jerome S. Bruner, *The Process of Education*, 33.

34. Ibid.

35. Jerome S. Bruner, *Toward a Theory of Instruction* (Cambridge, MA: The Belknap Press, 1966): 74.

36. Ibid., 93.

37. Dow, *Schoolhouse Politics*, 135.

38. Schaffarzick & Sykes, *Value Conflicts and Curriculum Issues: Lessons from, Research and Experience* (Berkeley, CA: McCutchan Publishing Corporation, 1979): 9.

39. Dow, *Schoolhouse Politics*, 178–190.

40. Schaffarzick & Sykes, *Value Conflicts*, 10.

41. Dow, *Schoolhouse Politics*, 178.

42. Todd Gitlin, *The Twilight of Common Dreams: Why America Is Wracked by Culture Wars* (New York: Henry Holt & Company, 1995); James A. La Spina, *The Visual Turn and the Transformation of the Textbook* (Mahwah, NJ: Lawrence Erlbaum Associates, 1998).

43. Gary B. Nash, Charlotte Crabtree, & Ross E. Dunn, *History on Trial: Culture Wars and the Teaching of the Past* (New York: Alfred A. Knopf, 1997); Linda Symcox, "A Case Study in the Politics of American Educational Reform in the U.S.: The Storm over the National Standards for History," in *Annali di Storia Moderna e Contemporanea*, 4 (1998): 479–502.

Chapter Two

1. Joyce Appleby, Lynn Hunt, & Margaret Jacob, *Telling the Truth About History* (New York: W.W. Norton & Company, 1994): 73.

2. Thomas S. Kuhn, *The Copernican Revolution: Planetary Astronomy in the Development of Western Thought* (Cambridge, MA: Harvard University Press, 1957).

3. Kuhn, *The Structure of Scientific Revolutions*, 3rd ed. (Chicago: University of Chicago Press, 1962).

4. Ibid., 10–34.

5. Appleby, Hunt, & Jacob, *Telling the Truth About History*, 28.

6. Discussion with Geoffrey Symcox.

7. Ibid.

8. Alice Kessler-Harris, "The New Social History," *The New American History*, Eric Foner, ed. (Philadelphia: Temple University Press, 1990): 163–184.

9. Eric Foner, ed., *The New American History* (Philadelphia: Temple University Press, 1990): ix.

10. Kessler-Harris, "The New Social History," 165.

11. Gary B. Nash, *Red, White, and Black: The Peoples of Early North America*, 3rd. ed. (Englewood Cliffs, NJ: Prentice Hall, 1974/1992).

12. Thomas T. Bender, "Wholes and Parts: The Need for Synthesis in American History," *Journal of American History*, 73, 1 (June 1986): 120–136.

13. Thomas C. Holt, "African-American History," in *The New American History*, Eric Foner, ed. (Philadelphia: Temple University Press, 1990): 212.

14. See John Blassingame, *The Slave Community: Plantation Life in the Antebellum South*, rev. ed. (New York: Oxford University Press, 1979); Eugene Genovese, *Roll, Jordan, Roll: The World the Slaves Made* (New York: Pantheon Books, 1974); Herbert G. Gutman, *The Black Family in Slavery and Freedom, 1750–1925* (New York: Pantheon Books, 1974); and Lawrence W. Levine, *Black Culture, Black Consciousness: Afro-American Folk Thought from Slavery to Freedom* (New York: Oxford University Press, 1977).

15. Holt, "African-American History," 215.

16. Ibid., 229.

17. Nash, Crabtree, & Dunn, *History on Trial*, 78.

18. Linda Gordon, "U.S. Women's History," in *The New American History*, Eric Foner, ed. (Philadelphia: Temple University Press, 1990): 189.

19. Ibid., 197.

20. Ibid., 198.

21. Joyce Appleby, "The Power of History," *The American Historical Review* 103, 1 (1998): 1–14.

22. Foner, *The New American History*, x.

23. Gilbert Allardyce, "Toward World History: American Historians and the Coming of the World History Course," *Journal of World History*, 1, 1 (Spring 1990): 24.

24. Arnold Toynbee, *The World and the West* (New York: Oxford University Press, 1953), and countless other volumes on regional history.

25. Allardyce, "Toward World History," 67.

26. William McNeill, "What We Mean by the West," *American Educator*, 48, 49 (Spring 2000): 10–15.

27. Allardyce, "Toward World History," 48.

28. Ibid., 40–41.

29. Marshall Hodgson, "Hemispheric Interregional History as an Approach to World History," in Ross Dunn, ed., *The New World History: A Teacher's Companion* (Boston: Bedford St. Martin's Press, 2000): 121.

30. Ross Dunn, ed., *The New World History: A Teacher's Companion* (Boston: Bedford St. Martin's Press, 2000): 109.

31. William H. McNeill, *Mythistory and Other Essays* (Chicago: The University of Chicago Press, 1986): 67.

32. Ibid., 71.

33. William McNeill, "What We Mean by the West," 17.

34. Hayden White, *The Content of the Form: Narrative Discourse and Historical Representation* (Baltimore: The Johns Hopkins University Press, 1987): 27.

35. Ibid., 57.

36. Appleby et al., *Telling the Truth*, 89.

37. For pioneering studies of microhistory see the classic works of Carlo Ginzburg, *The Cheese and the Worms: The Cosmos of a Sixteenth-Century Miller*, trans. John & Anne Tedeschi (New York: Penguin Books, 1982); Ginzburg, *Ecstasies: Deciphering the Witches' Sabbath*, 1st American ed., trans. Raymond

Rosenthal (New York: Pantheon, 1991); and Ginzburg, "Microhistory: Two or Three Things That I Know About It," *Critical Inquiry*, 20, 1 (Autumn 1993): 10–35.

38. Natalie Z. Davis, *The Return of Martin Guerre* (Cambridge, MA: Harvard University Press, 1983). For a general overview of this methodology see Edward Muir & Guido Ruggiero, eds., *Microhistory and the Lost Peoples of Europe* (Baltimore: The Johns Hopkins University Press, 1991).

39. Natalie Z. Davis, *Fiction in the Archives: Pardon Tales and Their Tellers in Sixteenth-Century France* (Stanford, CA: Stanford University Press, 1987).

40. These pardons were petitions from criminals to the king outlining their crimes, explaining extenuating circumstances, and therefore asking for pardon.

41. Lynn Hunt, ed., *The New Cultural History* (Berkeley, CA: University of California Press, 1989): 20.

42. Ibid.

43. Peter Novick, *That Noble Dream: The "Objectivity Question" and the American Historical Profession* (Cambridge, MA: Cambridge University Press, 1988): 682.

Chapter Three

1. Karl Mannheim, *Ideology and Utopia* (New York: Harvest Books, 1936, Preface by Louis Wirth): xxiii.

2. Terrel H. Bell, "Reflections One Decade After *A Nation at Risk*," *Phi Delta Kappan*, 74, 9 (April 1993): 592–597.

3. Theodore Roosevelt first coined the term "bully pulpit." He was referring to the rhetorical power that could be wielded by people holding high positions.

4. Joel Spring, *Conflicts of Interest*, 102.

5. William Bennett, "Completing the Reagan Revolution," Heritage Lecture #62 (Washington, D.C.: The Heritage Foundation, 1986): 3.

6. Richard Jung & Michael Kirst, "Beyond Mutual Adaptation, into the Bully Pulpit: Recent Research on the Federal Role in Education," *Educational Administration Quarterly*, 22, 3 (Summer 1986): 95.

7. Foucault, *Power/Knowledge*.

8. Jung & Kirst, "Beyond Mutual Adaptation," 80.

9. Bell, "Reflections, One Decade After *A Nation at Risk*," 593.

10. National Commission on Excellence in Education, *A Nation at Risk*. 1983.

11. Terrel H. Bell, *Report by the Secretary on the Regional Forums on Excellence in Education* (Washington, D.C.: U.S. Department of Education, December 1983): 2.

12. Dennis A. Williams et al., "Can the Schools Be Saved?," *Newsweek*, May 9, 1983: 50–58.

13. *Newsweek*, 6–8.

14. Terrel Bell, "Reflections One Decade After *A Nation at Risk*," 593.

15. *A Nation at Risk*, 5.

16. David C. Berliner & Bruce J. Biddle, *The Manufactured Crisis: Myths, Frauds, and the Attack on America's Public Schools* (New York: Longman, 1995): 8–9.

17. Ibid., 23.

18. William W. Wayson et al., *Up From Excellence: The Impact of the Excellence Movement on Schools* (Bloomington, IN: Phi Delta Kappa Educational Foundation, 1986): 91.

19. Stanley Aronowitz & Henry Giroux, *Education Under Siege: The Conservative, Liberal, and Radical Debate Over Schooling* (South Hadley, MA: Bergin & Garvey Publishers, Inc., 1985): 201.

20. Ira Shor, *Culture Wars: School & Society in the Conservative Restoration, 1969–1984* (Boston: Routledge & Kegan Paul, 1986).

21. Task Force on Education for Economic Growth, *Action for Excellence: A Comprehensive Plan to Improve Our Nation's Schools* (Denver: Education Commission of the States, 1983).

22. Shor, *Culture Wars*, 110.

23. College Board Educational Equity Project, *Academic Preparation for College* (New York: College Entrance Examination Board, 1983); Twentieth Century Fund Task Force on Federal Elementary and Secondary Education Policy, *Making the Grade* (New York: Twentieth Century Fund, 1983); Carnegie Corporation of New York, *Education and Economic Progress: Toward a National Educational Policy* (New York: Carnegie Corporation, 1983).

24. Jeannie Oakes, "Tracking, Inequality, and the Rhetoric of Reform: Why Schools Don't Change," *Journal of Education*, 168, 1 (1986): 70.

25. As cited in Oakes, 71.

26. Shor, *Culture Wars*, 151. All this may have had a more sinister side, too. Michael Lind, a former conservative turned critic of the right, was positively cynical in his analysis of neo-conservative motives. In his 1996 book, *Up from Conservatism: Why the Right Is Wrong for America*, he argued that conservative Republicans had launched a culture war against public schools as a way of deflecting "the wrath of wage-earning populist voters from Wall St. and corporate America to other targets: the universities, the media, racial minorities, homosexuals, and immigrants." According to Lind, the neo-conservative claim of a crisis in public education amounted to "a great policy hoax leading many Americans to believe that the schools were failing the nation, rather than the other way around." As cited in Joel Spring, *Political Agendas for Education: From the Christian Coalition to the Green Party* (Mahwah, New Jersey: Lawrence Erlbaum Associates, Publishers, 1997): 1.

27. As cited in Shor, 143.

28. *A Nation at Risk*, 5.

29. Chester E. Finn Jr., *We Must Take Charge: Our Schools and Our Future* (New York: The Free Press, 1991).

30. Paul E. Peterson, "Did the Education Commissions Say Anything?," *The Brookings Review*, 2, 2 (Winter 1983): 3–11.

31. Theodore Sizer, *Horace's Compromise: The Dilemma of the American High School* (Boston: Houghton Mifflin, 1984): 214.

32. Thomas J. Peters & Robert H. Waterman, *In Search of Excellence: Lessons From America's Best-Run Companies* (New York: Harper & Row, 1982).

33. Aronowitz & Giroux, *Education Under Siege*, 200.

34. Michael W. Apple, "Being Popular About National Standards: A Review of National Standards in American Education: A Citizen's Guide," *Education Policy Analysis Archives*, 4, 10 (June 30, 1996): 5. [http://clam.ed.asu.edu/epaa/v4n10.html].

35. Spring, *Political Agendas*, 25.

36. As cited in Spring, *Political Agendas*, 27

37. Charles L. Heatherly, *Mandate for Leadership: Policy Management in a Conservative Administration* (Washington, D.C.: The Heritage Foundation, 1981).

38. Ibid., 187, 190–1.

39. Ibid., 197.

40. Stuart M. Butler, Michael Sanera, & W. Bruce Weinrod, *Mandate for Leadership II: Continuing the Conservative Revolution* (Washington, D.C.: The Heritage Foundation, 1984); Charles L. Heatherly & Burton Yale Pines, co-editors, *Mandate for Leadership III: Policy Strategies for the 1990s* (Washington, D.C.: The Heritage Foundation, 1989).

41. Eileen M. Gardner, *A New Agenda for Education* (Washington, D.C.: The Heritage Foundation, 1985).

42. As cited in Spring, *Political Agendas*, 44.

43. According to Joel Spring, this was part of a larger strategy that began with Reagan's 1980 presidential campaign. "The Republican Party developed its education policy by forming a network of interest groups promoting private schools, vouchers, school prayer, and moral values in the curriculum. This coalition drew its membership from what was then called the Moral Majority and was organized under the umbrella organization the Committee for the Survival of a Free Congress. Later, when William Bennett was appointed to his position as Secretary of Education in 1986, he admitted that he had been interviewed for the position by twelve conservative organizations grouped under that umbrella." (Spring, *Political Agendas*, 34).

44. Free Congress Research and Education Foundation, *Cultural Conservatism: Toward a New National Agenda* (Lanham, MD: UPA Inc., 1987); Valarie Scatamburlo, *Soldiers of Misfortune: The New Right's Culture War and the Politics of Political Correctness* (New York: Peter Lang, 1998): 52.

45. Spring, *Political Agendas*, 27.

46. Harvey J. Kaye, *The Powers of the Past: Reflections On the Crisis and the Promise of History* (New York: Harvester Wheatsheaf, 1991): 90–91.

47. Valarie Scatamburlo, *Soldiers of Misfortune*, 54–55.

48. Ibid. 112–114.

49. Ibid., 112–115.

50. Diane Ravitch, *Left Back: A Century of Failed School Reform* (New York: Simon & Schuster, 2000).

51. Diane Ravtich, *The Troubled Crusade: American Education 1945–1980* (New York: Basic Books, 1983): 324.

52. Ibid., 328.

53. Chester E. Finn, Jr., Diane Ravitch, & Robert T. Fancher, *Against Mediocrity: The Humanities in America's High Schools* (New York: Holmes Meier, 1984) x.

54. Ibid., 238, 244.

55. National Assessment Governing Board. *National Assessment for Educational Progress*. (Washington, D.C.: U.S. Department of Education, 1986).

56. Diane Ravitch & Chester E. Finn, Jr., *What Do Our 17-Year-Olds Know?: A Report on the First National Assessment of History and Literature* (New York: Harper & Row, 1987): 46.

57. Ibid., 49–50.

58. David C. Berliner & Bruce J. Biddle, *The Manufactured Crisis*, 34.

59. Christopher Hitchens, "Goodbye to All That: Why Americans Are Not Taught History," *Harper's Magazine*, 297 (November, 1998): 39.

60. Arthur E. Bestor, *Educational Wastelands: The Retreat from Learning in Our Public Schools* (Urbana, IL: University of Illinois Press, 1953); Richard Hofstadter, *Anti-Intellectualism in American Life* (New York: Alfred A. Knopf, 1963).

61. William J. Bennett and Chester Finn Jr., *What Works: Research About Teaching and Learning* (Washington, D.C.: 1986): 115.

62. William J. Bennett, *To Reclaim a Legacy: A Report on the Humanities in Higher Education* (Washington, D.C.: National Endowment for the Humanities, November 1994): 113.

63. Harvey J. Kaye, *The Powers of the Past*: 115.

64. Alexis de Tocqueville, *The Old Regime and the French Revolution*, trans., Stuart Gilbert (Gloucester, MA: Peter Smith, 1978): 113.

65. E. D. Hirsch Jr., *Cultural Literacy: What Every American Needs to Know* (Boston: Houghton Mifflin Company, 1987): x.

66. Ibid., 9.

67. Ibid., xiv.

68. Ibid.

69. Ibid., xvi. Hirsch's choice of the word "polis" is interesting here. Consider the implications of equating the United States with Periclean Athens, which, incidentally, had no system of public education.

70. Ibid., xvii. This argument sounds Geertzian.

71. Ibid., 7.

72. Ibid., 33–34.

73. Ibid., 63.

74. Ibid., 108.

75. Ibid., 18.

76. Ibid., 182–183.

77. Noah de Lissovoy, "Understanding the Standards Movement," unpublished paper (Los Angeles: University of California, Los Angeles, 2000): 12–14.

78. Note, however, that Hirsch has profited handsomely from the sale of his lists.

79. Benedict Anderson, *Imagined Communities: Reflections on the Origin and Spread of Nationalism* (London: Verso, 1983).

80. Ernest P. Gellner, *Nations and Nationalism* (Ithaca, NY: Cornell University Press, 1983) :7.

81. Ibid.

82. Ibid., 34.

83. Ibid., 64.

84. Allan Bloom, *The Closing of the American Mind: How Higher Education Has Failed Democracy and Impoverished the Souls of Today's Students* (New York: Simon & Schuster, 1987).

85. "The Thought Police," *Newsweek,* (December 24, 1990): 48–55.

86. Paul Gottfried, "Populism vs. Neoconservatism," *Telos,* 90 (Winter 1991/92): 186.

87. Dinesh D'Souza, *Illiberal Education: The Politics of Race and Sex on Campus* (New York: Vintage Books, 1992).

88. Roger Kimball, *Tenured Radicals: How Politics Has Corrupted Our Higher Education* (New York: Harper & Row, Publishers, 1990).

89. Russell Jacoby, *Dogmatic Wisdom: How the Culture Wars Divert Education and Distract America* (New York: Anchor Books, 1994).

90. Ibid., 6.

91. Indeed, the *L.A. Times* carried an article in 1998 confirming Jacoby's worst fears. Elaine Woo, *Times* education writer, wrote an article titled, "Hire Education: Colleges Design 'Contract' Courses to Meet Employers' Needs." She warned, "Forget Multiculturalism 101 and alcohol-free fraternities. The new frontier in higher education is 'hire education'—courses custom-designed by colleges to fit the needs of employers."

92. Lawrence Levine, *The Opening of the American Mind: Canons, Culture, and History* (Boston: Beacon Press, 1996): 15.

93. Ibid., 15.

94. Ibid., 91.

95. Gitlin, *The Twilight of Common Dreams,* 35.

96. Ibid., 134.

97. Ibid., 135.

98. As cited in Scatamburlo, *Soldiers of Misfortune,* 162–163.

Chapter Four

1. California State Department of Education, *History–Social Science Framework* (Sacramento, CA: California State Department of Education, 1988).

2. James Guthrie et al., *Conditions of Education in California, 1990* (CA: Policy Analysis for California Education [Berkeley, CA: PACE], 1990): 40.

3. Bill Honig, telephone interview, January 1998.

4. Bill Honig, *Last Chance for Our Children: How You Can Help Save Our Schools* (Reading, MA: Addison-Wesley Publishing Company, Inc., 1985): 47.

5. The members of the *Framework* advisory committee were: Zoe Acosta, R. Freeman Butts, Henry Chambers, Todd Clark, F. Michael Couch, Matthew Downey, Paul Gagnon, Paula Gilette, Joyce Harper, Milton A. Kato, Carol S.

Katzman, David Kennedy, Juan Francisco Lara, Carol Marquis, Page Miller, Diane Ravitch, Christopher Salter, and Ted Yanak.

6. To understand how Crabtree defined the field of social studies in 1983, see Charlotte Crabtree, "A Common Curriculum for the Social Studies," in *Individual Differences and the Common Curriculum*, eds. Gary D. Fenstermacher & John I. Goodland (Chicago: National Society for the Study of Education, 1983): 248–281.

7. Bradley Commission on History in the Schools, *Building a History Curriculum: Guidelines for Teaching History in the Schools* (Education Excellence Network, 1988): 16.

8. Ravitch, e-mail interview with author and James La Spina, January 17, 1998.

9. Matthew Downey, telephone interview, February 1998. According to Downey, Ravitch quoted from Bruno Bettelheim's *The Uses of Enchantment: The Meaning and Importance of Fairy Tales* (New York: Vintage Books, 1986) to support her position. Ravitch also cites Bettelheim extensively in her 1987 article "Tot Sociology" (*The American Scholar*, Summer 1987: 343–354). Here she claims that according to Bettelheim, there is no basis for the expanding environments approach either in cognitive or developmental psychology, 349.

10. Jean Claugus, telephone interview with author and James La Spina, January 1998.

11. Diane Ravitch, e-mail interview with author and James LaSpina, January 17, 1998.

12. Hazel Hertzberg, *Social Studies Reform: 1880–1980* (Boulder, CO: Social Sciences Educational Consortium, 1981): 12.

13. National Council for the Social Studies, "Curriculum Guidelines for Multicultural Education," *Social Education*, 55 (September 1992): 274–294.

14. As cited in Hertzberg, *Social Studies Reform*, 13.

15. John Dewey, *Democracy and Education: An Introduction to the Philosophy of Education* (New York: The Macmillan Co., 1916).

16. Michael B. Lybarger, "Need as Ideology: Social Workers, Social Settlements and Social Studies," in *The Formation of School Subjects: The Struggle for Creating an American Institution*, ed. T. S. Popkewitz (London: Falmer Press, 1987): 176–190.

17. As cited in Nash et al., *History on Trial*, 37.

18. Charles A. Beard, *The Nature of the Social Sciences in Relation to Objectives of Instruction* (New York: Charles Scribner's Sons, 1934).

19. Many of these debates were chronicled by Alberta M. Dougan in, "The Search for a Definition of the Social Studies: A Historical Overview," *Indiana Journal of Social Education*, 3 (1985): 13–35.

20. Bestor, *Educational Wastelands*, 144.

21. Bruner, *The Process of Education*, 17.

22. Bestor, *Educational Wastelands*, 134.

23. Kieran Egan, *Teaching as Story Telling: An Alternative Approach to Teaching and Curriculum in the Elementary School* (Ontario: The Althouse Press, 1986).

24. National Council for the Social Studies, "Curriculum Guidelines for Multiethnic Education: Position Statement," in *Social Education*, 40, 6 (October 1976): special supplement.

25. National Council for the Social Studies, "Curriculum Guidelines for Multicultural Education," in *Social Education*, 55 (September, 1992): 274–294.

26. Nathan Glazer, "New Name for an Old Problem: Multicultural 'School Wars' Date to the 1840s," in David J. Flinders & Stephen J. Thornton, eds., *The Curriculum Studies Reader* (New York: Routledge, 1997): 274.

27. Ravitch, e-mail interview, January 17, 1998.

28. California State Department of Education, *History–Social Science Framework* (Sacramento, CA: California State Department of Education, 1988): 20.

29. Lawrence A. Blum, "Anti-Racist Civic Education in the *California History–Social Science Framework*," in Robert K. Fullinwider, ed., *Public Education in a Multicultural Society: Policy, Theory, Critique* (New York: Cambridge University Press, 1996): 23–48.

30. As cited in Lawrence A. Blum, "Anti-Racist Civic Education," 38.

31. Catherine Cornbleth & Dexter Waugh, *The Great Speckled Bird: Multicultural Politics and Education Policymaking* (New York: St. Martin's Press, 1995): 59. This book, and the article on which it was based, became very controversial among the humanities reformers. *Educational Researcher* published an article entitled "An Exchange of Views on 'The Great Speckled Bird'" in which Bill Honig rebutted the article and Cornbleth and Waugh responded (Ursula Casanova, ed., August-September, 1995): 22–27.

32. Cornbleth & Waugh, *The Great Speckled Bird*, 66.

33. As cited in Gary B. Nash, "Multiculturalism and History: Historical Perspectives and Present Prospects," in R. K. Fullinwider, ed., *Public Education in a Multicultural Society* (New York: Cambridge University Press, 1996): 183–202.

34. As cited in Joel Spring, *Political Agendas*, 38.

35. Cornbleth & Waugh, *The Great Speckled Bird*, 13.

36. As cited in ibid., 13.

37. Diane Ravitch, "Multiculturalism in the Curriculum," Presentation before the Manhattan Institute, New York, 11/27/89: 4.

38. As cited in Cornbleth & Waugh, *The Great Speckled Bird*, 86.

39. As cited in ibid., 86.

40. Bradley Commission, *Building a History Curriculum*, 1.

41. Other members included John M. Arevalo, Marjorie Wall Bingham, Louise Cox Byron, Gordon A. Craig, Robert H. Ferrell, Hazel Whitman Hertzberg, Claudia Hoone, Nathan I. Huggins, Michael Kammen, William E. Leuchtenburg, Leon F. Litwack, William H. McNeill, Charles Shotland, and C. Vann Woodward.

42. Bradley Commission, *Building a History Curriculum*.

43. Ibid., 2.

44. As cited in Robert K. Fullinwider, "Patriotic History," in Robert K. Fullinwider, ed., *Public Education in a Multicultural Society* (New York: Cambridge University Press, 1996): 204.

45. Bradley Commission, *Building a History Curriculum*, 16.

46. Cornbleth & Waugh, *The Great Speckled Bird*, 17.

47. American Textbook Council, *History Textbooks: A Standard Guide* (New York: American Textbook Council, 1994): 63.

48. National Commission on Social Studies in the Schools, *Charting a Course: Social Studies for the 21st Century* (Washington, D.C.: National Commission on Social Studies in the Schools, 1989): vi.

49. Ibid, vi.

50. Members of this Commission were William O. Baker, The Honorable Lindy Boggs, Paul Bohannan, William J. Bouwsma, The Honorable Bill Bradley, Ronalda Cadiente, Albert Camarillo, Muncel Chang, Carol Hamilton Cobb, The Honorable Martha Layne Collins, Jean Craven, Thomas E. Cronin McHugh, Roy L. Crumly, Matthew T. Downey, Edmund W. Gordon, Donald M. Graham, Don Ian Gray, Zenda Gutierrez, Leslie M. Handley, W. Lee Hansen, The Honorable Gary K. Hart, Hazel Whitman Hertzberg, Thomas C. Holt, Bill Honig, Dell H. Hymes, Lillian G. Katz, Myron Marty, William H. McNeill, Howard Mehlinger, Fred Newman, Kevin O'Reilly, Christopher L. Salter, and John D. Toma. Staff members were Fay D. Metcalf, David Jenness, and Mary E. Kennedy.

51. National Commission on Social Studies in the Schools, *Charting a Course*.

52. Ibid., ix.

53. Ibid., 8.

54. Ibid., 14–18.

55. Lynne V. Cheney, *American Memory: A Report on the Humanities in the Nation's Public Schools* (Washington, D.C.: National Endowment for the Humanities, 1987).

56. Ibid., 8–9.

57. Ibid., 7.

58. Ibid., 10

59. Robert Rothman, "$1.5 Million Awarded for Center on History," *Education Week*, March 30, 1988.

60. Ibid.

61. Lynne V. Cheney, *NCHS Newsletter* (Los Angeles: University of California, Los Angeles, Fall 1991): 3.

62. Center Scholars were Kathleen Conzen, University of Chicago; Don Fehrenbacher, Stanford; Paul Gagnon, Univesity of Massachusetts; Nikki Keddie, UCLA; Bill Rowe, Johns Hopkins University; Richard Saller, University of Chicago; Thaddeus Tate, The College of William and Mary; Scott Waugh, UCLA; and Michael Winston, Howard University.

63. Rothman, *Education Week*, March 30, 1987.

64. *Application to the National Endowment for the Humanities for a Cooperative Agreement to Establish a UCLA Research Center on the Teaching and Learning of History in Elementary and Secondary Schools.* Submitted by: Charlotte Crabtree, Professor, University of California, Los Angeles, Graduate School of Education, December 8, 1987 (UCLA-University Archives, Record Series #667, unprocessed records, box 85), 6.

65. Ibid., 7

66. Ibid., 4.

67. Advisory panel members were Francie Alexander, associate super-intendent of the California State Department of Education; historian Gordon Craig, Stanford University; teacher Wayne Ginety, Lockport, NY; teacher David Millstone, Norwich, VT; teacher Marguerite Navarrete, Cerritios, CA; historian Gordon Wood, Brown University. Center Scholars were historian Kathleen Conzen, University of Chicago; historian Don Fehrenbacher, Stanford; historian Paul Gagnon, University of Massachusetts; historian Nikki Keddie, UCLA; historian Bill Rowe, Johns Hopkins; historian Richard Saller, University of Chicago; historian Thaddeus Tate, The College of William and Mary; historian Scott Waugh, UCLA; and historian Michael Winston, Howard University.

68. Charlotte Crabtree, et al., eds., *Lessons from History: Essential Understandings and Historical Perspectives Students Should Acquire* (Los Angeles: Regents, University of California, 1992).

69. Ibid., x.

70. Linda Symcox, *Selected Teaching Materials for United States and World History: An Annotated Bibiography* (Los Angeles: University of California, 1990).

71. Jim Pearson, *Women in the American Revolution* (Los Angeles: University of California, 1991): 32.

72. Berliner & Biddle, *The Manufactured Crisis*, 88.

73. As cited in Robert M. Huelsdamp, "Perspectives on Education in America," *Phi Delta Kappan*, 74, 9 (1993): 718–720.

74. National Center for History in the Schools, *National Standards for United States History*, iii.

75. Harvey J. Kaye, *The Powers of the Past*, 142–143.

76. Fukuyama, as cited in Kaye, 143.

77. Ibid., 142.

78. Ibid, 143.

79. Cornbleth & Waugh, *The Great Speckled Bird*, 95.

80. Nathan Glazer, *We Are All Multiculturalists Now* (Cambridge: Harvard University Press, 1997): 23.

81. As cited in Cornbleth & Waugh, *The Great Speckled Bird*, 96.

82. As cited in ibid., 100.

83. Glazer, *We Are All Multiculturalists Now*, 24.

84. Cornbleth & Waugh, *The Great Speckled Bird*, 131.

85. New York State Social Studies Review and Development Committee, *One Nation, Many Peoples: A Declaration of Cultural Independence* (New York: New York State Department of Education, June 1991) and Cornbleth & Waugh, *The Great Speckled Bird*, 122.

86. Gitlin, *The Twilight of Common Dreams*.

87. Note the rhetoric of international competition in the term "world-class."

88. National Council on Education Standards and Testing, *Raising Standards for American Education, A Report to Congress, the Secretary of Education, the*

National Education Goals Panel, and the American People (Washington: D.C.: U.S. Government Printing Office, 1992): i.

Chapter Five

1. Adapted from, National Center for History in the Schools, *National Standards for United States History: Exploring the American Experience* (Los Angeles: University of California, Los Angeles, 1994).

2. Council members consisted of Charlotte Anderson, NCSS President; Joyce Appleby, UCLA historian; Samuel Banks, Executive Director for Compensatory and Funded Programs, Baltimore; David Battini, New York teacher; David Baumbach, Pittsburgh teacher; Earl Bell, President, Organization of History Teachers; Mary Bicouvaris, Newport News teacher; Diane Brooks, CSSSS President; Pedro Castillo, UC Santa Cruz historian; Ainslie T. Embree, Columbia historian; Elizabeth Fox-Genovese, Emory historian; Carol Gluck, Columbia historian; Darlene Clark Hine, Michigan State historian; Bill Honig, President, CCSSO, 1992; Akira Iriye, Harvard historian; Barbara Talbert Jackson, President, ASCD; Kenneth Jackson, Columbia historian; Morton Keller, Brandeis historian; Bernard Lewis, Princeton historian; William McNeill, University of Chicago historian; Alan D. Morgan, President, CCSSO, 1993; Stephanie Pace-Marshall, President, ASCD, 1993; John J. Patrick, Director, SSDC, Indiana University; Theodore K. Rabb, Princeton historian; C. Frederick Risinger, Associate Director, SSDC, Indiana University; Denny Schillings, President, NCSS, 1994; Gilbert T. Sewall, Director, American Textbook Council; Warren Solomon, Curriculum Consultant for Social Studies, Missouri Department of Education; and Michael R. Winston, Vice President Emeritus and historian, Howard University. Ex officio members were Charlotte Crabtree and Gary B. Nash, Co-directors, and Linda Symcox, Assistant Director.

3. The National Forum consisted of representatives from the following organizations: The National Association of Elementary School Principals, the National Congress of Parents and Teachers, the National Association for Asian and Pacific American Education, the League of United Latin American Citizens, the Atlantic Council of the United States, the National Education Association, the Council for Basic Education, the Education Excellence Network, the Quality Education for Minorities Network, the National Association of Secondary School Principals, the Council of Great City Schools, the Council for American Private Education, the National Catholic Educational Association, the American Association of State and Local History, the National Alliance of Black School Educators, the Association for the Study of Afro-American Life and History, the Lutheran Schools, the Center for Civic Education, the National Council for Geographic Education, the National Association of State Boards of Education, the American Association of School Librarians, the Native American Heritage Commission, the National Association for Asian and Pacific American Education, and the American Federation of Teachers.

4. U.S. CURRICULUM TASK FORCE MEMBERS: Kirk S. Ankeney, Earl Bell, Charlotte Crabtree, Mark W. Gale, Melvin Garrison, Stan Miesner, Lawrence A. Miller, Lori Lee Morton, Gary B. Nash, Minna Novick, John J. Patrick, Daniel A. Preston, John M. Pyne, Angeline Rinaldo, William C. Schultheis, Gloria Sesso, Linda Symcox, Helen Tracey, and David Vigilante. WORLD HISTORY TASK FORCE MEMBERS: Joann Alberghini, John Arevalo, Joan Arno, David Baumbach, Edward Berenson, Margaret Binnaker, Jacqueline Brown-Frierson, Richard Bulliet, Stanley Burstein, Anne Chapman, Peter Cheoros, Charlotte Crabtree, Sammy Crawford, Ross Dunn, Benjamin Elman, Jean Fleet, Jana Flores, Michele Forman, Charles Frazee, Marilynn Jo Hitchens, Jean Johnson, Henry G. Kiernan, Carrie McIver, Susan Meisler, Gary B. Nash, Joe Palumbo, Sue Rosenthal, Heidi Roupp, Irene Segade, Geoffrey Symcox, Linda Symcox, David Vigilante, Scott Waugh, Julia Werner, and Donald Woodruff.

5. Charlotte Crabtree, *Application to the National Endowment for the Humanities, Division of Education Programs. From the National Center for History in the Schools: A Cooperative UCLA/NEH Research Program. To Support the Center's National K–12 History Standards Project and Continue its Developmental and Dissemination Activities.* University of California, Los Angeles, November 5, 1991. (UCLA—University Archives, Record Series #667, unprocessed records, box 85): 4.

6. Crabtree, *Application to Support History Standards*, 4–5.

7. Ellen K. Coughlin, "Scholars Confront Fundamental Question: Which Vision of America Should Prevail?: Multiculturalism Issue Draws Historians into Debates over Framing the Nation's Past," *Chronicle of Higher Education*, 38, 21 (January 29, 1992): A8, 2.

8. Ibid., 2.

9. OAH Focus Group Report, May 14, 1992, 2. (UCLA—University Archives, Record Series #667, unprocessed records, box 85): 2.

10. Crabtree, *Application to Support National Standards*, November 5, 1991: 2.

11. Lynne V. Cheney, *National Tests: What Other Countries Expect Their Students to Know* (Washington, D.C.: National Endowment for the Humanities, 1991): 2.

12. As cited in Nash et al., *History on Trial*, 153–154.

13. Crabtree, *Application to Support National Standards*, 13.

14. ASCD Focus Group Report, May, 1992. (UCLA—University Archives, Record Series #667, unprocessed records, box 60): 4.

15. AHA U.S. History Focus Group Report, May 1992 (UCLA—University Archives, Record Series #667, unprocessed records, box 60): 4.

16. OAH Focus Group Report, May 19, 1993 (UCLA—University Archives, Record Series #667, unprocessed records, box 75): 4.

17. AHA World History Focus Group Report, May 1992 (UCLA—University Archives, Record Series #667, unprocessed records, box 60): 1.

18. Ibid., 10.

19. Ibid., 5.

20. Ibid., 2.

21. In the final *Standards* document Criterion 13 became Criterion 15 because two other criteria were added toward the end of the consensus project.

22. Forum meeting, February 1992.

23. William McNeill to Charlotte Crabtree, May 8, 1992 (UCLA—University Archives, Record Series #667, unprocessed records, box 60).

24. "ASCD Focus Group Report, May 1992" (UCLA—University Archives, Record Series #667, unprocessed records, box 60): 3.

25. "AHA World History Focus Group Report, May 5, 1992" (UCLA—University Archives, Record Series #667, unprocessed records, box 62): 2.

26. William McNeill to Charlotte Crabtree, May 8, 1992 (UCLA—University Archives, Record Series #667, unprocessed records, box 63).

27. Jim Gardner to Charlotte Crabtree, July 14, 1992 (UCLA—University Archives, Record Series #667, unprocessed records, box 60).

28. Robert Blackey to Crabtree and Nash, Dec. 2, 1992 (UCLA—University Archives, Record Series #667, unprocessed records, box 60).

29. Lousie Tilly et al. to Charlotte Crabtree and Gary Nash (UCLA—University Archives, Record Series #667, unprocessed records, box 60).

30. Lynne Cheney to Charlotte Crabtree, October 6, 1992 (UCLA—University Archives, Record Series #667, unprocessed records, box 54).

31. "Cheney Resigns," *Los Angeles Times*, Dec. 11, 1992.

32. Michael Winston et al., *Draft Four of the Organizing Questions for Standards in World History*, May 23, 1993 (UCLA—University Archives, Record Series #667, unprocessed records, box 68).

33. Jerry H. Bentley, "The Quest for World-Class Standards in World History," in *The History Teacher*, 28, 3 (May 1995): 450.

34. Dunn, *The New World History*, 360.

35. Vice-President Robert J. Stahl, NCSS annual meeting, Nov. 1993.

36. Gerald A. Danzer & Mark Newman, *Tuning In: Primary Sources in the Teaching of History* (Chicago: The University of Illinois at Chicago, 1991): 7.

37. This section is adapted from National Center for History in the Schools, *National Standards for History, Basic Edition* (Los Angeles: University of California, Los Angeles, 1996), 17–33.

38. Linda S. Levstik, "NCSS and the Teaching of History," in *NCSS in Retrospect,* Bulletin 92 (Washington, D.C.: National Council for the Social Studies, 1996): 21, 34.

39. Ibid., 25.

40. NCSS Focus Group Report, May 1993 (UCLA—University Archives, Record Series #667, unprocessed records, box 60): 10.

41. AHA Focus Group Report, May 7, 1993 (UCLA—University Archives, Record Series #667, unprocessed records, box 60): 2.

42. Adapted from National Center for History in the Schools, UCLA, *National Standards for United States History: Exploring the American Experience* (Los Angeles: Regents, University of California, 1994): 82–85.

43. Karen Diegmueller & Debra Viadero, "Playing Games with History," *Education Week,* November 15, 1995: 29–34.

44. Chester Finn, Jr., Notes for National Forum Meeting, Education Excellence Network, May 19, 1994 (UCLA—University Archives, Record Series #667, unprocessed records, Box 74): 2.

45. Ibid., 3.

46. NHSP tape recording, May 21, 1994, Washington, D.C. (UCLA—University Archives, Record Series #667, unprocessed records, Box 74).

47. Paul Gagnon, "Paul Gagnon's Review," July 7, 1994 (UCLA—University Archives, Record Series #667, unprocessed records, box 68).

48. Memorandum from Chester Finn Jr. to Charlotte Crabtree and Gary Nash, July 7, 1994, p. 2 (UCLA—University Archives, Record Series #667, unprocessed records, box 74).

49. Carole Innerst, "Finn Leads War for Tough Education," *The Washington Times*, August 24, 1994.

50. Gilbert Sewall to Charlotte Crabtree and Gary Nash, July 1994 (UCLA—University Archives, Record Series #667, unprocessed records, box 71).

51. Albert Shanker to Charlotte Crabtree and Gary Nash, (UCLA—University Archives, Record Series #667, unprocessed records, box 74): 3.

Chapter Six

1. Note the reference to Francis Fukuyama's book, *The End of History*, discussed earlier.

2. Jon Wiener, "History Lesson," *The New Republic* (January 2, 1995): 9–11.

3. "Plan to Teach U.S. History Is Said to Slight White Males," *New York Times*, October 26, 1994.

4. Charles Krauthammer, "History Hijacked," *The Washington Post* (November 4, 1994). Krauthammer's claim that it was the historians who had hijacked history made his piece absurd.

5. As cited in Wiener, "History Lesson," 10.

6. Ibid., 10.

7. "Maligning the History Standards," Editorial, *New York Times* (February 13, 1995): A14.

8. Gary B. Nash, "Talking Points" (UCLA—University Archives, Record Series #667, unprocessed records, box 70): 3.

9. *National Standards for United States History*, 82–90.

10. Ibid., 82.

11. Ross Dunn, "A History of the History Standards: The Making of a Controversy of Historic Proportions," *UCLA Magazine* (Winter 1995): 32–35.

12. National Center for History in the Schools, *National Standards for United States History: Exploring the American Experience* (Los Angeles: Regents, University of California, Los Angeles, 1994): 79.

13. Ibid., 76.

14. Elizabeth Fox-Genovese, Bill Honig, Arnita Jones, Ruth Wattenberg, James Gardner, Elaine Wisley Reed, Fran Haley, Pedro Castillo, Charlotte Crabtree, Linda Levstick, and John Patrick were also members of the NHSP Council, Focus Groups, and Forum.

15. U.S. Department of Education Office of Educational Research and Improvement, National Center for Education Statistics, *NAEP 1994 U.S. History: A First Look: Findings From the National Assessment of Educational Progress* (November 1995), 33, 48–50.

16. John Pyne & Gloria Sesso, Letter to the Editor, *The New York Times*, February 7, 1995.

17. This argument is adapted from Ross Dunn's analysis in "A History of the History Standards," 33.

18. John Leo, "History Standards Are Bunk," *U.S. News and World Report* (February 6, 1995): 23.

19. Carol Gluck, "History According to Whom? Let the Debate Continue," *The New York Times* (February 6, 1995): 15.

20. Kirk Ankeney, "A History Lesson," *The San Diego Union*, November 21, 1994.

21. Patricia Avery & Theresa Johnson, "How Newspapers Framed the U.S. History Standards Debate," *Social Education*, 63,4 (May–June, 1999): 220–224.

22. The only forum available to K–12 teachers was a quarterly journal called *The History Teacher*, with a circulation of 2000 readers, a quarter of whom were high school history teachers. Devoting two separate issues to the controversy (Volume 18, Number 3, [May 1995], and Volume 30, Number 4, [November 1997]), the journal gave voice to K–12 teachers, academic historians, and policy makers.

23. "Maligning the History Standards;" Editorial, *The New York Times*, February 13, 1995; "Now a History for the Rest of Us: New Standards Look to Common People's Roles," Editorial, *The Los Angeles Times*, October 27, 1994; "A Blueprint of History for American Students," Editorial, *The San Francisco Chronicle* November 1994; "A History Lesson," *The Christian Science Monitor*, November 7, 1994; "Living History: New Standards Reflect Vital Reality," Editorial, *The Star Tribune*, November 14, 1994.

24. Diane Ravitch, "Standards in U.S. History: Solid Material Interwoven with Political Bias," *Education Week*, December 7, 1994: 48.

25. Ibid.

26. Ross E. Dunn, e-mail, H-NET, January 25, 1995.

27. Joyce Appleby to Bob Wheeler, e-mail, December 6, 1994 (UCLA—University Archives, Record Series #667, unprocessed records, box 67).

28. Representing the NCHS were Joyce Appleby, Gary Nash, Ross Dunn, and Donald Woodruff, and representing the critics were Diane Ravitch, Ruth Wattenberg, Gilbert Sewall, Al Shanker, Elizabeth Fox-Genovese, Joy Hakim, and John Fonte, Cheney's deputy. Note that several of the critics had originally been Council members.

29. Gary B. Nash & Charlotte Crabtree to "Dear Colleagues," January 20 1995 (UCLA—University Archives, Record Series #667, unprocessed records, box 74).

30. U.S. Senate, Senator Slade Gorton of Washington speaking on National History Standards, *Congressional Record*, January 18, 1995 (S1026).

31. Ibid.

32. The only other time the Congress took it upon itself to intervene in the Social Studies curriculum was when it censured the MACOS curriculum in 1975. When the NSF asked Congress for additional funds for teacher training and other promotions for the MACOS curriculum, the U.S. House of Representatives told the NSF that "it could not use any funds to promote or market MACOS or any other curriculum materials for elementary or secondary schools." (As discussed in Yvonne A. Davis, *The Relationship Between Pupil's Participation in Man: A Course of Study and Their Achievement in Social Studies,* Diss. (Los Angeles: UCLA, 1977).

33. *Congressional Record,* January 18, 1995.

34. *National Standards for United States History,* 245.

35. *National Standards for United States History,* 70–91.

36. *Congressional Record,* January 18, 1995.

37. Ibid.

38. The NCHS sold over 30,000 copies of the American and world history books in the first few months.

39. The Goals 2000 legislation provided for a National Education Standards and Improvement Council (NESIC) whose task would be to approve the various national standards. Since the panel would be appointed by Clinton, Republicans feared that members would be sympathetic to liberal curricula.

40. *Congressional Record,* S1030.

41. Press release by Sheldon Hackney, Chairman, NEH, January 19, 1995 (UCLA-University Archives, Record Series #667, unprocessed records, box 67).

42. Ross E. Dunn, e-mail, H-NET, March 12, 1995.

43. Ross E. Dunn, "A History of the History Standards," 35–36.

44. Lynne Cheney, "Kill My Old Agency, Please," *The Wall Street Journal,* January 24, 1995, 22.

45. Testimony of Lynne V. Cheney, W. H. Brady Jr. Distinguished Fellow, American Enterprise Institute; Chairman, National Endowment for the Humanities, 1986–1993, before the Interior Appropriations Subcommittee on January 24, 1995 (UCLA—University Archives, Record Series #667, unprocessed records, box 52).

46. Ibid.

47. Page Putnam-Miller, NCC Washington Update, 1, 4 January 24, 1995 (UCLA—University Archives, Record Series #667, unprocessed records, box 68).

48. The National Endowment for the Arts (NEA) had stirred up a controversy a few years earlier by funding several provocative works of art, including an exhibition of erotic homosexual photographs by Robert Mapplethorpe.

49. Frank Rich, "Eating Her Offspring," *The New York Times* (January 26, 1995): A19.

50. The Center's archives still contain the very drafts from 1992 that Cheney once praised and now castigated (UCLA—University Archives, Record Series #667, unprocessed records, box 67).

51. Lynne V. Cheney to Charlotte Crabtree, October 1992 (UCLA—University Archives, Record Series #667, unprocessed records, box 45).

52. UCLA—University Archives, Record Series #667, unprocessed records, box 64.

53. Fax from Charlotte Crabtree to Gary Nash and Ross Dunn, October 19, 1995 (UCLA—Archives, Record Series #667, unprocessed records, box 82).

54. UCLA—University Archives, Record Series #667, unprocessed records, box 64.

55. AHA, "Questions for Lynne Cheney RE: Role in Development of National History Standards," fax to NCHS January 23, 1995 (UCLA—University Archives, Record Series #667, unprocessed records, box 100): 4.

56. Glazer, *We Are All Multiculturalists Now*, 30.

57. Jo Thomas, "U.S. Panel's History Model Looks Beyond Europe," *The New York Times* (November 11, 1994).

58. Richard Riley, Press Release, September 4, 1995 (UCLA—University Archives, Record Series #667, unprocessed records, box 100).

59. Letter to Richard Riley, September 5, 1995 (UCLA—University Archives, Record Series #667, unprocessed records, box 100).

60. Sandi Cooper to Senator Daniel Moynihan, March 1, 1995 (UCLA—University Archives, Record Series #667, unprocessed records, box 100).

61. Letter, Stanford History Department to Academic Senate (UCLA—University Archives, Record Series #667, unprocessed records, box 92).

62. Resolution for UCLA Faculty Senate (UCLA—University Archives, Record Series #667, unprocessed records, box 87).

63. The site is: http://www.tntech.edu/www/acad/hist/natstan.hstand.

64. E-mail, December 8, 1994, from G. L. Seligmann, (UCLA—University Archives, Record Series #667, unprocessed records, box 69).

65. Jean Johnson to Patrick Moynihan, January 25, 1995 (UCLA—University Archives, Record Series #667, unprocessed records, box 75).

66. "Christian Coalition Presents The Contract With the American Family" (http://www.cc.org/publications/ca/speech/contract.html): 402.

67. Ibid., 402–404.

68. Richard Jensen, "The Culture Wars, 1965–1995: A Historian's Map," *Journal of Social History*, 29 (October 1995): 17–37.

69. Gary L. Bauer, "National History Standards: Clintonites Miss the Moon." Advertisement, *The Washington Times*, March 25, 1999.

70. Gary L. Bauer, "National History Standards: Clintonites Miss the Moon," *Perspective* (http://www.frc.org/perspective/1995.html).

71. Hazel Hertzberg, *Social Studies Reform*, 95.

72. U.S. History panelists were: The Hon. Albert Quie, Chair; Cary Carson; Evelyn Brooks Higginbotham; David Hollinger; Jeannette LaFors; Diane Ravitch; Rex Shepard; Stephan Thernstrom; Reed Ueda; and Maris A. Vinovskis. World History panelists were: Steven Muller, Chair; Hilary Ainger; Robert Bain; Allison Blakely; A. Lee Blitch; Philip D. Curtin; Prasenjit Duara; Michael F. Jimenez; Ramsay MacMullen; Marjorie Malley; Joan Wallach Scott; and John Obert Voll.

73. Council for Basic Education, *History in the Making: An Independent Review of the Voluntary National History Standards* (Washington, D.C.: Council for Basic Education, January 1996): i.

74. Richard Riley, press release, June 1995 (UCLA—University Archives, Record Series #667, unprocessed records, box 73).

75. Council for Basic Education, *History in the Making*, ii.

76. Ibid., i.

77. Ibid., 25.

78. Page-Putnam Miller, NCC Washington Update, Vol. 1, #54 (UCLA—University Archives, Record Series #667, unprocessed records, box 67).

79. Elaine Woo, "History Standards Flawed But Can Be Saved, Panels Say," *Los Angeles Times* (October 12, 1995).

80. Ibid.

81. Lynne Cheney, "The National History (Sub) Standards," *The Wall Street Journal* (October 23, 1995): A16.

82. Gary B. Nash, "Report on Revisions to the National History Standards," undated, 1996 (UCLA—University Archives, Record Series #667, unprocessed records, box 24).

83. National Center for History in the Schools, *National Standards for History: Basic Edition* (Los Angeles: Regents, University of California, 1996).

84. Diane Ravitch & Arthur M. Schlesinger Jr., "The New, Improved History Standards," *The Wall Street Journal* (April 3, 1996): A22.

Chapter Seven

1. William J. Bennett, Willard Fair, Chester E. Finn Jr., Rev. Floyd Flake, E. D. Hirsch, Will Marshall, Diane Ravitch, et al., *A Nation Still at Risk: An Education Manifesto* (Dayton, OH: Heritage Foundation, 1998).

2. *Crossfire* is the name of a confrontational talk show on CNN.

3. Among the leaders, William Bennett, Lynne V. Cheney, E. D. Hirsch, Allan Bloom, and Chester Finn were trained in English literature. Diane Ravitch, the only exception, holds a doctorate in history.

4. Lawrence W. Levine, "Clio, Canons, and Culture," *Journal of American History*, 80, 3 (December 1993): 852.

5. Dow, *Schoolhouse Politics*, 228.

6. Sandra Stotsky, *What's at Stake in the Standards Wars*, xv.

References

PUBLISHED SOURCES

Allardyce, Gilbert. "Toward World History: American Historians and the Coming of the World History Course." *Journal of World History*, 1,1 (Spring 1990): 23–76.

American Textbook Council. *History Textbooks: A Standard Guide*. New York: American Textbook Council, 1994.

Anderson, Benedict. *Imagined Communities: Reflections on the Origin and Spread of Nationalism*. London: Verso, 1983.

Apple, Michael W. *Ideology and Curriculum,* 2nd ed. New York: Routledge & Kegan Paul, 1990.

Apple, Michael W. *Cultural Politics and Education*. New York: Teachers College Press, 1996.

Apple, Michael W. "Being Popular About National Standards: A Review of National Standards in American Education: A Citizen's Guide." *Education Policy Analysis Archives* 4,10 (June 30, 1996): [http://clam.ed.asu.edu/epaa/v4n10.html].

Apple, Michael W. "Are Markets and Standards Democratic?" *Educational Researcher*, 27,6 (August–September, 1998): 24–28.

Appleby, Joyce. "The Power of History." *The American Historical Review*, 103, 1 (1998): 1–14.

Appleby, Joyce, Lynn Hunt, & Margaret Jacob. *Telling the Truth About History*. New York: W.W. Norton & Company, 1994.

Armstrong, Orlen K. "Treason in Textbooks." *The American Legion Magazine* (September 1940): 70–72.

Arnold, Matthew. *Culture and Anarchy*. New Haven: Yale University Press, 1869/1995.

Aronowitz, Stanley & Henry Giroux. *Education Under Siege: The Conservative, Liberal, and Radical Debate Over Schooling*. South Hadley, MA: Bergin & Garvey Publishers, Inc., 1985.

Aronowitz, Stanley & Henry Giroux. *Postmodern Education: Politics, Culture and Social Criticism*. Minneapolis, MN: University of Minnesota Press, 1991.

Avery, Patricia G. & Theresa Johnson. "How Newspapers Framed the U.S. History Standards Debate." *Social Education*, 63, 4 (May–June 1999): 220–224.

Beard, Charles A. *The Nature of the Social Sciences in Relation to Objectives of Instruction*. New York: Charles Scribner's Sons, 1934.

Bell, Terrel H. "Reflections One Decade After *A Nation at Risk.*" *Phi Delta Kappan*, 74, 9 (April 1993): 592–597.

Bender, Thomas. "Wholes and Parts: The Need for Synthesis in American History." *Journal of American History*, 73, 1 (June 1986): 120–136.

Bennett, William J. "Completing the Reagan Revolution." *Heritage Lecture #62.* Washington, D.C.: The Heritage Foundation, 1986.

Bennett, William, Willard Fair, Chester Finn Jr., Rev. Floyd Flake, E. D. Hirsch, Will Marshall, Diane Ravitch, et al. *A Nation Still at Risk: An Education Manifesto.* Dayton: OH: Heritage Foundation, 1998.

Bentley, Jerry H. "The Quest for World-Class Standards in World History." *The History Teacher*, 28, 3 (May 1995): 449–456.

Berliner, David C. & Bruce J. Biddle. *The Manufactured Crisis: Myths, Frauds, and the Attack on America's Public Schools.* New York: Longman, 1995.

Bestor, Arthur E. *Educational Wastelands: The Retreat from Learning in Our Public Schools.* Urbana, IL: University of Illinois Press, 1953.

Bettelheim, Bruno. *The Uses of Enchantment: The Meaning and Importance of Fairy Tales.* New York: Vintage Books, 1975.

Blassingame, John. *The Slave Community: Plantation Life in the Antebellum South,* rev. ed. New York: Oxford University Press, 1979.

Bloom, Allan. *The Closing of the American Mind: How Higher Education Has Failed Democracy and Impoverished the Souls of Today's Students.* New York: Simon & Schuster, 1987.

Blum, Lawrence A. "Anti-Racist Civic Education in the California History-Social Science Framework." In Robert K. Fullinwider (Ed.), *Public Education in a Multicultural Society: Policy, Theory, Critique.* New York: Cambridge University Press, 1996: 23–48.

Bobbit, Franklin J. "The Elimination of Waste in Education," *The Elementary School Teacher*, 12: 259–271.

Bradley Commission on History in the Schools. *Building a History Curriculum: Guidelines for Teaching History in the Schools.* Washington, D.C.: Education Excellence Network, 1988.

Bruner, Jerome S. *The Process of Education.* Cambridge, MA: Harvard University Press, 1963.

Bruner, Jerome. *Toward a Theory of Instruction.* Cambridge: The Belknap Press of Harvard University Press, 1966.

Butler, Stuart M., Michael Sanera, & W. Brude Weinrod. *Mandate for Leadership II: Continuing the Conservative Revolution.* Washington, D.C.: The Heritage Foundation, 1984.

Carnegie Corporation of New York. *Education and Economic Progress: Toward a National Educational Policy.* New York: Carnegie Corporation, 1983.

Casanova, Ursula, ed. "An Exchange of Views on 'The Great Speckled Bird.'" *Educational Researcher* (August–September, 1995): 22–27.

Christian Coalition. *Contract with the American Family, A Bold Plan by the Christian Coalition to Strengthen the Family and Restore Common-Sense Values.* Nashville, TN: Moorings, 1995.

College Board Educational Equity Project. *Academic Preparation for College: What Students Need to Know and Be Able to Do.* New York: The College Board, 1983.

Cornbleth, Catherine & Dexter Waugh. *The Great Speckled Bird: Multicultural Politics and Education Policymaking.* New York: St. Martin's Press, 1995.

Council for Basic Education. *History in the Making: An Independent Review of the Voluntary National History Standards*. Washington, D.C.: Council for Basic Education, 1996.

Counts, George S. *Dare the Schools Build a New Social Order?* New York: John Day Co., 1932.

Counts, George S. *The Social Foundations of Education*. New York: Scribners, 1934.

Crabtree, Charlotte A. "A Common Curriculum for the Social Studies." In Gary D. Fenstermacher & John I. Goodland (Eds.), *Individual Differences and the Common Curriculum*. Chicago: National Society for the Study of Education, 1983: 248–281.

Crabtree, Charlotte, Paul Gagnon, Gary B. Nash, & Scott Waugh, eds. *Lessons from History: Essential Understandings and Historical Perspectives Students Should Acquire*. Los Angeles: Regents, University of California, 1992.

Danzer, Gerald A. & Mark Newman. *Tuning In: Primary Sources in the Teaching of History*. Chicago: The University of Illinois at Chicago, 1991.

Davis, Natalie Z. *The Return of Martin Guerre*. Cambridge, MA: Harvard University Press, 1983.

Davis, Natalie Z. *Fiction in the Archives: Pardon Tales and Their Tellers in Sixteenth-Century France*. Stanford: Stanford University Press, 1987.

Davis, Yvonne A. *The Relationship Between Pupils' Participation in Man: A Course of Study and Their Achievement in Social Studies*. Dissertation. Los Angeles: University of California, 1977.

de Lissovoy, Noah. "Understanding the Standards Movement." Unpublished paper. Los Angeles: University of California, Los Angeles, 2000.

de Tocqueville, Alexis. *The Old Regime and the French Revolution* (Stuart Gilbert, trans.). Gloucester, MA: Peter Smith, 1978.

Dewey, John. *The Child and the Curriculum*. Chicago: University of Chicago Press, 1902.

Dewey, John. *Democracy and Education: An Introduction to the Philosophy of Education*. New York: The Macmillan Co., 1916.

Dougan, Alberta M. "The Search for a Definition of the Social Studies: A Historical Overview." *Indiana Journal of Social Education*, 3 (1985): 13–35.

Dow, Peter B. *Schoolhouse Politics: Lessons from the Sputnik Era*. Cambridge, MA: Harvard University Press, 1991.

D'Souza, Dinesh. *Illiberal Education: The Politics of Race and Sex on Campus*. New York: Vintage Books, 1992.

Dunn, Ross E. "A History of the History Standards: The Making of a Controversy of Historic Proportions." *UCLA Magazine* (Winter 1995): 32–35.

Dunn, Ross E. *The New World History: A Teacher's Companion*. Boston: Bedford St. Martin's, 2000.

Egan, Kieran. *Teaching as Story Telling: An Alternative Approach to Teaching and Curriculum in the Elementary School*. Ontario: The Althouse Press, 1986.

Eisner, Elliott W. & Elizabeth Vallance, eds. *Conflicting Conceptions of Curriculum*. Berkeley, CA: McCutchen, 1974.

Family Research Council. *Let Freedom Ring!: A Basic Outline of American History*. Boulder, CO: Family Research Council, 1995.

Finn, Chester E. Jr. *We Must Take Charge: Our Schools and Our Future*. New York: The Free Press, 1991.

Finn, Chester E. Jr., Diane Ravitch, & Robert T. Fancher. *Against Mediocrity: The Humanities in America's High Schools*. New York: Holmes & Meier, 1984.

Foner, Eric, ed. *The New American History*. Philadelphia: Temple University Press, 1990.

Foucault, Michel. *Power/Knowledge: Selected Interviews & Other Writings, 1972–1977*. (Colin Gordon, Ed.). New York: Pantheon Books, 1980.

Free Congress Research and Education Foundation. *Cultural Conservatism: Toward a New National Agenda*. Lanham, MD: UPA Inc., 1987.

Freire, Paulo. *Pedagogy of the Oppressed*, revised 20th Anniversary ed. (M. B. Ramos, trans.). New York: Continuum, 1997.

Fukuyama, Francis. *The End of History and the Last Man*. New York: Avon, 1992.

Fullinwider, Robert K. "Patriotic History." In Robert K. Fullinwider (Ed.), *Public Education in a Multicultural Society: Policy, Theory, Critique*. New York: Cambridge University Press, 1996: 203–230.

Gardner, Eileen M. *A New Agenda for Education*. Washington, D.C.: The Heritage Foundation, 1985.

Gellner, Ernest. *Nations and Nationalism*. Ithaca, NY: Cornell University Press, 1983.

Genovese, Eugene. *Roll, Jordan, Roll: The World the Slaves Made*. New York: Pantheon Books, 1974.

Gillespie, Ed & Bob Schellas, eds. *Contract with America, The Bold Plan by Rep. Newt Gingrich, Rep. Dick Armey, and the House Republicans to Change the Nation*. New York: Times Books, 1994.

Ginzburg, Carlo. *The Cheese and the Worms: The Cosmos of a Sixteenth-Century Miller* (John & Anne Tedeschi, trans.). New York: Penguin Books, 1982.

Ginzburg, Carlo. *Ecstasies: Deciphering the Witches' Sabbath*, 1st American ed. (Raymond Rosenthal, trans.). New York: Pantheon, 1991.

Ginzburg, Carlo. "Microhistory: Two or Three Things That I Know About It." *Critical Inquiry*, 20, 1 (Autumn 1993): 10–35.

Gitlin, Todd. *The Twilight of Common Dreams: Why America Is Wracked by Culture Wars*. New York: Henry Holt & Company, 1995.

Glazer, Nathan. "New Name for an Old Problem: Multicultural 'School Wars' Date to the 1840s." In David J. Flinders & Stephen J. Thornton (Eds.), *The Curriculum Studies Reader*. New York: Routledge, 1997: 274–278.

Glazer, Nathan. *We Are All Multiculturalists Now*. Cambridge, MA: Harvard University Press, 1997.

Gordon, Linda. "U.S. Women's History." In Eric Foner (Ed.), *The New American History*. Philadelphia: Temple University Press, 1990: 185–210.

Gottfried, Paul. "Populism vs. Neoconservatism." *Telos*, 90 (Winter, 1991/92): 184–188.

Guthrie, James, W., M. W. Kirst, A .R. Odden, J. E. Koppich, G. R. Hayward, J. E. Adams, Jr., G. Geeting, & F. R. Webb. *Conditions of Education in California, 1989*. Berkeley, CA: Policy Analysis for California Education, 1989.

Guthrie, James, et al. *Conditions of Education in California, 1990*. Berkeley, CA: Policy Analysis for California Education, 1990.

Gutman, Herbert G. *The Black Family in Slavery and Freedom, 1750–1925*. New York: Pantheon Books, 1974.

Heatherly, Charles L., ed. *Mandate for Leadership: Political Management in a Conservative Administration*. Washington, D.C.: The Heritage Foundation, 1981.

Heatherly, Charles L. & Burton Yale Pines, eds. *Mandate for Leadership III: Policy Strategies for the 1990s*. Washington, D.C.: The Heritage Foundation, 1989.

Hertzberg, Hazel. *Social Studies Reform: 1880–1980*. Boulder, CO: Social Sciences Educational Consortium, 1981.

Hirsch, E. D., Jr. *Cultural Literacy: What Every American Needs to Know*. Boston: Houghton Mifflin Company, 1987.

Hitchens, Christopher. "Goodbye to All That: Why Americans Are Not Taught History." *Harper's Magazine*, 297 (November 1998): 37–47.

Hodgson, Marshall G. S. "Hemispheric Interregional History as an Approach to World History." In Ross E. Dunn (Ed.), *The New World History: A Teacher's Companion*. Boston: Bedford/St. Martin's, 2000: 113–122.

Hofstadter, Richard. *Anti-Intellectualism in American Life*. New York: Alfred A. Knopf, 1963.

Holt, Thomas C. *Thinking Historically: Narrative, Imagination, and Understanding*. New York: College Examination, 1990.

Holt, Thomas C. "African-American History." In Eric Foner (Ed.), *The New American History*. Philadelphia: Temple University Press, 1990: 211–232.

Honig, Bill. *Last Chance for Our Children: How You Can Help Save Our Schools*. Reading, MA: Addison-Wesley Publishing Company, Inc., 1985.

Huelsdamp, Robert M. "Perspectives on Education in America." *Phi Delta Kappan*, 74, 9 (1993): 718–720.

Hunt, Lynn, ed. *The New Cultural History*. Berkeley, CA: University of California Press, 1989.

Jacoby, Russell. *Dogmatic Wisdom: How the Culture Wars Divert Education and Distract America*. New York: Anchor Books, 1994.

Jensen, Richard. "The Culture Wars, 1965–1995: A Historian's Map," *Journal of Social History*, 29 (October 1995): 17–37.

Jung, Richard & Michael Kirst. "Beyond Mutual Adaptation, into the Bully Pulpit: Recent Research on the Federal Role in Education." *Educational Administration Quarterly*, 22, 3 (Summer 1986): 80–109.

Kaye, Harvey J. *The Powers of the Past: Reflections on the Crisis and the Promise of History*. New York: Harvester Wheatsheaf, 1991.

Kessler-Harris, Alice. "The New Social History." In Eric E. Foner (Ed.), *The New American History*. Philadelphia: Temple University Press, 1990: 163–184.

Kimball, Roger. *Tenured Radicals: How Politics Has Corrupted Our Higher Education*. New York: Harper & Row, Publishers, 1990.

Kirst, Michael W. *Who Controls Our Schools?: American Values in Conflict*. New York: W.H. Freeman and Company, 1984.

Kliebard, Herbert M. "Constructing a History of the American Curriculum." In Phillip Jackson (Ed.), *Handbook of Research on Curriculum*. New York: Macmillan, 1992: 157–184.

Kliebard, Herbert M. *The Struggle for the American Curriculum: 1893–1958*. New York: Routledge, 1995.

Kuhn, Thomas S. *The Copernican Revolution: Planetary Astronomy in the Development of Western Thought*. Cambridge, MA: Harvard University Press, 1957.

Kuhn, Thomas S. *The Structure of Scientific Revolutions*, 3rd ed. Chicago: University of Chicago Press, 1962.

La Spina, James A. *The Visual Turn and the Transformation of the Textbook*. Mahwah, NJ: Lawrence Erlbaum Associates, 1998.

Lemann, Nicholas. *The Big Test: The Secret History of the American Meritocracy*. New York: Farrar, Straus, and Giroux, 1999.

Levine, Lawrence W. *Black Culture, Black Consciousness: Afro-American Folk Thought from Slavery to Freedom*. New York: Oxford University Press, 1977.

Levine, Lawrence W. "Clio, Canons, and Culture." *Journal of American History*, 80, 3 (December 1993): 849–867.

Levine, Lawrence W. *The Opening of the American Mind: Canons, Culture, and History*. Boston: Beacon Press, 1996.

Levstick, Linda S. "NCSS and the Teaching of History." In *NCSS in Retrospect, Bulletin 92*. Washington D.C.: National Council for the Social Studies, 1996: 21, 34.

Lind, Michael. *Up from Conservatism: Why the Right Is Wrong for America*. New York: The Free Press, 1996.

Lybarger, Michael B. "Need as Ideology: Social Workers, Social Settlements and Social Studies." In T. S. Popkewitz, (Ed.), *The Formation of School Subjects: The Struggle for Creating an American Institution*. London: Falmer Press, 1987: 176–190.

Mannheim, Karl. *Ideology and Utopia*. New York: Harvest Books, 1936.

McHoul, Alec & Wendy Grace, eds., *A Foucault Primer: Discourse, Power and the Subject*. Melbourne, Australia: Melbourne University Press, 1993.

McLaren, Peter. *Critical Pedagogy and Predatory Culture: Oppositional Politics in a Postmodern Era*. New York: Routledge, 1995.

McNeill, William H. *Mythistory and Other Essays*. Chicago: The University of Chicago Press, 1986.

McNeill, William H. "The Rise of the West After Twenty-Five Years." *Journal of World History*, 1,1 (Spring 1990): 1–22.

McNeill, William H. "What We Mean by the West." *American Educator*, 48,49 (Spring 2000): 10–15.

Muir, Edward & Guido Ruggiero, eds. *Microhistory and the Lost Peoples of Europe*. Baltimore: The Johns Hopkins University Press, 1991.

Nash, Gary B. *Red, White, and Black: The Peoples of Early North America*, 3rd. ed. Englewood Cliffs, NJ: Prentice Hall, 1974/1992.

Nash, Gary B. "Multiculturalism and History: Historical Perspectives and Present Prospects." In Robert K. Fullinwider (Ed.), *Public Education in a Multicultural Society: Policy, Theory and Critique*. New York: Cambridge University Press, 1996: 183–202.

Nash, Gary B., Charlotte Crabtree, & Ross E. Dunn. *History on Trial: Culture Wars and the Teaching of the Past*. New York: Alfred A. Knopf, 1997.

Nash, Gary B. & Ross E. Dunn. "National History Standards: Controversy and Commentary." *Social Studies Review*, (Winter 1995): 4–12.

National Center for History in the Schools. *Newsletter*. Los Angeles: University of California, Los Angeles, March/April, 1991.

National Center for History in the Schools. "Organizing Questions for Standards in World History." Unpublished report, May 1993.

National Center for History in the Schools. *National Standards for United States History: Exploring the American Experience*. Los Angeles: Regents, University of California, Los Angeles, 1994.

National Center for History in the Schools. *National Standards for World History: Exploring Paths to the Present*. Los Angeles: Regents, University of California, Los Angeles, 1994.

National Center for History in the Schools. *National Standards for History for

Grades K–4: Expanding Children's World in Time and Space. Los Angeles: Regents, University of California, Los Angeles, 1994.

National Center for History in the Schools. *National Standards for History: Basic Edition*. Los Angeles: National Center for History in the Schools, 1996.

National Commission on Social Studies in the Schools. *Charting a Course: Social Studies for the 21st Century*. Washington, D.C.: National Commission on Social Studies in the Schools, 1989.

National Council for the Social Studies. "Curriculum Guidelines for Multiethnic Education: Position Statement." *Social Education*, 40, 6 (October 1976): special supplement.

National Council for the Social Studies. "Curriculum Guidelines for Multicultural Education." *Social Education*, 55 (September, 1992): 274–294.

National Society for the Study of Education. *The Twenty-Sixth Yearbook*. Bloomington, IL: Public School Publishing Company, 1926.

Newman, John Henry. *The Idea of the University*. New Haven, CT: Yale University Press, 1869/1996.

Novick, Peter. *That Noble Dream: The "Objectivity Question" and the American Historical Profession*. Cambridge, MA: Cambridge University Press, 1988.

Oakes, Jeannie. "Tracking, Inequality, and the Rhetoric of Reform: Why Schools Don't Change." *Journal of Education*, 168, 1 (1986): 60–80.

Pearson, Jim. *Women in the American Revolution*. Los Angeles: University of California, 1991.

Peters, Thomas J. & Robert H. Waterman. *In Search of Excellence: Lessons from America's Best-Run Companies*. New York: Harper & Row, 1982.

Peterson, Paul E. "Did the Education Commissions Say Anything?" *The Brookings Review*, 2, 2 (Winter 1983), 3–11.

Ravitch, Diane. *The Troubled Crusade: American Education, 1945–1980*. New York: Basic Books, 1983.

Ravitch, Diane. "Tot Sociology: Or What Happened to History in the Grade Schools?" *The American Scholar*, 56 (Summer 1987): 343–354.

Ravitch, Diane. "Multiculturalism in the Curriculum." Paper presented before the Manhattan Institute, New York, NY, November 27, 1989.

Ravitch, Diane. *Left Back: A Century of Failed School Reform*. New York: Simon & Schuster, 2000.

Ravitch, Diane & Chester E. Finn. *What Do Our 17-Year-Olds Know?: A Report on the First National Assessment of History and Literature*. New York: Harper & Row, 1987.

Reisenger, Frederick C. "The National History Standards: A View from the Inside." *The History Teacher*, 28, 3 (May 1995): 387–393.

Rockefeller Brothers Fund. *The Pursuit of Excellence: Education and the Future of America. Panel Report V of the Special Studies Project*. New York: Doubleday & Company, Inc., 1958.

Rugg, Harold. "Needed Changes in the Committee Procedure of Reconstructing the Social Studies." *The Elementary School Journal*, 21 (1921): 690–710.

Rugg, Harold. *The Great Technology: Public Chaos and the Public School*. New York: John Day, 1933.

Rugg, Harold. *That Men May Understand: An American in the Long Armistice*. New York: Doubleday, Doran, 1941.

Scatamburlo, Valerie L. *Soldiers of Misfortune: The New Right's Culture War and the Politics of Political Correctness*. New York: Peter Lang, 1998.

Schaffarzick, Jon and Gary Sykes. *Value Conflicts and Curriculum Issues: Lessons from Research and Experience.* Berkeley, CA: McCutchan Publishing Corporation, 1979.

Shor, Ira. *Culture Wars: School and Society in the Conservative Restoration, 1969–1984.* Boston: Routledge & Kegan Paul, 1986.

Simon, William F. *A Time for Truth.* New York: Reader's Digest Press, 1978.

Sizer, Theodore. *Horace's Compromise: The Dilemma of the American High School.* Boston: Houghton Mifflin, 1984.

Sleeter, Christine & Carl A. Grant. "Race, Class, Gender, and Disability in Current Textbooks." In Michael W. Apple & Linda K. Christian-Smith (Eds.), *Politics of the Textbook.* New York: Routledge, 1991.

Spring, Joel. *Conflict of Interests: The Politics of American Education,* 2nd ed. New York: Longman, 1993.

Spring, Joel. *Political Agendas for Education: From the Christian Coalition to the Green Party.* Mahwah, New Jersey: Lawrence Erlbaum Associates, Publishers, 1997.

Stotsky, Sandra, ed. *What's at Stake in the K–12 Standards Wars: A Primer for Educational Policy Makers.* New York: Peter Lang, 2000.

Symcox, Linda S. *Selected Teaching Materials for United States and World History: An Annotated Bibliography.* Los Angeles: Regents, University of California, 1990.

Symcox, Linda S. "Thinking Historically: Critical Engagement with the Past." *ICSS Journal,* 10, 1 (Fall 1997): 1–6.

Symcox, Linda S. "A Case Study in the Politics of American Educational Reform in the U.S.: The Storm over the National Standards for History." *Annali di Storia Moderna e Contemporanea,* 4 (1998): 479–502.

Symcox, Linda S. & James A. La Spina. "The Untroubled Crusaders: Development of California's Social-Science Framework and Its National Impact: The Genealogy of a Curriculum Reform." Los Angeles: Unpublished AERA paper, April 1998.

Task Force on Education for Economic Growth. *Action for Excellence: A Comprehensive Plan to Improve Our Nation's Schools.* Denver: Education Commission of the States, 1983.

Taylor, Frederick Winslow. *Principles of Factory Management.* New York: Harper and Brothers, 1911.

Toynbee, Arnold. *The World and the West.* New York: Oxford University Press, 1953.

Twentieth Century Fund Task Force on Federal Elementary and Secondary Education Policy. *Making the Grade.* New York: Twentieth Century Fund, 1983.

Tyack, David & Larry Cuban. *Tinkering Toward Utopia: A Century of Public School Reform.* Cambridge, MA: Harvard University Press, 1995.

Ward, Lester F. *Dynamic Sociology,* New York: D. Appleton, 1883.

Wayson, William W. et al. *Up from Excellence: The Impact of the Excellence Movement on Schools.* Bloomington, IN: Phi Delta Kappa Educational Foundation, 1986.

Weaver, Richard M. *Ideas Have Consequences.* Chicago: University of Chicago Press, 1948.

Weber, William A. & Richard H. Wilde, eds. "Exploring the National Standards for United States and World History." *The History Teacher,* 28, 3 (May 1995).

White, Hayden. *The Content of the Form: Narrative Discourse and Historical Representation.* Baltimore: The Johns Hopkins University Press, 1987.

OFFICIAL AND GOVERNMENT PUBLICATIONS

America 2000: Excellence in Education Act. H.R. 2460, 102nd Congress, October 24, 1991.

Bell, Terrel H. *Report by the Secretary on the Regional Forums on Excellence in Education.* Washington, D.C.: U.S. Department of Education, December 1983.

Bennett, William J. *To Reclaim a Legacy: A Report on the Humanities in Higher Education.* Washington, D.C.: National Endowment for the Humanities, November 1994.

Bennett, William J. & Chester Finn Jr. *What Works: Research About Teaching and Learning.* Washington, D.C.: U.S. Department of Education, 1986.

Cheney, Lynne V. *American Memory: A Report on the Humanities in the Nation's Public Schools.* Washington, D.C.: National Endowment for the Humanities, 1987.

Cheney, Lynne V. *National Tests: What Other Countries Expect Their Students to Know.* Washington, D.C.: National Endowment for the Humanities, 1991.

Congressional Record. S1080, 104th Congress, January 18, 1995.

Goals 2000: Educate America Act, Public Law 103-227, 103rd Congress, March 31, 1994.

History-Social Science Framework Committee. *History-Social Science Framework for California Public Schools, Kindergarten Through Grade Twelve.* Sacramento, CA: California State Board of Education, 1981.

History-Social Science Framework Committee. *History-Social Science Framework for California Public Schools, Kindergarten Through Grade Twelve.* Sacramento, CA: California State Board of Education, 1988.

Mehan, Hugh. *Sociological Foundations Supporting the Study of Cultural Diversity.* Washington, D.C.: Office of Educational Research and Improvement of the U.S. Department of Education, 1991. [*http://ncbe.gwu.edu/miscpubs/ncrcds11/rr1.htm*].

National Assessment Governing Board. *U.S. History Framework for the 1994 National Assessment of Educational Progress.* Washington, D.C.: U.S. Department of Education, 1994.

National Center for Education Statistics. *NAEP 1994 U.S. History: A First Look: Findings from the National Assessment of Educational Progress.* Washington, D.C.: Office of Educational Research and Improvement, U.S. Department of Education, November 1995.

National Commission on Excellence in Education. *A Nation at Risk: The Imperative for Educational Reform.* Washington, D.C.: U.S. Department of Education, April 1983.

National Council on Education Standards and Testing. *Raising Standards for American Education: A Report to Congress, the Secretary of Education, the National Education Goals Panel, and the American People.* Washington, D.C.: U.S. Department of Education, 1992.

New York State Social Studies Review and Development Committee. *One Nation, Many Peoples: A Declaration of Cultural Independence.* New York: New York Department of Education, June 1991.

NEWSPAPERS AND MAGAZINES

Ankeney, Kirk. "A History Lesson." *The San Diego Union* (Nov. 21, 1994).

Bauer, Gary L. "National History Standards: Clintonites Miss the Moon." Advertisement. *The Washington Times* (March 25, 1995).

Bauer, Gary L. "National History Standards: Clintonites Miss the Moon." *Perspective* [*http://www.frc.org/perspective/1995.html*].

"A Blueprint of History for American Students." Editorial. *The San Francisco Chronicle* (Nov. 1994).

"Cheney Resigns." *Los Angeles Times* (December 11, 1992).

Cheney, Lynne V. "The End of History." *The Wall Street Journal* (Oct. 20, 1994): A22, A26–A27.

Cheney, Lynne V. "Kill My Old Agency, Please." *The Wall Street Journal* (Jan. 24, 1995): A22.

Cheney, Lynne V. "The National History (Sub) Standards." *The Wall Street Journal* (Oct. 23, 1995): A16.

"Christian Coalition Presents The Contract With the American Family." [*http://www.cc.org/publications/ca/speech/contract.html*].

Coughlin, Ellen K. "Scholars Confront Fundamental Question: Which Vision of America Should Prevail?: Multicultualism Issue Draws Historians into Debates over Framing the Nation's Past." *Chronicle of Higher Education*, 38, 21 (January 29, 1992): A8.

Diegmueller, Karen & Debra Viadero. "Playing Games with History." *Education Week* (November 15, 1995): 29–34.

Gluck, Carol. "History According to Whom?: Let the Debate Continue." *The New York Times* (November 19, 1994): 15.

"A History Lesson." *The Christian Science Monitor.* (November 7, 1994).

Innerst, Carole. "Finn Leads War for Tough Education." *The Washington Times* (August 24, 1994).

Krauthammer, Charles. "History Hijacked." *Washington Post* (November 4, 1994): A25.

Leo, John. "History Standards Are Bunk." *U.S. News and World Report* (February 6, 1995): 23.

"Living History: New Standards Reflect Vital Reality." *The Star Tribune.* (Minneapolis: November 14, 1994).

"Maligning the History Standards." *The New York Times* (February 13, 1995): A14.

"Now a History for the Rest of Us: New Standards Look to Common People's Roles." *The Los Angeles Times* (October 27, 1994): B6.

"Plan to Teach U.S. History Is Said to Slight White Males." *The New York Times* (October 26, 1994).

Pyne, John & Gloria Sesso. "Letter to the Editor." *The New York Times* (February 7, 1995).

Ravitch, Diane. "Standards in U.S. History: Solid Material Interwoven with Political Bias." *Education Week* (December 7, 1994): 48.

Ravitch, Diane. "Revise, but Don't Abandon, the History Standards." *The Chronicle of Higher Education* (February 17, 1995): A52.

Ravitch, Diane and Arthur M. Schlesinger Jr. "The New, Improved History Standards." *The Wall Street Journal* (April 3, 1996): A22.

Rich, Frank. "Eating Her Offspring." *The New York Times* (January 26, 1995): A19.

Rothman, Robert. "$1.5 Million Awarded for Center on History." *Education Week* (March 30, 1988).

Thomas, Jo. "U.S. Panel's History Model Looks Beyond Europe." *The New York Times* (November 11, 1994).

"The Thought Police." *Newsweek*, (December 24, 1990): 48–55.

Wiener, Jon. "History Lesson." *The New Republic* (January 2, 1995): 9–11.

Williams, Dennis A. et al. "Can the Schools Be Saved?" *Newsweek* (May 9, 1983): 50–58.

Woo, Elaine. "History Standards Flawed but Can Be Saved, Panels Say." *The Los Angeles Times* (October 12, 1995).

Woo, Elaine. "Hire Education: Colleges Design 'Contract' Courses to Meet Employers' Needs." *Los Angeles Times* (Feb 15, 1998) Record Edition: 10

ARCHIVAL SOURCES

All of the archival sources are from the UCLA—University Archives: Record Series #667, unprocessed boxes 40–109, and processed boxes 1–20. The box numbers I have used are provisional, due to the fact that when I did my archival work in 1999 the items were being processed and reconfigured into smaller boxes. These boxes contained the full gamut of materials generated from the NCHS between 1988 and 1996. They included the following types of materials: correspondence and memoranda; grant applications; focus group reports; drafts of standards; congressional records; newspaper and magazine articles; e-mail records; and drafts of teaching units. Most of the boxes contained unprocessed documents.

Supplementary Bibliography

WORKS CONSULTED BUT NOT CITED

PUBLISHED SOURCES

Adler, Louise & Kip Tellez. "Curriculum Challenge from the Religious Right: The *Impressions* Reading Series." *Urban Education*, 27, 2 (July 1992): 152–173.

Adler, Mortimer J. "The Paideia Proposal: Rediscovering the Essence of Education." *American School Board Journal*, 169, 7 (July 1982): 17–20.

Adler, Mortimer J. "Understanding the U.S.A." *Journal of Teacher Education*, 34,6 (Nov–Dec 1983): 35–37.

Apple, Michael W. "What Counts as Legitimate Knowledge: The Social Production and Use of Reviews." *Review of Educational Research*, 69, 4 (Winter 1999): 343–346.

Atlas, James. "Chicago's Grumpy Guru: Best-Selling Professor Allan Bloom and the Chicago Intellectuals." In Robert L. Stone (Ed.), *Essays on the Closing of the American Mind*. Chicago: Chicago Review Press, 1989: 68–72.

Bain, Robert B. "Beyond the Standards Wars: Politics and Pedagogy in the National History Standards' Controversy." [*www.iac.net/~pfilio/bain.htm*].

Barber, Benjamin. "The Philosopher Despot: Allan Bloom's Elitist Agenda." In Robert L. Stone (Ed.), *Essays on the Closing of the American Mind*. Chicago: Chicago Review Press, 1989: 81–88.

Bell, Terrel H. *The Thirteenth Man: A Reagan Cabinet Memoir*. New York: The Free Press, 1988.

Bennett, William J. *The Devaluing of America: The Fight for Our Culture and Our Children*. New York: Summit Books, 1992.

Bentley, Jerry H. *Shapes of World History in Twentieth-Century Scholarship*. Washington, D.C.: American Historical Association, 1996.

Berliner, David C. "Educational Psychology Meets the Christian Right: Differing Views of Children, Schooling, Teaching, and Learning." *Teachers College Record*, 98, 3 (Spring 1997): 381–416.

Bobbit, Franklin J. *The Curriculum*. Boston: Houghton Mifflin Co., 1918.

Browder, Lesley H. Jr. "The Religious Right, the Secular Left, and Their Shared Dilemma: The Public School" *International Journal of Educational Reform*, 7, 4 (October 1998): 309–318.

Bruner, Jerome. *Actual Minds, Possible Worlds*. Cambridge, MA: Harvard University Press, 1986.

Bruner, Jerome. *Acts of Meaning*. Cambridge, MA: Harvard University Press, 1990.

Bruner, Jerome. "The Narrative Construction of Reality." *Critical Inquiry*, 18 (1991): 1–21.

Cheney, Lynne V. "Telling the Truth: A Report on the State of the Humanities in Higher Education." *Humanities*, 13, 5 (Sept.–Oct. 1992): 4–9.

Cohen, Saul. "The History of the History of American Education: The Uses of the Past." Unpublished paper, 1997.

Coleman, James. "Rawls, Nozick, and Educational Equality." *The Public Interest*, 43, 48 (Spring 1976): 121–128.

Conlan, John B. & Peter B. Dow. "Pro/Con Forum: The MACOS Controversy. The Push for a Uniform National Curriculum [And] MACOS Revisited: A Commentary on the Most Frequently Asked Questions About *Man: A Course of Study*." *Social Education* 39, 6 (Oct. 1975): 388–396.

Cromer, Alan. "The Science Standards Wars: What Is the Basis for Scientific Inquiry?" In Sandra Stotsky, (Ed.), *What's at Stake in the Standards Wars: A Primer for Educational Policy Makers*. New York: Peter Lang, 2000: 99–113.

Cronon, W., J. P. Diggins, E. Foner, J. Higham, D. A. Hollinger, L. K. Kerber, J. Lukacs, W. A. McDougall, E. Morgan, D. Ravitch, & C. Vann Woodward. "Teaching American History." *The American Scholar* (Winter 1998): 91–106.

Cross, Patricia K. "The Rising Tide of School Reform Reports." *Phi Delta Kappan*, 66 (November 1984): 167–172.

Cuban, Larry. "School Reform by Remote Control: SB 813 in California." *Phi Delta Kappan*, 66 (November, 1984): 213–215.

Darling-Hammond, Linda. "The Right to Learn and the Advancement of Teaching: Research, Policy, and Practice for Democratic Education." *Educational Researcher*, 25, 6 (1996): 5–17.

Davis, O. J. Jr., ed. *NCSS in Retrospect, Bulletin 92*. Washington, D.C.: National Council for the Social Studies, 1996.

Dow, Peter B. "*Man: A Course of Study* in Retrospect: A Primer for Curriculum in the 70s." *Theory into Practice*, 10, 3 (June, 1971): 168–177.

Dow, Peter B. *MACOS Controversy: Responses to Charges by John Conlan*. Newton, MA: Education Development Center, Inc., 1975.

Dow, Peter B. "MACOS: Social Studies in Crisis." *Educational Leadership*, 34, 1 (Oct. 1976): 35–39.

Egan, Kieran. "John Dewey and the Social Studies Curriculum." *Theory and Research in Social Education*, 8 (1980): 37–53.

Feinberg, Walter. *Reason and Rhetoric: The Intellectual Foundations of 20th Century Liberal Educational Policy*. New York: John Wiley & Sons, 1975.

Finn, Chester E. Jr. & Diane Ravitch, "Educational Reform 1995–96, Introduction," *www.edexcellence.net* (February 1999).

Foshay, Arthur W. "How Fare the Disciplines?" *Phi Delta Kappan*. LI, 4 (March 1970): 349–352.

Franklin, Barry M. "Discourse, Rationality, and Educational Research: A Historical Perspective of RER." *Review of Educational Research*, 69, 4 (Winter 1999): 347–363.

Fukuyama, Francis. "Are We at the End of History?" *Fortune*, 121, 2 (January 15, 1990): 75–77.

Gagnon, Paul. *Democracy's Half-Told Story: What American History Textbooks Should Add*. Washington, D.C.: American Federation of Teachers, 1989.

Gagnon, Paul, ed. *Historical Literacy: The Case for History in American Education*. Boston: Houghton Mifflin, 1989.

Gagnon, Paul. "What Children Should Learn: National Standards Have Been Thwarted but State-Mandated Academic Standards and Local Action Can Yet Save the Schools." *The Atlantic Monthly* (December 1995): 65–78.

Gallagher, Mary Campbell. "Lessons from the Sputnik-Era Curriculum Reform Movement: The Institutions We Need for Educational Reform." In Sandra Stotsky (Ed.), *What's At Stake in the Standards Wars: A Primer for Educational Policy Makers*. New York: Peter Lang, 2000: 281–312.

Gellner, Ernest. *Nationalism*. New York: New York University Press, 1997.

Gibson, Rich. "History on Trial in the Heart of Darkness." *Theory and Research in Social Education*, 26, 4 (Fall 1998).

Giroux, Henry. *Border Crossings: Cultural Workers and the Politics of Education*. New York: Routledge, 1992.

Graham, Patricia A. "Assimilation, Adjustment, and Access." In Diane Ravitch & Maris A. Vinovskis (Eds.), *Learning From the Past: What History Teaches Us About School Reform*. Baltimore: The Johns Hopkins University Press: 3–24.

Grant, Carl A. & Christine E. Sleeter. *Making Choices for Multicultual Education: Five Approaches to Race, Class, and Gender*. New Jersey: Merrill, 1994.

Greider, William. "Bloom and Doom." In Robert L. Stone (Ed.), *Essays on the Closing of the American Mind*. Chicago: Chicago Review Press, 1989: 244–247.

Habermas, Jurgen. "Modernity: An Incomplete Project." *The Anti-Aesthetic: Essays on Postmodern Culture*. Seattle: Bay Press, 1983.

Hatcher, Ed. "The Center Holds: The National Standards for World History and the Triumph of Historical Method." Unpublished paper, May 8, 1995.

Hobsbawm, Eric & Terence Ranger, eds. *The Invention of Tradition*. Cambridge, England: Cambridge University Press, 1983.

Hollinger, David. *Post-ethnic America: Beyond Multiculturalism*. New York: Basic Books, 1995.

Honig, Bill. "California's Experience with Textbook Improvement." *Educational Policy*, 3, 2 (1986): 125–135.

Iggers, Georg G. *Historiography in the Twentieth Century: From Scientific Objectivity to the Postmodern Challenge*. Hanover, NH: Wesleyan University Press, 1997.

Jenkins, Keith, ed. *The Postmodern History Reader*. London: Routledge, 1997.

Kammen, Michael. *Mystic Chords of Memory: The Transformation of Tradition in American Culture*. New York: Alfred A. Knopf, 1991.

Kammen, Michael. *In the Past Lane: Historical Perspectives on American Culture*. New York: Oxford University Press, 1997.

Kaye, Harvey J. "From *Lessons From History* to *National Standards:* Questions of Class, Labor and American Radicalism," draft copy of book review for *Review of Education*, 1995.

Kelly, Elizabeth A. *Education, Democracy & Public Knowledge*. Boulder: Westview Press, 1995.

Kliebard, Herbert M. "Bestor Agonistes." *Educational Studies*, 17, 4 (Winter 1986): 542–549.

Kliebard, Herbert M. "What Is a Knowledge Base, and Who Would Use It If We Had One?" *Review of Educational Research*, 63, 3 (Fall 1993): 295–303.

Kozol, Jonathan. *Savage Inequalities: Children in America's Schools*. New York: HarperCollins, 1991.

Labaree, David F. "Politics, Markets, and the Compromised Curriculum." *Harvard Educational Review,* 57 (November 1987): 483–494.

Labaree, David. "Power, Knowledge, and the Rationalization of Teaching: A Genealogy of the Movement to Professionalize Teaching." *Harvard Educational Review*, 62, 2 (1992): 123–154.

Lagemann, Ellen Condliffe. *An Elusive Science: The Troubling History of Educational Research*. Chicago: University of Chicago Press, 2000.

La Spina, James A. "Closing the Multicultural Frontier in a Land of Buried Cultures: Nation-Building Without Natives in a Global Age." Unpublished manuscript, 1999.

Lerner, Gerda. *Why History Matters: Life and Thought*. New York: Oxford University Press, 1997.

Levine, Lawrence, W. *The Unpredictable Past: Explorations in American Cultural History*. New York: Oxford University Press, 1993.

Linenthal, Edward T. & Tom Engelhardt, eds. *History Wars: The Enola Gay and Other Battles for the American Past*. New York: Henry Holt and Company, 1996.

Lobes, Loretta. "Surveying State Standards: National History Education Network's 1997 Report on State Social Studies Standards." Washington, D.C.: National History Education Network, 1998.

Lowen, James W. *Lies My Teacher Told Me: Everything Your American History Textbook Got Wrong*. New York: New Press, 1995.

Lund, Leonard & Cathleen Wild. *Ten Years After "A Nation at Risk."* New York: The Conference Board, 1993.

Lutz, Sabrina W. M. "Whose Standards?: Conservative Citizen Groups and Standards-based Reform." *Educational Horizons*, 75 (1997): 133–142.

McCarthy, Cameron. *The Uses of Culture*. New York: Routledge, 1998.

McKeown, Michael, David Klein, & Chris Patterson. "The National Science Foundation Systemic Initiatives: How a Small Amount of Federal Money Promotes Ill-Designed Mathematics and Science Programs in K–12 and Undermines Local Control of Education." In Sandra Stotsky (Ed.), *What's At Stake in the Standards Wars: A Primer for Educational Policy Makers*. New York: Peter Lang, 2000: 313–369.

McNeill, William H. "The Rise of the West After Twenty-Five Years." *Journal of World History*, 1, 1 (Spring 1990): 1–22.

Oakes, Jeannie & Martin Lipton. *Teaching to Change the World*. Boston: McGraw-Hill, 1999.

O'Malley, Michael & Roy Rosenzweig. "Brave New World or Blind Alley? American History on the World Wide Web." *Journal of American History*, 84, 1 (June 1997): 132–155.

Piaget, Jean. *The Child's Conception of Physical Causality*. Originally published: London: K. Paul, Trench, Trubner & Co. Ltd., 1930. New Brunswick, NJ: Transaction Publishers, 2000.

Piaget, Jean & Bärbel Inhelder. *The Child's Conception of Space* (F. J. Langdon & J. L. Lunzer, trans.). London: Routledge & Kegan Paul, 1956.

Pinar, William F., William M. Reynolds, Patrick Slattery, & Peter M. Taubman. *Understanding Curriculum: An Introduction to the Study of Historical and Contemporary Curriculum Discourses.* New York: Peter Lang, 1995.

Poster, Mark. *Cultural History & Postmodernity: Disciplinary Readings and Challenges.* New York: Columbia University Press, 1997.

Puddington, Arch. *Better Ways to Tell Our Story: A Critique of the Proposed National History Standards.* Washington, D.C.: American Federation of Teachers, December 1995.

Ravitch, Diane. *The Great School Wars: New York City, 1805–1973: A History of the Public Schools as Battlefield of Social Change.* New York: Basic Books, 1974.

Ravitch, Diane. "The Meaning of the New Coleman Report." *Phi Delta Kappan,* 62, 10 (June 1981): 718–720.

Ravitch, Diane. "Forgetting the Questions: The Problem of Educational Reform." *American Scholar,* 50, 3 (Summer 1981): 329–340.

Ravitch, Diane. "The New Right and the Schools: Why Mainstream America Is Listening to Our Critics." *American Educator,* (Fall 1982): 9–14.

Ravitch, Diane. *The Schools We Deserve: Reflections on the Educational Crises of Our Times.* New York: Basic Books, 1985.

Ravitch, Diane. "The Precarious State of History." *American Educator,* 9, 1 (1985): 10–17.

Ravitch, Diane. "A Culture in Common." *Educational Leadership,* 49, 4 (Dec. 1991): 8–11.

Ravitch, Diane. "Launching a Revolution in Standards and Assessments." *Phi Delta Kappan,* 74, 10 (June 1993): 767–772.

Ravitch, Diane. *National Standards in American Education: A Citizen's Guide.* Washington, D.C.: Brookings Institution Press, 1995.

Ravitch, Diane. "50 States, 50 Standards?: The Continuing Need for National Voluntary Standards in Education." *The Brookings Review,* 14, 3 (Summer 1996): 6–9.

Ravitch, Diane & Maris A. Vinovskis, eds. *Learning from the Past: What History Teaches Us About School Reform.* Baltimore: The John Hopkins University Press, 1995.

Reisenger, Frederick C. "The National History Standards: A View from the Inside." *The History Teacher,* 28, 3 (May 1995): 387–393.

Rieff, David. "The Colonel and the Professor." In Robert L. Stone, (Ed.), *Essays on the Closing of the American Mind.* Chicago: Chicago Review Press, 1989: 290–295.

Rorty, Richard. "Straussianism, Democracy, and Allan Bloom: That Old Time Philosophy." In Robert L. Stone (Ed.), *Essays on the Closing of the American Mind.* Chicago: Chicago Review Press, 1989: 194.

Rosenau, Pauline M. *Post-Modernism and the Social Sciences: Insights, Inroads, and Intrusions.* Princeton: Princeton University Press, 1995).

Sarason, Seymour. *The Predictable Failure of Educational Reform.* San Francisco: Jossey-Bass, 1990.

Schlesinger, Arthur M. Jr. *The Disuniting of America: Reflections on a Multicultural Society.* Originally published by Whittle Direct Books, Knoxville, TN, 1991. New York: W. W. Norton, 1992.

Shabbas, Audrey. "Good Guys, Bad Guys, and Stifling the Spirit of Inquiry." *www.Washington report.org/backissues/0389/8903022.html*.

Showalter, Elaine. "Lynne Cheney, Feminist Intellectual?" *The Chronicle of Higher Education* [*http://chronicle.com/free/v47/i05/05b01101.htm*] (September 29, 2000).

Slattery, Patrick. *Curriculum Development in the Postmodern Era*. New York: Garland Publishing, Inc., 1995.

Smith, Marshall S., Jennifer O'Day, & D. K. Cohen. "National Curriculum Style: Can It Be Done?, What Might It Look Like?" *American Educator* (Winter 1990): 10–47.

Spring, Joel. *The Sorting Machine Revisited: National Educational Policy Since 1945*. New York: Longman, 1989.

Spring, Joel. *Education and the Rise of the Global Economy*. Mahwah, NJ: Lawrence Erlbaum Associates, Inc, 1998.

Stainton, Catherine & Gaea Leinhardt. "Telling the Tale: Narrative Explanation in History." Pittsburgh: Learning Research and Development Center, University of Pittsburgh, AERA paper, April, 1994.

Stern, Sheldon M. "Why the Battle over History Standards?" In Sandra Stotsky (Ed.), *What's at Stake in the Standards Wars: A Primer for Educational Policy Makers*. New York: Peter Lang, 2000: 149–168.

Stone, Lawrence. "Prosopography." *Daedalus: Journal of the American Academy of Arts and Sciences* 100, 1 (Winter 1971): 46–79.

Stone, Robert L., ed. *Essays on the Closing of the American Mind*. Chicago: Chicago Review Press, 1989.

Symcox, Linda S. & James A. La Spina. "The Untroubled Crusaders: Development of California's Social-Science Framework and Its National Impact: The Genealogy of a Curriculum Reform." Los Angeles: Unpublished AERA paper, April 1998.

Tanner, Daniel. "The Textbook Controversies." In Margaret J. Early & Kenneth J. Rehage, (Eds.), *Issues in Curriculum: Selected Chapters from NSSE Yearbooks, Ninety-Eighth Yearbook for the National Society for the Study of Education, Part II*. Chicago: University of Chicago Press, 1999: 115–140.

Toch, Thomas. "The Dark Side of the Excellence Movement." *Phi Delta Kappan*, 66 (November 1984): 173–176.

Tyack, David. *The One Best System: A History of American Urban Education*. Cambridge, MA: Harvard University Press, 1974.

Tyack, David & James Banks. "Moral Majorities and the School Curriculum: Historical Perspectives on the Legalization of Virtue." *Teacher's College Record*, 86, 4 (1985): 513–535.

VanBurkleo, Sandra F. "The National History Standards and the Culture Wars of Our Times." *Michigan Historical Review*, 22, 2 (Fall 1996): 167–188.

Van Sledright, Bruce A. "Arbitrating Competing Claims in the Classroom Culture Wars." Organization of American Historians (Feb. 1999) [*http://www.indiana.edu/~oah/nl/99feb/vansledright.htm*]

Venezky, Richard. "Textbooks in School and Society." In Phillip Jackson (Ed.), *Handbook of Research on Curriculum*. New York: Macmillan, 1992: 436–461.

Weber, Eugen. "Western Civilization." In (Anthony Molho & Gordon S. Wood, Eds.), *Imagined Histories: American Historians Interpret the Past*. Princeton, NJ: Princeton University Press, 1998.

Wineberg, Samuel S. "On the Reading of Historical Texts: Notes on the Reach Between School and Academy." *American Educational Research Journal*, 28 (1991): 495–519.

Wineberg, Samuel S. "The Cognitive Representation of Historical Text." In Gaea Leinhardt, Isabel L. Beck, & Catherine Stainton (Eds.), *Teaching and Learning History*. Hillsdale, NJ: Lawrence Erlbaum Associates, Publishers, 1994.

Wineberg, Samuel S. "Historical Thinking and Other Unnatural Acts." *Phi Delta Kappan*, 80, 7 (1999): 448–499.

OFFICIAL AND GOVERNMENT PUBLICATIONS

Cheney, Lynne V. *Tyrannical Machines: A Report on Educational Practices Gone Wrong and Our Best Hopes of Setting Them Right*. Washington, D.C.: National Endowment for the Humanities, 1990.

National Commission on Excellence in Education. *Meeting the Challenge: Recent Efforts to Improve Education Across the Nation*. Washington, D.C.: U.S. Department of Education, November 1983.

National Education Association. *A Guide from Teachers to* A Nation At Risk *and Other Studies*. Washington, D.C.: National Education Association, 1983.

United States Department of Education. *Report by the Secretary on the Regional Forums on Excellence in Education*. Washington, D.C.: United States Department of Education, December 1983.

United States Department of Education. *The Nation Responds: Recent Efforts to Improve Education*. Washington, D.C.: United States Department of Education, 1984.

Index

215

About the Author

Linda Symcox is an assistant professor of curriculum and instruction at the College of Education, California State University, Long Beach. She was formerly the associate director of the National Center for History in the Schools (NCHS) at the University of California, Los Angeles (UCLA) and director of the Options for Youth 21st Century Curriculum Laboratory at UCLA. She was an elementary school teacher in Los Angeles Unified School District and has served as a curriculum designer for the Huntington Library in Pasadena, California. Her research focuses on the interplay between curriculum theory, policy, and reform. She examines how educational policy is shaped by the competing agendas of academics, politicians, and the media; how different interest groups use their positions of power to advance their intellectual and ideological programs; and how their efforts drive curricular policy.

DATE DUE

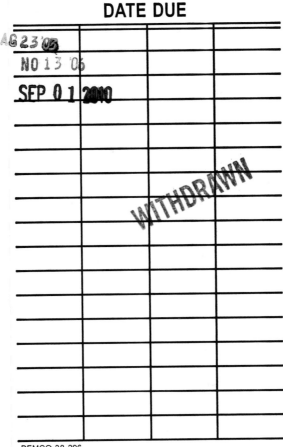

AG 23 '05			
NO 13 06			
SEP 0 1 2010			